baking
&
desserts

baking
&
desserts

Bath New York Singapore Hong Kong Cologne Delhi Melbourne

This edition published by Parragon in 2009

Parragon
Queen Street House
4 Queen Street
Bath BA1 1HE, UK

Copyright © Parragon Books Ltd 2009
Designed by Terry Jeavons & Company
Additional text written by Linda Doeser

ISBN: 978-1-4075-4760-2

Printed in Indonesia

Notes for the Reader
This book uses both metric and imperial measurements. Follow the same units of measurement throughout; do not mix metric and imperial. All spoon measurements are level: teaspoons are assumed to be 5 ml, and tablespoons are assumed to be 15 ml. Unless otherwise stated, milk is assumed to be full fat, eggs and individual vegetables are medium and pepper is freshly ground black pepper.

The times given are an approximate guide only. Preparation times differ according to the techniques used by different people and the cooking times may also vary from those given. Optional ingredients, variations or serving suggestions have not been included in the calculations.

Recipes using raw or very lightly cooked eggs should be avoided by infants, the elderly, pregnant women, convalescents and anyone suffering from an illness. Pregnant and breastfeeding women are advised to avoid eating peanuts and peanut products. Sufferers from nut allergies should be aware that some of the ready-made ingredients used in the recipes in this book may contain nuts. Always check the packaging before use.

contents

introduction

Whether rhythmically rolling out pastry, vigorously kneading bread dough, inhaling the spicy aroma of a fruit cake in the oven or neatly arranging lines of cookies on a wire rack, baking is an intensely sensuous and satisfying type of cooking. While preparing family meals day after day can sometimes feel like a chore, baking is always fun and appeals to the creative instincts of cooks. Home-baked cakes and biscuits, tarts and pies, breads and savoury snacks are always greeted with enthusiasm.

Home-baked goods are surprisingly easy to make. After all, helping Mum by spooning cake batter into paper cases or stamping out shapes of cookie dough is, for many children, their first experience of cooking. Rustling up a batch of muffins or whisking up a sponge cake takes very little time and making more elaborate, special occasion gâteaux, tortes, cheesecakes and other desserts

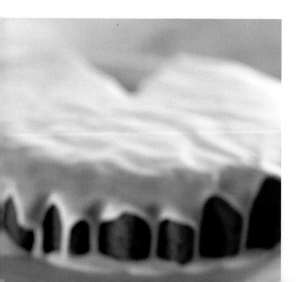

is so rewarding that any extra effort involved seems negligible. Some, although not all, breads require plenty of time to rise before baking, but as you can just leave them to get on with it, this is hardly a problem.

It's probably more important with baking than with any other kind of cooking to use the specified ingredients, measure them accurately and follow the recipe carefully. Different flours, for example, vary in their characteristics and if you use the wrong one, the results are likely to be disappointing. However, if you have decided to make a cake that requires self-raising flour and have run out of it, you can make a satisfactory, although not a perfect substitute by sifting $2^1/_2$ teaspoons of baking powder with 250 g/ 9 oz plain flour. Similarly, don't substitute soft tub margarine if the recipe specifies butter or block margarine, as the texture of the mixture will become much wetter.

The proportions of the ingredients are critical and, if you use too much fat or flour or too many eggs when making cakes, they will fail to rise and be dull and stodgy. Paradoxically, too much raising agent will cause a cake to sink when you remove it from the oven. Weigh dry ingredients accurately and measure liquids in a calibrated jug. Use a set of proper measuring spoons for small quantities. When

measuring dry ingredients, such as baking powder or dried yeast, scoop up a heaped spoonful, then level it off with the blade of a knife. Don't measure any ingredient directly over the mixing bowl as accidental spillage can result in disaster.

Following the recipes is very straightforward. Don't skip any instructions, such as sifting the flour and raising agent together, preheating the oven to the correct temperature or lining the tin. Even if you buy ready-sifted flour, this should be sifted again before use in fine baking. Do be careful not to overheat liquids when baking with yeast as this will kill it and the bread will not rise. Also bear in mind that the rising time may vary depending on external factors, such as the temperature. Always leave the dough long enough to reach the required stage, such as doubled in size. It is important, too, to use the right sized tin – otherwise cakes and loaves may crack or collapse. Set the oven timer for the baking time specified and resist the temptation to open the door during cooking.

All this is really just common sense, but there are a few 'tricks

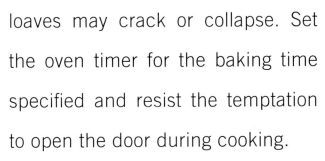

of the trade' that are worth knowing. If the recipe requires eggs, remove them from the refrigerator 30 minutes or so before you want to use them so that they can come to room temperature. Adding cold eggs to a creamed mixture is likely to result in their curdling. It's also better to add them gradually. Remember that adding liquid to a dry mixture containing baking powder or bicarbonate of soda activates the raising agent immediately, so don't leave the mixture standing around. You can speed up the rising process, sometimes called proving, for yeast doughs in the microwave. Put the kneaded dough into a clean non-metallic bowl, cover with clingfilm and heat on high for 10 seconds. Leave the dough in a warm place or in the microwave for about 20 minutes by which time it will have doubled in size. If not, heat on high for a further 10 seconds, then leave to rise for another 10 minutes.

Finally, when testing cakes to see if they are cooked, warm a skewer and then insert it into the centre of the cake. If it comes out clean, the cake is ready.

cakes

Home-baked cakes are always a special treat, whether you have decided to make a quick and easy Victoria sponge simply dusted with sugar or an impressive multi-layered gâteau elaborately decorated with melt-in-the-mouth icing and chocolate curls. The choice is immense and there are delicious confections for all tastes and dozens of occasions. There are cakes for kids, perfect partners for morning coffee or afternoon tea, luscious dinner party desserts, wonderful home-baked gifts, great any-time-of-day snacks and mouthwatering centrepieces for celebrations and special occasions. Even those watching their weight can enjoy an occasional moment of self-indulgence with a fat-free whisked sponge. Recipes feature cakes flavoured with coffee, plain chocolate, milk chocolate, white chocolate, nuts, fresh fruit, dried fruit, glacé fruit, spices, seeds, honey and liqueurs. They may be plain, iced, dredged with sugar or cocoa powder, drenched with syrup, smothered with chocolate or lavishly coated with cream.

The great thing is that they are not difficult to make, although some will take more time than others. Many are based on the technique of creaming, that is beating fat, usually butter, and sugar together until light and fluffy. This is most easily done with an electric mixer, but be careful not to overmix or the cake will end up with uneven air pockets and look like Swiss cheese

when it's sliced. Fold in the flour gradually using a metal spoon or rubber spatula in a gentle figure-of-eight movement to avoid knocking out the air. Nothing could be simpler – you might say, it's a piece of cake.

coffee & walnut cake

ingredients

SERVES 8

175 g/6 oz unsalted butter,
    plus extra for greasing
175 g/6 oz light muscovado
    sugar
3 large eggs, beaten
3 tbsp strong black coffee
175 g/6 oz self-raising flour
1$\frac{1}{2}$ tsp baking powder
115 g/4 oz walnut pieces
walnut halves, to decorate

frosting

115 g/4 oz unsalted butter
200 g/7 oz icing sugar
1 tbsp strong black coffee
$\frac{1}{2}$ tsp vanilla extract

method

1 Preheat the oven to 180°C/350°F/Gas Mark 4. Grease and base-line two 20-cm/8-inch sandwich tins.

2 Cream together the butter and muscovado sugar until pale and fluffy. Gradually add the eggs, beating well after each addition. Beat in the coffee.

3 Sift the flour and baking powder into the mixture, then fold in lightly and evenly with a metal spoon. Fold in the walnut pieces.

4 Divide the mixture between the prepared cake tins and smooth level. Bake in the preheated oven for 20–25 minutes, or until golden brown and springy to the touch. Turn out onto a wire rack to cool.

5 For the frosting, beat together the butter, icing sugar, coffee and vanilla extract, mixing until smooth and creamy.

6 Use about half the mixture to sandwich the cakes together, then spread the remaining frosting on top and swirl with a palette knife. Decorate with walnut halves.

mocha layer cake

ingredients

SERVES 8

butter, for greasing
200 g/7 oz self-raising flour
1/4 tsp baking powder
4 tbsp cocoa powder
100 g/3 oz caster sugar
2 eggs
2 tbsp golden syrup
150 ml/5 fl oz corn oil
150 ml/5 fl oz milk

filling

1 tsp instant coffee
1 tbsp boiling water
300 ml/10 fl oz double cream
2 tbsp icing sugar

to decorate

50 g/1 3/4 oz plain chocolate,
    grated
chocolate caraque
icing sugar, for dusting

method

1 Preheat the oven to 180°C/350°F/Gas Mark 4. Lightly grease three 18-cm/7-inch cake tins.

2 Sift the flour, baking powder and cocoa powder into a large bowl, then stir in the sugar. Make a well in the centre and stir in the eggs, golden syrup, oil and milk. Beat with a wooden spoon, gradually mixing in the dry ingredients to make a smooth batter. Divide the mixture between the tins.

3 Bake in the preheated oven for 35–45 minutes, or until springy to the touch. Leave to stand in the tins for 5 minutes, then turn out and leave to cool completely on a wire rack.

4 To make the filling, dissolve the instant coffee in the boiling water and place in a large bowl with the cream and icing sugar. Whip until the cream is just holding its shape, then use half the cream to sandwich the three cakes together. Spread the remaining cream over the top and sides of the cake. Press the grated chocolate into the cream round the edge of the cake. Transfer the cake to a serving plate. Lay the chocolate caraque over the top of the cake. Cut a few thin strips of baking paper and place on top of the chocolate caraque. Dust lightly with icing sugar, then carefully remove the paper and serve.

coffee caramel cake

ingredients

SERVES 8

175 g/6 oz butter, softened,
     plus extra for greasing
200 g/7 oz golden caster sugar
3 eggs, beaten
225 g/8 oz self-raising flour,
     sifted
125 ml/4 fl oz strong black
     coffee
chocolate-covered coffee
     beans, to decorate

frosting

125 ml/4 fl oz milk
125 g/4¹/₂ oz butter
3 tbsp golden caster sugar
650 g/1 lb 7 oz icing sugar

method

1 Preheat the oven to 180°C/350°F/Gas Mark 4, then grease and base-line two 20-cm/8-inch sponge tins. Place the butter and sugar in a bowl and beat together until light and fluffy. Gradually beat in the eggs, then fold in the flour and coffee. Divide the batter between the prepared tins and bake in the preheated oven for 30 minutes, or until well risen and springy when pressed in the centre. Leave to cool in the tins for 5 minutes, then turn out and peel off the lining paper. Transfer to wire racks to cool completely.

2 To make the frosting, put the milk and butter into a saucepan, place over a low heat, and stir until the butter has melted. Remove the pan from the heat and set aside. Place the caster sugar in a separate, heavy-based saucepan and place over a low heat, stirring constantly, until the sugar dissolves and turns a golden caramel. Remove from the heat and stir in the warm milk mixture. Return to the heat and stir until the caramel dissolves.

3 Remove from the heat and gradually stir in the icing sugar, beating until the frosting is a smooth spreading consistency. Join the cakes together with some of the frosting and spread the rest over the top and sides. Decorate with chocolate-covered coffee beans.

victoria sponge cake

ingredients

SERVES 8–10

175 g/6 oz butter, at room
    temperature, plus extra for
    greasing
175 g/6 oz caster sugar
3 eggs, beaten
175 g/6 oz self-raising flour
pinch of salt
3 tbsp raspberry jam and
    1 tbsp caster or icing
    sugar, to serve

method

1 Preheat the oven to 180°C/350°F/Gas Mark 4. Grease two 20-cm/8-inch sponge tins and base-line with greaseproof paper.

2 Cream the butter and sugar together in a mixing bowl, using a wooden spoon or a hand-held mixer, until the mixture is pale in colour and light and fluffy.

3 Add the eggs a little at a time, beating well after each addition.

4 Sift the flour and salt and carefully add to the mixture, folding it in with a metal spoon or a spatula.

5 Divide the mixture between the tins and smooth over with the spatula.

6 Place them on the same shelf in the centre of the oven and bake for 25–30 minutes, until well risen, golden brown and beginning to shrink from the sides of the tin.

7 Remove from the oven and allow to stand for 1 minute. Loosen the cakes from around the edge of the tins using a palette knife. Turn the cakes out onto a clean tea towel, remove the paper and invert them onto a wire rack.

8 When completely cool, sandwich together with the jam and sprinkle with the sugar. The cake is delicious when freshly baked, but any remaining cake can be stored in an airtight tin for up to 1 week.

sticky toffee cake

ingredients

SERVES 9

175 g/6 oz stoned dates, chopped
175 ml/6 fl oz boiling water
1/2 tsp bicarbonate of soda
85 g/3 oz butter, plus extra for greasing
140 g/5 oz caster sugar
1 large egg, beaten
1/2 tsp vanilla extract
175 g/6 oz self-raising flour

toffee sauce
85 g/3 oz light muscovado sugar
40 g/1 1/2 oz butter
2 tbsp single cream or milk

method

1 Preheat the oven to 180°C/350°F/Gas Mark 4. Grease and line a 20-cm/8-inch square cake tin.

2 Put the dates in a small saucepan with the boiling water and bicarbonate of soda. Heat gently for about 5 minutes, without boiling, until the dates are soft.

3 Cream together the butter and caster sugar in a bowl until light and fluffy. Beat in the egg, vanilla extract and date mixture.

4 Fold in the flour using a metal spoon, mixing evenly. Pour the mixture into the prepared cake tin. Bake in the preheated oven for 40–45 minutes, or until firm to the touch and just starting to shrink away from the sides of the tin.

5 For the toffee sauce, combine the muscovado sugar, butter and cream in a saucepan and heat gently, until the sugar has dissolved. Simmer gently, stirring, for about 2 minutes.

6 Remove the cake from the oven and prick all over the surface with a skewer or fork. Pour the hot toffee sauce evenly over the surface. Leave it to cool in the tin, then cut into squares.

madeira cake

ingredients

SERVES 8–10

175 g/6 oz unsalted butter,
    plus extra for greasing
175 g/6 oz caster sugar
finely grated rind of 1 lemon
3 large eggs, beaten
115 g/4 oz plain flour
115 g/4 oz self-raising flour
2–3 tbsp brandy or milk
2 slices of citron peel

method

1 Preheat the oven to 160°C/325°F/Gas Mark 3. Grease and line an 18-cm/7-inch round deep cake tin.

2 Cream together the butter and sugar until pale and fluffy. Add the lemon rind and gradually beat in the eggs. Sift in the flours and fold in evenly, adding enough brandy to make a soft dropping consistency.

3 Spoon the mixture into the prepared tin and smooth the surface. Lay the slices of citron peel on top of the cake.

4 Bake in the preheated oven for 1–1¼ hours, or until well risen, golden brown and springy to the touch.

5 Cool in the tin for 10 minutes, then turn out and cool completely on a wire rack.

classic cherry cake

ingredients

SERVES 8

250 g/9 oz glacé cherries,
    quartered
85 g/3 oz ground almonds
200 g/7 oz plain flour
1 tsp baking powder
200 g/7 oz unsalted butter,
    plus extra for greasing
200 g/7 oz caster sugar
3 large eggs
finely grated rind and juice of
    1 lemon
6 sugar cubes, crushed

method

1 Preheat the oven to 180°C/350°F/Gas Mark 4. Grease and base-line a 20-cm/8-inch round cake tin.

2 Stir together the cherries, ground almonds and 1 tablespoon of the flour. Sift the remaining flour into a separate bowl with the baking powder.

3 Cream together the butter and sugar until light in colour and fluffy in texture. Gradually add the eggs, beating hard with each addition, until evenly mixed.

4 Add the flour mixture and fold lightly and evenly into the creamed mixture with a metal spoon. Add the cherry mixture and fold in evenly. Finally, fold in the lemon rind and juice.

5 Spoon the mixture into the prepared cake tin and sprinkle with the crushed sugar cubes. Bake in the preheated oven for 1–1¼ hours, or until risen, golden brown and the cake is just beginning to shrink away from the sides of the tin.

6 Cool in the tin for about 15 minutes, then turn out to finish cooling on a wire rack.

rich fruit cake

ingredients

SERVES 8

butter, for greasing
140 g/5 oz stoned
     unsweetened dates
100 g/3½ oz dried prunes
225 ml/8 fl oz unsweetened
     orange juice
2 tbsp treacle
1 tsp finely grated lemon rind
1 tsp finely grated orange rind
270 g/9½ oz wholemeal self-
     raising flour
1 tsp mixed spice
100 g/3½ oz seedless raisins
100 g/3½ oz sultanas
115 g/4 oz currants
100 g/3½ oz dried cranberries
3 large eggs, separated
1 tbsp apricot jam, warmed

frosting

115 g/4½ oz icing sugar, plus
     extra for dusting
1–2 tsp water
1 tsp vanilla extract
orange rind strips and lemon
     rind strips, to decorate

method

1 Preheat the oven to 160°C/325°F/Gas Mark 3. Grease and line a deep 20-cm/8-inch round cake tin. Chop the dates and prunes and place in a saucepan. Pour over the orange juice and leave to simmer for 10 minutes. Remove the pan from the heat and beat the fruit mixture until puréed. Add the treacle and citrus rinds and leave to cool.

2 Sift the flour and spice into a bowl, adding any bran that remains in the sieve. Add the dried fruits. When the date and prune mixture is cool, whisk in the egg yolks. Whisk the egg whites in a separate, clean bowl until stiff. Spoon the fruit mixture into the dry ingredients and mix together.

3 Gently fold in the egg whites. Transfer to the prepared tin and bake in the preheated oven for 1½ hours. Leave to cool in the tin.

4 Remove the cake from the tin and brush the top with apricot jam. To make the frosting, sift the sugar into a bowl and mix with enough water and the vanilla extract to form a soft frosting. Lay the frosting over the top of the cake and trim the edges. Decorate with orange and lemon rind strips.

crispy-topped fruit bake

ingredients

SERVES 10

butter, for greasing

350 g/12 oz cooking apples

3 tbsp lemon juice

350 g/12 oz self-raising
    wholemeal flour

1/2 tsp baking powder

1 tsp ground cinnamon, plus
    extra for dusting

115 g/4 oz prepared
    blackberries, thawed,
    if frozen

115 g/4 oz light muscovado
    sugar

1 egg, beaten

200 ml/7 fl oz low-fat natural
    yogurt

55 g/2 oz white or brown sugar
    lumps, lightly crushed

method

1 Preheat the oven to 190°C/375°F/Gas Mark 5. Grease and line a 900-g/2-lb loaf tin.

2 Peel, core and finely dice the apples. Place them in a saucepan with the lemon juice, bring to the boil, cover and simmer for about 10 minutes, until soft and pulpy. Beat well and set aside to cool.

3 Sift the flour, baking powder and cinnamon into a bowl, adding any husks that remain in the sieve. Stir in 70 g/2^1/$_2$ oz of the blackberries and the sugar.

4 Make a well in the centre of the ingredients and add the egg, yogurt and cooled apple purée. Mix well to incorporate thoroughly. Spoon the mixture into the prepared tin and smooth the top.

5 Sprinkle with the remaining blackberries, pressing them down into the cake mixture, and top with the crushed sugar lumps. Bake in the preheated oven for 40–45 minutes. Remove from the oven and set aside in the tin to cool.

6 Remove the cake from the tin and peel away the lining paper. Serve dusted with cinnamon.

gingerbread

ingredients

SERVES 12–16

450 g/1 lb plain flour
3 tsp baking powder
1 tsp bicarbonate of soda
3 tsp ground ginger
175 g/6 oz butter
175 g/6 oz soft light brown
    sugar
175 g/6 oz black treacle
175 g/6 oz golden syrup
1 egg, beaten
300 ml/10 fl oz milk
cream or warmed golden
    syrup, to serve

method

1 Line a 23-cm/9-inch square cake tin, 5 cm/ 2 inches deep, with greaseproof or baking paper.

2 Preheat the oven to 160°C/325°F/Gas Mark 3. Sift the dry ingredients into a large mixing bowl.

3 Place the butter, sugar, treacle and syrup in a medium-sized saucepan and heat over a low heat until the butter has melted and the sugar has dissolved. Allow to cool a little.

4 Mix the beaten egg with the milk and add to the cooled syrup mixture.

5 Add all the liquid ingredients to the flour mixture and beat well, using a wooden spoon until the mixture is smooth and glossy.

6 Pour the mixture into the prepared tin and bake in the centre of the oven for $1^1/_2$ hours, until well risen and just firm to the touch. A skewer inserted into the cake should come out clean. This gives a lovely sticky gingerbread, but if you like a firmer cake cook for a further 15 minutes.

7 Remove from the oven and leave the cake to cool in the tin. When cool, remove the cake from the tin with the lining paper. Overwrap with foil and place in an airtight tin for up to 1 week to allow the flavours to mature.

8 Cut into wedges and serve for tea or serve with cream as a pudding. Extra warmed syrup is an added extravagance.

sticky ginger marmalade loaf

ingredients

SERVES 10

175 g/6 oz butter, softened,
    plus extra for greasing

85 g/3 oz ginger marmalade

200 g/7 oz brown sugar

3 eggs, beaten

225 g/8 oz self-raising flour

1/2 tsp baking powder

1 tsp ground ginger

85 g/3 oz pecan nuts, coarsely
    chopped

method

1 Preheat the oven to 180°C/350°F/Gas Mark 4. Grease and line the base and sides of a 900-g/2-lb loaf tin. Place 1 tablespoon of the ginger marmalade in a small saucepan and reserve. Place the remaining marmalade in a bowl with the butter, sugar and eggs.

2 Sift in the flour, baking powder, and ground ginger and beat together until smooth. Stir in three quarters of the nuts. Spoon the mixture into the prepared loaf tin and smooth the top. Sprinkle with the remaining nuts and bake in the preheated oven for 1 hour, or until well risen and a skewer inserted into the centre comes out clean.

3 Leave to cool in the tin for 10 minutes, then turn out and peel off the lining paper. Transfer to a wire rack to cool until warm. Place the pan of reserved marmalade over a low heat to warm, then brush it over the loaf. Serve in slices.

carrot cake

ingredients

SERVES 16

butter, for greasing

2 eggs

150 g/5^1/$_2$ oz molasses sugar

225 ml/8 fl oz sunflower oil

140 g/5 oz carrots, coarsely
  grated

350 g/12 oz wholemeal flour

1 tsp bicarbonate of soda

2 tsp ground cinnamon

1 tsp grated nutmeg

85 g/3 oz walnuts, roughly
  chopped

1 tsp grated lemon rind and
  1 tsp grated orange rind,
  to decorate

topping

115 g/4 oz cream cheese

55 g/2 oz butter, softened

85 g/3 oz icing sugar

method

1 Preheat the oven to 190°C/375°F/Gas Mark 5. Grease and line a 23-cm/9-inch square cake tin. In a mixing bowl, beat the eggs until well blended and add the sugar and oil. Mix well. Add the grated carrot.

2 Sift in the flour, bicarbonate of soda and spices, then add the walnuts. Mix everything together until well incorporated.

3 Spread the mixture into the prepared cake tin and bake in the centre of the preheated oven for 40–50 minutes until the cake is nicely risen and firm to the touch, and has begun to shrink away slightly from the edge of the tin.

4 Remove from the oven and leave to cool in the tin until just warm, then turn out onto a wire rack to cool completely.

5 To make the topping, put all the ingredients into a mixing bowl and beat together for 2–3 minutes until really smooth.

6 When the cake is completely cold, spread over the topping, smooth with a fork, and sprinkle with grated lemon rind and orange rind. Leave to firm up a little before cutting into 16 portions. Store in an airtight container in a cool place for up to 1 week.

banana & chocolate loaf

ingredients

SERVES 8

115 g/4 oz butter, softened,
    plus extra for greasing
2 ripe bananas
75 g/2³/₄ oz golden caster
    sugar
2 eggs
225 g/8 oz self-raising flour
25 g/1 oz cocoa powder
1 tsp baking powder
1–2 tbsp milk
85 g/3 oz plain chocolate
    chips
butter, to serve (optional)

method

1 Preheat the oven to 180°C/350°F/Gas Mark 4. Grease and line a 900-g/2-lb loaf tin. Peel the bananas, place in a large bowl and mash with a fork.

2 Add the butter, sugar and eggs, then sift the flour, cocoa powder and baking powder into the bowl. Beat vigorously until smooth, adding enough milk to give a reluctant dropping consistency. Stir in the chocolate chips.

3 Spoon the mixture into the prepared tin and bake in the preheated oven for 50–60 minutes, or until well risen and the tip of a knife inserted in the centre comes out clean. Leave to stand in the tin for 5 minutes, then turn out onto a wire rack to cool completely. Serve sliced, with butter, if using.

battenberg cake

ingredients

SERVES 6–8

115 g/4 oz butter or
    margarine, softened,
    plus extra for greasing
115 g/4 oz caster sugar,
    plus extra for sprinkling
2 eggs, lightly beaten
1 tsp vanilla extract
115 g/4 oz self-raising flour,
    sifted
a few drops of pink edible
    food colouring
2–3 tbsp apricot jam
300 g/10$^{1}/_{2}$ oz marzipan

method

1 Preheat the oven to 180°C/350°F/Gas Mark 4. Grease and line an 18-cm/7-inch shallow square baking tin. Cut a strip of double baking paper, grease it and use to divide the tin in half.

2 Cream the butter and sugar in a mixing bowl until pale and fluffy. Gently beat in the eggs and vanilla extract, gradually adding in the flour. Spoon half the mixture into a separate bowl and colour it with a few drops of food colouring.

3 Spoon the plain mixture into half the prepared baking tin. Spoon the coloured mixture into the other half of the tin, trying to make the divide as straight as possible. Bake in the preheated oven for 35–40 minutes. Turn out and leave to cool on a wire rack.

4 When cool, trim the edges and cut the cake portions in half lengthways. Warm the jam in a small saucepan. Brush two sides of each cake portion with some of the jam and stick them together to give a chequerboard effect.

5 Knead the marzipan with a few drops of food colouring to colour it a subtle shade of pink. Roll out the marzipan to a rectangle wide enough to wrap around the cake. Brush the outside of the cake with the remaining jam. Place the cake on the marzipan and wrap the marzipan around the cake, making sure that the seam is on one corner of the cake. Trim the edges neatly. Crimp the top edges of the cake, if desired, and sprinkle with sugar.

angel food cake

ingredients

SERVES 10

115 g/4 oz plain flour,
    plus extra for dusting
sunflower oil, for greasing
8 large egg whites
1 tsp cream of tartar
1 tsp almond extract
250 g/9 oz caster sugar
250 g/9 oz summer berries
1 tbsp lemon juice
2 tbsp icing sugar, to serve

method

1 Preheat the oven to 160°C/325°F/Gas Mark 3. Brush the inside of a 1.7-litre/3-pint ring tin with oil and dust lightly with flour.

2 In a clean, grease-free bowl, whisk the egg whites until they hold soft peaks. Add the cream of tartar and whisk again until the whites are stiff but not dry.

3 Whisk in the almond extract, then add the sugar, a tablespoon at a time, whisking hard between each addition. Sift in the flour and fold in lightly and evenly, using a large metal spoon.

4 Spoon the mixture into the prepared cake tin and tap on the work surface to remove any large air bubbles. Bake in the preheated oven for 40–45 minutes, or until golden brown and firm to the touch.

5 Run the tip of a small knife around the edges of the cake to loosen from the tin. Leave to cool in the tin for 10 minutes, then turn out onto a wire rack to finish cooling.

6 To serve, place the berries, lemon juice and icing sugar in a saucepan and heat gently until the sugar has dissolved. Serve with the cake.

moroccan orange & almond cake

ingredients

SERVES 8

115 g/4 oz butter, softened, plus extra for greasing

1 orange

100 g/3½ oz golden caster sugar

2 eggs, beaten

150 g/5½ oz semolina

100 g/3½ oz ground almonds

1½ tsp baking powder

icing sugar, for dusting

Greek-style yogurt, to serve

syrup

300 ml/10 fl oz orange juice

150 g/5½ oz caster sugar

8 cardamom pods, crushed

method

1 Preheat the oven to 180°C/350°F/Gas Mark 4. Grease and base-line a 20-cm/8-inch cake tin. Grate the rind from the orange, reserving some for the decoration, and squeeze the juice from one half. Place the butter, orange rind and caster sugar in a bowl and beat together until light and fluffy. Gradually beat in the eggs. In a separate bowl, mix together the semolina, ground almonds and baking powder, then fold into the creamed mixture with the orange juice. Spoon the batter into the prepared tin and bake in the preheated oven for 30–40 minutes, or until well risen and a skewer inserted into the centre comes out clean. Leave to cool in the tin for 10 minutes.

2 To make the syrup, place the orange juice, sugar and cardamom pods in a saucepan over a low heat and stir until the sugar has dissolved. Bring to the boil and simmer for 4 minutes, or until syrupy.

3 Turn the cake out into a deep serving dish. Using a skewer, make holes over the surface of the warm cake. Strain the syrup into a separate bowl and spoon three quarters of it over the cake, then leave it to stand for 30 minutes. Dust the cake with icing sugar and cut into slices. Serve with the remaining syrup drizzled around, accompanied by yogurt.

caribbean coconut cake

ingredients

SERVES 9

280 g/10 oz butter, softened,
   plus extra for greasing
200 g/7 oz golden caster sugar
3 eggs
200 g/7 oz self-raising flour
1$1/2$ tsp baking powder
$1/2$ tsp freshly grated nutmeg
55 g/2 oz desiccated coconut
5 tbsp coconut cream
300 g/10$1/2$ oz icing sugar
5 tbsp pineapple jam
desiccated coconut, toasted,
   to decorate

method

1 Preheat the oven to 180°C/350°F/Gas Mark 4. Grease and base-line two 20-cm/8-inch sponge tins. Place 175 g/6 oz of the butter in a bowl with the sugar and eggs and sift in the flour, baking powder and nutmeg. Beat together until smooth, then stir in the coconut and 2 tablespoons of the coconut cream.

2 Divide the mixture between the prepared tins and smooth the tops. Bake in the preheated oven for 25 minutes, or until golden and firm to the touch. Leave to cool in the tins for 5 minutes, then turn out onto a wire rack, peel off the lining paper and leave to cool completely.

3 Sift the icing sugar into a bowl and add the remaining butter and coconut cream. Beat together until smooth. Spread the pineapple jam on one of the cakes and top with just under half of the buttercream. Place the other cake on top. Spread the remaining buttercream on top of the cake and scatter over the toasted coconut.

honey spice cake

ingredients

SERVES 8

150 g/5$^1/_2$ oz butter, plus extra
   for greasing
100 g/3$^1/_2$ oz brown sugar
150 g/5$^1/_2$ oz honey
1 tbsp water
225 g/8 oz self-raising flour
$^1/_2$ tsp ground ginger
$^1/_2$ tsp ground cinnamon
$^1/_2$ tsp caraway seeds
seeds from 8 cardamom pods,
   ground
2 eggs, beaten
400 g/14 oz icing sugar

method

1 Preheat the oven to 180°C/350°F/Gas Mark 4. Grease a fluted cake tin. Place the butter, sugar, honey and water into a heavy-based saucepan. Place over low heat and stir until the butter has melted and the sugar has dissolved. Remove from the heat and leave to cool for 10 minutes.

2 Sift the flour into a bowl and mix in the ginger, cinnamon, caraway seeds and cardamom. Make a well in the centre. Pour in the honey mixture and the eggs and beat well until smooth. Pour the batter into the prepared tin and bake in the preheated oven for 40–50 minutes, or until well risen and a skewer inserted into the centre comes out clean. Leave to cool in the tin for 5 minutes, then transfer to a wire rack to cool completely.

3 Sift the icing sugar into a bowl. Stir in enough warm water to make a smooth, flowing frosting. Spoon over the cake, allowing it to flow down the sides, then leave to set.

blueberry & lemon drizzle cake

ingredients

SERVES 12

225 g/8 oz butter, softened, plus extra for greasing

200 g/7 oz golden caster sugar

4 eggs, beaten

280 g/10 oz self-raising flour, sifted

finely grated rind and juice of 1 lemon

55 g/2 oz ground almonds

200 g/7 oz fresh blueberries

topping

juice of 2 lemons

100 g/3¹/₂ oz golden caster sugar

method

1 Preheat the oven to 180°C/350°F/Gas Mark 4, then grease and base-line a 20-cm/8-inch square cake tin. Place the butter and sugar in a bowl and beat together until light and fluffy. Gradually beat in the eggs, adding a little flour towards the end to prevent curdling. Beat in the lemon rind, then fold in the remaining flour and almonds with enough of the lemon juice to give a good dropping consistency.

2 Fold in three quarters of the blueberries and turn into the prepared tin. Smooth the surface, then scatter the remaining blueberries on top. Bake in the preheated oven for 1 hour, or until firm to the touch and a skewer inserted in the centre comes out clean.

3 To make the topping, put the lemon juice and sugar in a bowl and mix together. As soon as the cake comes out of the oven, prick it all over with a fine skewer and pour over the lemon mixture. Leave to cool in the tin until completely cold, then cut into 12 squares to serve.

apple streusel cake

ingredients

SERVES 8

450 g/1 lb tart cooking apples
lemon juice
200 g/7 oz self-raising flour
1 tsp ground cinnamon
pinch of salt
115 g/4 oz butter, plus extra
    for greasing
100 g/3½ oz golden caster
    sugar
2 eggs
1–2 tbsp milk
icing sugar, for dusting

streusel topping
125 g/4½ oz self-raising flour
75 g/2¾ oz butter
100 g/3½ oz golden caster
    sugar

method

1 Preheat the oven to 180°C/350°F/Gas Mark 4, then grease a 23-cm/9-inch springform cake tin. To make the streusel topping, sift the flour into a bowl and rub in the butter until the mixture resembles coarse crumbs. Stir in the sugar and set aside.

2 Peel, core and thinly slice the apples. To make the cake, sift the flour into a bowl with the cinnamon and salt. Place the butter and sugar in a separate bowl and beat together until light and fluffy. Gradually beat in the eggs, adding a little of the flour mixture with the last addition of egg. Gently fold in half the remaining flour mixture, then fold in the rest with the milk.

3 Spoon the batter into the prepared tin and smooth the top. Cover with the sliced apples and sprinkle the streusel topping evenly over the top. Bake in the preheated oven for 1 hour, or until browned and firm to the touch. Leave to cool in the tin before releasing the side. Dust the cake with icing sugar before serving.

banana & lime cake

ingredients

SERVES 10

butter, for greasing

300 g/10½ oz plain flour

1 tsp salt

1½ tsp baking powder

175 g/6 oz brown sugar

1 tsp grated lime rind

1 egg, beaten

1 banana, mashed with 1 tbsp
    lime juice

150 g/5½ oz low-fat
    mascarpone cheese

115 g/4 oz sultanas

banana chips and finely grated
    lime rind, to decorate

topping

115 g/4 oz icing sugar

1–2 tsp lime juice

½ tsp finely grated lime rind

method

1 Preheat the oven to 180°C/350°F/Gas Mark 4. Grease and line a deep 18-cm/7-inch round cake tin. Sift the flour into a large bowl with the salt and baking powder and stir in the sugar and lime rind.

2 Make a well in the centre of the dry ingredients and add the egg, banana, mascarpone cheese and sultanas. Mix well until thoroughly incorporated. Spoon the batter into the prepared tin and smooth the surface.

3 Bake in the preheated oven for 40–45 minutes, until firm to the touch or until a skewer inserted in the centre comes out clean. Leave to cool in the tin for 10 minutes, then turn out onto a wire rack to cool completely.

4 To make the topping, sift the icing sugar into a small bowl and mix with the lime juice to form a soft, but not too runny topping. Stir in the grated lime rind. Drizzle the topping over the cake, letting it run down the sides. Decorate the cake with banana chips and lime rind. Leave the cake to stand for 15 minutes so that the topping sets.

pear & ginger cake

ingredients

SERVES 6

225 g/8 oz unsalted butter,
    softened, plus extra for
    greasing
150 g/5¹/₂ oz caster sugar
200 g/7 oz self-raising flour,
    sifted
1 tbsp ground ginger
3 eggs, beaten lightly
450 g/1 lb pears, peeled,
    cored, and thinly sliced,
    then brushed with lemon
    juice
1 tbsp brown sugar
ice cream or double cream,
    lightly whipped, to serve

method

1 Preheat the oven to 180°C/350°F/Gas Mark 4. Lightly grease and base-line a 20-cm/8-inch deep round cake tin.

2 Mix all but 2 tablespoons of the butter with the caster sugar, flour, ginger and eggs in a bowl. Beat with a whisk until the mixture forms a smooth consistency.

3 Spoon the cake batter into the prepared tin and level out the surface with a spatula.

4 Arrange the pear slices over the cake batter. Sprinkle with the brown sugar and dot with the remaining butter.

5 Bake in the preheated oven for 35–40 minutes, or until the cake is golden on top and feels springy to the touch.

6 Serve the pear and ginger cake warm, with ice cream.

banana loaf

ingredients

SERVES 8

butter, for greasing

125 g/4$^{1}/_{2}$ oz white self-raising
   flour

100 g/3$^{1}/_{2}$ oz wholemeal
   self-raising flour

150 g/5$^{1}/_{2}$ oz demerara sugar

pinch of salt

$^{1}/_{2}$ tsp ground cinnamon

$^{1}/_{2}$ tsp ground nutmeg

2 large ripe bananas, peeled

175 ml/6 fl oz orange juice

2 eggs, beaten

4 tbsp rapeseed oil

method

1 Preheat the oven to 180°C/350°F/Gas Mark 4. Lightly grease and line a 900-g/2-lb loaf tin.

2 Sift the flours, sugar, salt and the spices into a large bowl. In a separate bowl mash the bananas with the orange juice, then stir in the eggs and oil. Pour into the dry ingredients and mix well.

3 Spoon into the prepared tin and bake in the preheated oven for 1 hour. Test to see if the loaf is cooked by inserting a skewer into the centre. If it comes out clean, the loaf is done. If not, bake for a further 10 minutes and test again.

4 Remove from the oven and leave to cool in the tin. Turn out the loaf, slice and serve.

lemon polenta cake

ingredients

SERVES 8

200 g/7 oz unsalted butter,
    plus extra for greasing
200 g/7 oz caster sugar
finely grated rind and juice of
    1 large lemon
3 eggs, beaten
140 g/5 oz ground almonds
100 g/3½ oz quick-cook
    polenta
1 tsp baking powder
crème fraîche, to serve

syrup
juice of 2 lemons
55 g/2 oz caster sugar
2 tbsp water

method

1 Preheat the oven to 180°C/350°F/Gas Mark 4. Lightly grease and base-line a 20-cm/8-inch deep round cake tin.

2 Beat together the butter and sugar until pale and fluffy. Beat in the lemon rind, lemon juice, eggs and ground almonds. Sift in the polenta and baking powder and stir until evenly mixed.

3 Spoon the mixture into the prepared tin and spread evenly. Bake in the preheated oven for 30–35 minutes, or until just firm to the touch and golden brown. Remove the cake from the oven and leave to cool in the tin for 20 minutes.

4 For the syrup, place the lemon juice, sugar and water in a small saucepan. Heat gently, stirring until the sugar has dissolved, then bring to the boil and simmer for 3–4 minutes, or until slightly reduced and syrupy.

5 Turn out the cake onto a wire rack then drizzle half of the syrup evenly over the surface. Leave to cool completely.

6 Cut the cake into slices, drizzle the extra syrup over the top and serve with crème fraîche.

apple cake with streusel topping

ingredients

SERVES 8

500 g/1 lb 2 oz eating apples, peeled, cored and cut into 1-cm/$\frac{1}{2}$-inch dice

1 tbsp lemon juice

125 g/4$\frac{1}{2}$ oz unsalted butter, plus extra for greasing

125 g/4$\frac{1}{2}$ oz golden caster sugar

2 large eggs, beaten

225 g/8 oz plain flour

3 tsp baking powder

1 tsp ground cinnamon

$\frac{1}{2}$ tsp ground nutmeg

3 tbsp cider or apple juice

streusel topping

40 g/1$\frac{1}{2}$ oz hazelnuts, skinned and finely chopped

40 g/1$\frac{1}{2}$ oz plain flour

25 g/1 oz light muscovado sugar

$\frac{1}{2}$ tsp ground cinnamon

25 g/1 oz unsalted butter, melted

method

1 Preheat the oven to 180°C/350°F/Gas Mark 4. Grease and base-line a 20-cm/8-inch round loose-based cake tin. Toss the apples in the lemon juice.

2 Cream together the butter and caster sugar until pale and fluffy, then gradually add the eggs, beating thoroughly after each addition. Sift together the flour, baking powder, cinnamon and nutmeg into the mixture and fold in lightly and evenly using a metal spoon. Stir in the cider.

3 Stir the apples into the mixture to distribute evenly, then spoon into the prepared tin and level the surface.

4 For the streusel topping, mix together the hazelnuts, flour, sugar and cinnamon, then stir in the melted butter, mixing until crumbly. Spread over the cake.

5 Bake the cake in the preheated oven for 1–1$\frac{1}{4}$ hours, or until firm and golden brown. Cool for 10 minutes in the tin, then remove carefully and finish cooling on a wire rack.

honey & almond cake

ingredients

SERVES 12–16

150 g/5½ oz unsalted butter,
    plus extra for greasing
115 g/4 oz light muscovado
    sugar
175 g/6 oz clear honey
1 tbsp lemon juice
2 eggs, beaten
200 g/7 oz self-raising flour
15 g/½ oz flaked almonds
warmed honey, for glazing

method

1 Preheat the oven to 180°C/350°F/Gas Mark 4. Grease and base-line a 20-cm/8-inch deep square cake tin.

2 Place the butter, sugar, honey and lemon juice in a saucepan and stir over a medium heat, without boiling, until melted and smooth. Remove the pan from the heat and quickly beat in the eggs with a wooden spoon. Sift in the flour and stir lightly and evenly with a metal spoon.

3 Pour the mixture into the prepared tin and scatter the flaked almonds over the top. Bake in the preheated oven for 35–40 minutes, until risen, firm and golden brown.

4 Leave the cake to cool in the tin for about 15 minutes, then turn out and cool completely on a wire rack. Brush with the warmed honey and cut into slices to serve.

pineapple upside-down cake

ingredients

SERVES 10

4 eggs, beaten

200 g/7 oz golden caster sugar

1 tsp vanilla extract

200 g/7 oz plain flour

2 tsp baking powder

125 g/4$^{1}/_{2}$ oz unsalted butter, melted, plus extra for greasing

topping

40 g/1$^{1}/_{2}$ oz unsalted butter

4 tbsp golden syrup

425 g/15 oz canned pineapple rings, drained

4–6 glacé cherries, halved

method

1 Preheat the oven to 160°C/325°F/Gas Mark 3. Grease and base-line a 23-cm/9-inch deep round cake tin.

2 For the topping, place the butter and golden syrup in a heavy-based saucepan and heat gently until melted. Bring to the boil and boil for 2–3 minutes, stirring, until slightly thickened and toffee-like.

3 Pour the syrup into the base of the prepared tin. Arrange the pineapple rings and glacé cherries in one layer over the syrup.

4 Place the eggs, sugar and vanilla extract in a large heatproof bowl over a saucepan of gently simmering water and whisk with an electric mixer for about 10–15 minutes, until thick enough to leave a trail when the whisk is lifted. Sift in the flour and baking powder and fold in lightly and evenly with a metal spoon.

5 Fold the melted butter into the mixture with a metal spoon until evenly mixed. Spoon into the prepared tin and bake in the preheated oven for 1–1$^{1}/_{4}$ hours, or until well risen, firm and golden brown.

6 Leave to cool in the tin for 10 minutes, then carefully turn out onto a serving plate. Serve warm or cold.

orange & poppy seed bundt cake

ingredients

SERVES 10

200 g/7 oz unsalted butter,
    plus extra for greasing
200 g/7 oz golden caster sugar
3 large eggs, beaten
finely grated rind of 1 orange
55 g/2 oz poppy seeds
300 g/10½ oz plain flour, plus
    extra for dusting
2 tsp baking powder
150 ml/5 fl oz milk
125 ml/4 fl oz orange juice
strips of orange zest,
    to decorate

syrup
140 g/5 oz golden caster sugar
150 ml/5 fl oz orange juice

method

1 Preheat the oven to 160°C/325°F/Gas Mark 3. Grease and lightly flour a Bundt ring tin, about 23 cm/9 inches in diameter and with a capacity of approximately 2 litres/3½ pints.

2 Cream together the butter and sugar until pale and fluffy, then add the eggs gradually, beating thoroughly after each addition. Stir in the orange rind and poppy seeds. Sift in the flour and baking powder, then fold in evenly. Add the milk and orange juice, stirring to mix evenly.

3 Spoon the mixture into the prepared tin and bake in the preheated oven for 45–50 minutes, or until firm and golden brown. Leave to cool in the tin for 10 minutes, then turn out onto a wire rack to cool.

4 For the syrup, place the sugar and orange juice in a saucepan and heat gently until the sugar melts. Bring to the boil and simmer for about 5 minutes, until reduced and syrupy.

5 Spoon the syrup over the cake while it is still warm. Top with the strips of orange zest and serve warm or cold.

hummingbird cake

ingredients

SERVES 10

250 g/9 oz plain flour

250 g/9 oz caster sugar

1 tsp ground cinnamon

1 tsp bicarbonate of soda

3 eggs, beaten

200 ml/7 fl oz sunflower oil,
    plus extra for greasing

100 g/3$^{1}/_{2}$ oz pecan nuts,
    roughly chopped, plus
    extra to decorate

3 ripe bananas (about
    375 g/13 oz peeled
    weight), mashed

85 g/3 oz canned crushed
    pineapple (drained weight),
    plus 4 tbsp juice from
    the can

frosting

175 g/6 oz full-fat soft cheese

55 g/2 oz unsalted butter

1 tsp vanilla extract

400 g/14 oz icing sugar

method

1 Preheat the oven to 180°C/350°F/Gas Mark 4. Lightly grease and base-line three 23-cm/9-inch sandwich tins.

2 Sift together the flour, caster sugar, cinnamon and bicarbonate of soda into a large bowl. Add the eggs, oil, pecan nuts, bananas, pineapple and pineapple juice, and stir with a wooden spoon until evenly mixed.

3 Divide the mixture between the prepared tins, spreading evenly. Bake in the preheated oven for 25–30 minutes, or until golden brown and firm to the touch.

4 Remove the cakes from the oven and leave to cool for 10 minutes in the tins before turning out onto wire racks to cool.

5 For the frosting, beat together the soft cheese, butter and vanilla extract in a bowl until smooth. Sift in the icing sugar and mix until smooth.

6 Sandwich the cakes together with half of the frosting, spread the remaining frosting over the top, then sprinkle with pecan nuts to decorate.

strawberry roulade

ingredients

SERVES 8

3 large eggs

125 g/4½ oz caster sugar

125 g/4½ oz plain flour

1 tbsp hot water

1 tbsp toasted flaked almonds,
    to decorate

filling

200 ml/7 fl oz low-fat fromage
    frais

1 tsp almond extract

225 g/8 oz small strawberries

method

1 Preheat the oven to 220°C/425°F/Gas Mark 7. Line a 35 x 25-cm/14 x 10-inch Swiss roll tin with baking paper.

2 Place the eggs in a mixing bowl with the caster sugar. Place the bowl over a saucepan of hot, but not boiling, water and whisk until pale and thick.

3 Remove the bowl from the pan. Sift in the flour and fold into the egg mixture with the hot water. Pour the mixture into the prepared tin and bake in the preheated oven for about 8–10 minutes, until golden and springy to the touch.

4 Remove from the tin and transfer to a sheet of baking paper. Peel off the lining paper and roll up the sponge tightly along with the baking paper. Wrap in a clean tea towel and set aside to cool.

5 For the filling, mix together the fromage frais and almond extract. Cover and chill in the refrigerator until required. Wash, hull and slice the strawberries.

6 Unroll the sponge, spread the fromage frais mixture over it and sprinkle with the sliced strawberries. Roll the sponge up again (without the baking paper this time) and transfer to a serving plate. Sprinkle with the toasted flaked almonds and serve.

citrus mousse cake

ingredients

SERVES 12

175 g/6 oz butter, plus extra
for greasing
175 g/6 oz caster sugar
4 eggs, lightly beaten
200 g/7 oz self-raising flour
1 tbsp cocoa powder
50 g/1¾ oz orange-flavoured
plain chocolate, melted
peeled orange segments, to
decorate

mousse

2 eggs, separated
50 g/1¾ oz caster sugar
200 ml/7 fl oz freshly
squeezed orange juice
2 tsp gelatine
3 tbsp water
300 ml/10 fl oz double cream,
whipped

method

1 Preheat the oven to 180°C/350°F/Gas Mark 4. Grease and base-line a 20-cm/8-inch round springform cake tin.

2 Beat the butter and sugar in a bowl until light and fluffy. Gradually add the eggs, beating well after each addition. Sift together the flour and cocoa and fold into the creamed mixture. Fold in the melted chocolate.

3 Pour into the prepared tin and level the top. Bake in the preheated oven for 40 minutes, or until springy to the touch. Leave to cool for 5 minutes in the tin, then turn out onto a wire rack and leave to cool completely. Cut the cold cake into two layers.

4 To make the orange mousse, beat the egg yolks and sugar until pale, then whisk in the orange juice. Sprinkle the gelatine over the water in a small bowl and allow to go spongy, then place over a saucepan of hot water and stir until dissolved. Stir into the egg yolk mixture.

5 Whisk the egg whites until standing in soft peaks, then fold into the whipped cream. Leave in a cool place until starting to set, stirring occasionally.

6 Place half of the cake in the tin. Pour in the mousse and press the second cake layer on top. Chill until set. Transfer to a serving plate, spoon teaspoonfuls of cream around the top and decorate the centre with orange segments.

chocolate fudge cake

ingredients

SERVES 9

175 g/6 oz unsalted butter,
  softened, plus extra
  for greasing
175 g/6 oz golden caster sugar
3 eggs, beaten
3 tbsp golden syrup
40 g/1½ oz ground almonds
175 g/6 oz self-raising flour
pinch of salt
40 g/1½ oz cocoa powder

icing

225 g/8 oz plain chocolate,
  broken into pieces
55 g/2 oz dark muscovado
  sugar
225 g/8 oz unsalted butter,
  diced
5 tbsp evaporated milk
½ tsp vanilla extract

method

1 Grease and base-line two 20-cm/8-inch round cake tins. To make the icing, place the chocolate, sugar, butter, evaporated milk and vanilla extract in a heavy-based saucepan. Heat gently, stirring constantly, until melted. Pour into a bowl and leave to cool. Cover and chill in the refrigerator for 1 hour, or until spreadable.

2 Preheat the oven to 180°C/350°F/Gas Mark 4. Place the butter and sugar in a bowl and beat together until light and fluffy. Gradually beat in the eggs. Stir in the syrup and ground almonds. Sift the flour, salt and cocoa powder into a separate bowl, then fold into the mixture. Add a little water, if necessary, to make a dropping consistency. Spoon the mixture into the prepared tins and bake in the oven for 30–35 minutes, or until springy to the touch and a skewer inserted in the centre comes out clean.

3 Leave the cakes in the tins for 5 minutes, then turn out on to wire racks to cool completely. When the cakes are cold, sandwich them together with half the icing. Spread the remaining icing over the top and sides of the cake, swirling it to give a frosted appearance.

chocolate truffle torte

ingredients

SERVES 10

butter, for greasing

55 g/2 oz golden caster sugar

2 eggs

25 g/1 oz plain flour

25 g/1 oz cocoa powder, plus
    extra to decorate

60 ml/2 fl oz strong black
    coffee

2 tbsp brandy

topping

600 ml/1 pint whipping cream

425 g/15 oz plain chocolate,
    melted and cooled

icing sugar,
    to decorate

method

1 Preheat the oven to 220°C/425°F/Gas Mark 7. Grease and base-line a 23-cm/9-inch springform cake tin. Place the sugar and eggs in a heatproof bowl and place over a saucepan of hot water. Whisk together until pale and mousse-like. Sift the flour and cocoa powder into a separate bowl, then fold gently into the cake batter. Pour into the prepared tin and bake in the preheated oven for 7–10 minutes, or until risen and firm to the touch.

2 Transfer to a wire rack to cool. Wash and dry the tin and replace the cooled cake in the tin. Mix the coffee and brandy together and brush over the cake. To make the topping, place the cream in a bowl and whip until very soft peaks form. Carefully fold in the cooled chocolate. Pour the chocolate mixture over the sponge. Leave to chill in the refrigerator for 4–5 hours, or until set.

3 To decorate the torte, sift cocoa over the top and carefully remove from the tin. Using strips of card or greaseproof paper, sift bands of icing sugar over the torte to create a striped pattern. To serve, cut into slices with a hot knife.

rich chocolate cake

ingredients

SERVES 10–12

85 g/3 oz raisins

finely grated rind and juice of 1 orange

175 g/6 oz butter, diced, plus extra for greasing

100 g/3½ oz plain chocolate, at least 70% cocoa solids, broken up

4 large eggs, beaten

100 g/3½ oz caster sugar

1 tsp vanilla extract

55 g/2 oz plain flour

115 g/4 oz ground almonds

½ tsp baking powder

pinch salt

55 g/2 oz blanched almonds, toasted and chopped

sifted icing sugar, to decorate

method

1 Preheat the oven to 180°C/350°F/Gas Mark 4. Put the raisins in a small bowl, add the orange juice and leave to soak for 20 minutes. Line a deep 25-cm/10-inch round loose-based cake tin with greaseproof paper and grease the paper; set aside.

2 Melt the butter and chocolate together in a small saucepan over a medium heat, stirring. Remove from the heat and set aside to cool.

3 Using an electric mixer beat the eggs, sugar and vanilla extract together for about 3 minutes until light and fluffy. Stir in the chocolate mixture.

4 Drain the raisins if they haven't absorbed all the orange juice. Sift over the flour, ground almonds, baking powder and salt. Add the raisins, orange rind, and almonds, and fold everything together.

5 Spoon into the cake tin and smooth the surface. Transfer to the preheated oven and bake for about 40 minutes, or until a cocktail stick inserted in the centre comes out clean and the cake starts to come away from the side of the tin. Leave to cool in the tin for 10 minutes, then remove from the tin and leave to cool completely on a wire rack. Dust the surface with icing sugar before serving.

devil's food cake

ingredients

SERVES 10–12

100 g/3¹/₂ oz plain chocolate
250 g/9 oz self-raising flour
1 tsp bicarbonate of soda
225 g/8 oz butter, plus extra
     for greasing
400 g/14 oz dark brown sugar
1 tsp vanilla extract
3 eggs
125 ml/4 fl oz buttermilk
225 ml/8 fl oz boiling water

frosting
300 g/10¹/₂ oz caster sugar
2 egg whites
1 tbsp lemon juice
3 tbsp orange juice
candied orange peel, to
     decorate

method

1 Preheat the oven to 190°C/375°F/Gas Mark 5. Lightly grease and base-line two 20-cm/8-inch shallow round cake tins. Place the chocolate in a heatproof bowl set over a saucepan of simmering water and heat until melted. Sift the flour and bicarbonate of soda together.

2 Place the butter and sugar in a large bowl and beat until pale and fluffy. Beat in the vanilla extract and the eggs, one at a time, beating well after each addition. Add a little flour if the mixture starts to curdle. Fold the melted chocolate into the mixture until well blended. Fold in the remaining flour, then stir in the buttermilk and the boiling water.

3 Divide the mixture between the prepared tins and level the tops. Bake in the preheated oven for 30 minutes, or until springy to the touch. Cool in the tin for 5 minutes, then transfer to a wire rack to cool completely.

4 Place the frosting ingredients in a large bowl set over a saucepan of simmering water. Using an electric whisk, whisk until thick and forming soft peaks. Remove from the heat and whisk until the mixture is cool.

5 Sandwich the two cakes together with a little of the frosting, then spread the remainder over the sides and top of the cake. Decorate with candied orange peel.

chocolate ganache cake

ingredients

SERVES 10

175 g/6 oz butter, plus extra
for greasing
175 g/6 oz caster sugar
4 eggs, beaten lightly
200 g/7 oz self-raising flour
1 tbsp cocoa powder
50 g/1³/₄ oz plain chocolate,
melted

ganache

450 ml/16 fl oz double cream
375 g/13 oz plain chocolate,
broken into pieces
200 g/7 oz chocolate-flavoured
cake covering, to finish

method

1 Preheat the oven to 180°C/ 350°F/Gas Mark 4. Lightly grease and base-line a 20-cm/8-inch springform cake tin. Beat the butter and sugar until light and fluffy. Gradually add the eggs, beating well. Sift the flour and cocoa together. Fold into the cake mixture, then fold in the melted chocolate.

2 Pour into the prepared tin and smooth the top. Bake in the preheated oven for 40 minutes or until springy to the touch. Cool for 5 minutes in the tin, then turn out onto a wire rack to cool completely. Cut into two layers.

3 To make the ganache, place the cream in a saucepan and bring to the boil, stirring. Add the chocolate and stir, until melted and combined. Pour into a bowl and whisk for about 5 minutes, or until fluffy and cool. Set aside one third of the ganache and use the rest to sandwich the cake together and spread smoothly and evenly over the top and sides of the cake.

4 Melt the cake covering and spread it over a large sheet of baking paper. Cool until just set. Cut into strips a little wider than the height of the cake. Place the strips around the edge of the cake, overlapping them slightly. Using a piping bag fitted with a fine tip, pipe the reserved ganache in tear drops or shells to cover the top of the cake. Chill for 1 hour in the refrigerator before serving.

chocolate cake with coffee syrup

ingredients

SERVES 12

225 g/8 oz plain chocolate, broken into pieces

115 g/4 oz unsalted butter, plus extra for greasing

1 tbsp strong black coffee

4 large eggs

2 egg yolks

115 g/4 oz golden caster sugar

55 g/2 oz plain flour

2 tsp ground cinnamon

50 g/1¾ oz ground almonds

chocolate-covered coffee beans, to decorate

syrup

300 ml/10 fl oz strong black coffee

115 g/4 oz golden caster sugar

1 cinnamon stick

method

1 Preheat the oven to 190°C/375°F/Gas Mark 5. Grease and base-line a 20-cm/8-inch round cake tin. Place the chocolate, butter and coffee in a heatproof bowl and place over a saucepan of gently simmering water until melted. Stir, then remove from the heat and cool slightly.

2 Place the eggs, egg yolks and sugar in a separate bowl and whisk together until thick and pale. Sift the flour and cinnamon over the egg mixture. Add the almonds and the chocolate mixture and fold in carefully. Spoon the batter into the prepared tin. Bake in the preheated oven for 35 minutes, or until the tip of a knife inserted into the centre comes out clean. Cool slightly before turning out onto a serving plate.

3 Meanwhile, make the syrup. Place the coffee, sugar and cinnamon stick in a heavy-based saucepan and heat gently, stirring, until the sugar has dissolved. Increase the heat and boil for 5 minutes, or until reduced and thickened slightly. Keep warm. Pierce the surface of the cake with a cocktail stick, then drizzle over half the coffee syrup. Decorate with chocolate-covered coffee beans and serve, cut into wedges, with the remaining coffee syrup.

white truffle cake

ingredients

SERVES 12

butter, for greasing

2 eggs

4 tbsp caster sugar

55 g/2 oz plain flour

50 g/1¾ oz white chocolate,
    melted

plain, milk or white chocolate
    caraque, to decorate

cocoa powder, for dusting

truffle topping

300 ml/10 fl oz double cream

350 g/12 oz white chocolate,
    broken into pieces

250 g/9 oz mascarpone
    cheese

method

1 Preheat the oven to 180°C/350°F/Gas Mark 4. Grease a 20-cm/8-inch springform cake tin and line with baking paper. Whisk the eggs and caster sugar in a mixing bowl for 10 minutes or until the mixture is very light and foamy and the whisk leaves a trail that lasts a few seconds when lifted. Sift the flour and fold in with a metal spoon. Fold in the melted white chocolate. Pour into the prepared tin and bake in the preheated oven for 25 minutes, or until springy to the touch. Cool slightly in the tin, then transfer to a wire rack until completely cold. Return the cold cake to the tin.

2 To make the topping, place the cream in a saucepan and bring to the boil, stirring to prevent it sticking to the base of the pan. Cool slightly, then add the white chocolate pieces and stir until melted and combined. Remove from the heat and stir until almost cool, then stir in the mascarpone cheese. Pour the mixture on top of the cake and chill for 2 hours.

3 Remove the cake from the tin and transfer to a plate. Decorate the top of the cake with the caraque. Dust with cocoa powder.

double chocolate gâteau

ingredients

SERVES 10

225 g/8 oz butter, softened,
      plus extra for greasing
225 g/8 oz golden caster sugar
4 eggs, beaten
175 g/6 oz self-raising flour
55 g/2 oz cocoa powder

filling

250 ml/9 fl oz whipping cream
225 g/8 oz white chocolate,
      broken into pieces

frosting

350 g/12 oz plain chocolate,
      broken into pieces
115 g/4 oz butter
85 ml/3 fl oz double cream

to decorate

chilled chocolate curls
2 tsp icing sugar
2 tsp cocoa powder

method

1 Preheat the oven to 180°C/350°F/Gas Mark 4. Grease and base-line a 20-cm/8-inch deep round cake tin. To make the filling, heat the cream to almost boiling. Place the white chocolate in a food processor and chop coarsely. With the motor running, pour the cream through the feed tube. Process for 10–15 seconds, or until the mixture is smooth. Transfer to a bowl to cool, then cover and chill for 2 hours, or until firm. Whisk the mixture until just starting to hold soft peaks.

2 To make the sponge, beat the butter and sugar together until light and fluffy. Gradually beat in the eggs. Sift the flour and cocoa into another bowl, then fold into the batter. Spoon into the prepared tin, level the surface, and bake in the preheated oven for 45–50 minutes, or until springy to the touch and the tip of a knife inserted into the centre comes out clean. Cool in the tin for 5 minutes, then cool completely on a wire rack.

3 To make the frosting, melt the chocolate. Stir in the butter and cream. Cool, stirring frequently, until the mixture is a spreading consistency. Slice the cake into three layers. Sandwich the layers together with the filling. Cover the cake with frosting and put chocolate curls on top. Mix together the icing sugar and cocoa and sift over the cake.

double chocolate roulade

ingredients

SERVES 8

4 eggs, separated

115 g/4 oz golden caster sugar

115 g/4 oz plain chocolate,
    melted and cooled

1 tsp instant coffee granules,
    dissolved in 2 tbsp hot
    water, cooled

icing sugar and cocoa powder,
    to decorate

fresh raspberries, to serve

filling

250 ml/9 fl oz whipping cream

140 g/5 oz white chocolate,
    broken into pieces

3 tbsp Tia Maria

method

1 Preheat the oven to 180°C/350°F/Gas Mark 4. Line a 23 x 33-cm/9 x 13-inch Swiss roll tin with non-stick baking paper. Whisk the egg yolks and sugar in a bowl until pale and mousse-like. Fold in the chocolate, then the coffee. Place the egg whites in a clean bowl and whisk until stiff but not dry. Stir a little of the egg white into the chocolate mixture, then fold in the remainder. Pour into the prepared tin and bake in the preheated oven for 15–20 minutes, or until firm. Cover the tin with a damp tea towel and set aside for at least 8 hours, or overnight.

2 Meanwhile, make the filling. Heat the cream until almost boiling. Place the chocolate in a food processor and chop coarsely. Pour the cream through the feed tube. Process until smooth. Stir in the Tia Maria. Transfer to a bowl to cool, then chill for 8 hours, or overnight.

3 To assemble the roulade, whip the chocolate cream until soft peaks form. Cut a sheet of greaseproof paper larger than the roulade, place on a work surface and sift icing sugar over it. Turn out the roulade onto the paper. Peel away the lining paper. Spread the chocolate cream over the roulade and roll up from the short side nearest to you. Transfer to a dish, seam-side down. Chill for 2 hours, then dust with cocoa. Serve with raspberries.

chocolate & walnut cake

ingredients

SERVES 8

4 eggs

125 g/4½ oz caster sugar

75 g/2¾ oz plain chocolate, broken into pieces

125 g/4½ oz plain flour

1 tbsp cocoa powder

25 g/1 oz butter, melted, plus extra for greasing

115 g/4 oz walnuts, finely chopped

icing

75 g/2¾ oz plain chocolate

115 g/4 oz butter

175 g/6 oz icing sugar

2 tbsp milk

walnut halves, to decorate

method

1 Preheat the oven to 160°C/325°F/Gas Mark 3. Grease and line an 18-cm/7-inch deep round cake tin. Place the eggs and caster sugar in a bowl and whisk with an electric whisk for 10 minutes, or until foamy and a trail is left when the whisk is dragged across the surface. Put the chocolate in a heatproof bowl set over a saucepan of gently simmering water, until melted.

2 Sift the flour and cocoa together and fold into the eggs and sugar with a spoon or a palette knife. Fold in the melted butter, melted chocolate and chopped walnuts. Pour into the tin and bake in the preheated oven for 30–35 minutes, or until springy to the touch.

3 Leave to cool in the tin for 5 minutes, then transfer to a wire rack and leave to cool completely.

4 To make the icing, melt the chocolate and leave to cool slightly. Beat together the butter, icing sugar and milk until the mixture is pale and fluffy. Whisk in the melted chocolate.

5 Cut the cake into 2 layers of equal thickness. Place the bottom half on a serving plate, spread with some of the icing and put the other half on top. Smooth the remaining icing over the top of the cake with a palette knife, swirling it slightly as you do so for a decorative effect. Decorate the cake with walnut halves, and serve.

chocolate slab cake

ingredients

SERVES 6

200 g/7 oz butter, plus extra
    for greasing
100 g/3$^{1}/_{2}$ oz plain chocolate,
    broken into pieces
75 ml/2$^{1}/_{2}$ fl oz water
350 g/12 oz plain flour
2 tsp baking powder
250 g/9 oz soft light brown
    sugar
75 ml/2$^{1}/_{2}$ fl oz soured cream
2 eggs, beaten

frosting

200 g/7 oz plain chocolate
6 tbsp water
3 tbsp single cream
1 tbsp butter, chilled

method

1 Preheat the oven to 190°C/375°F/Gas Mark 5. Grease and base-line a 33 x 20-cm/13 x 8-inch square cake tin. Melt the butter and chocolate with the water in a saucepan over a low heat, stirring frequently.

2 Sift the flour and baking powder into a mixing bowl and stir in the sugar.

3 Pour the hot chocolate liquid into the bowl and then beat well until all of the ingredients are evenly mixed. Stir in the soured cream, followed by the eggs.

4 Pour the mixture into the prepared cake tin and bake in the preheated oven for 40–45 minutes, until springy to the touch.

5 Leave the cake to cool slightly in the tin before turning it out on to a wire rack. Leave to cool completely.

6 To make the frosting, melt the chocolate with the water in a saucepan over a very low heat, stir in the cream and remove from the heat. Stir in the chilled butter, then pour the frosting over the cooled cake, using a palette knife to spread it evenly over the top of the cake.

chocolate passion cake

ingredients

SERVES 6

butter, for greasing
5 eggs
150 g/5½ oz caster sugar
150 g/5½ oz plain flour
40 g/1½ oz cocoa powder
175 g/6 oz carrots, peeled,
    finely grated, and
    squeezed until dry
50 g/1¾ oz walnuts, chopped
2 tbsp corn oil
350 g/12 oz medium-fat soft
    cheese
175 g/6 oz icing sugar
175 g/6 oz milk or plain
    chocolate, melted

method

1 Preheat the oven to 190°C/375°F/Gas Mark 5. Grease and base-line a 20-cm/8-inch deep round cake tin. Place the eggs and sugar in a large bowl set over a saucepan of gently simmering water and, using an electric whisk, whisk until the mixture is very thick and the whisk leaves a trail that lasts a few seconds when lifted.

2 Remove the bowl from the heat. Sift the flour and cocoa powder into the bowl and carefully fold in. Fold in the carrots, walnuts and corn oil until the cake batter is just blended.

3 Pour into the prepared tin and bake in the preheated oven for 45 minutes. Leave to cool slightly in the tin, then turn out onto a wire rack to cool completely.

4 Beat the soft cheese and icing sugar together until blended, then beat in the melted chocolate. Split the cake in half and sandwich together again with half the chocolate mixture. Cover the top of the cake with the remainder of the chocolate mixture, swirling it with a knife. Chill in the refrigerator or serve immediately.

chocolate & orange cake

ingredients

SERVES 8

175 g/6 oz caster sugar

175 g/6 oz butter or block
    margarine

3 eggs, beaten

175 g/6 oz self-raising flour,
    sifted

2 tbsp cocoa powder, sifted

2 tbsp milk

3 tbsp orange juice

grated rind of 1/2 orange

frosting

175 g/6 oz icing sugar

2 tbsp orange juice

a little melted chocolate

method

1 Preheat the oven to 190°C/375°F/Gas Mark 5. Grease and base-line a 20-cm/8-inch deep round cake tin. Beat the sugar and butter or margarine together in a bowl until light and fluffy. Gradually add the eggs, beating well after each addition. Carefully fold in the flour.

2 Divide the mixture in half. Add the cocoa and milk to one half, stirring until well combined. Flavour the other half with the orange juice and grated orange rind.

3 Place spoonfuls of each mixture into the prepared tin and swirl together with a skewer to create a marbled effect. Bake in the preheated oven for 25 minutes, or until the cake is springy to the touch. Leave to cool in the tin for a few minutes before transferring to a wire rack to cool completely.

4 To make the frosting, sift the icing sugar into a mixing bowl and mix in enough of the orange juice to form a smooth frosting. Spread the frosting over the top of the cake and leave to set. Pipe fine lines of melted chocolate in a decorated pattern over the top.

date & chocolate cake

ingredients

SERVES 6

115 g/4 oz plain chocolate

1 tbsp grenadine

1 tbsp golden syrup

115 g/4 oz unsalted butter,
    plus extra for greasing

55 g/2 oz caster sugar

2 large eggs

85 g/3 oz self-raising flour,
    plus extra for dusting

2 tbsp ground rice

1 tbsp icing sugar, to decorate

filling

115 g/4 oz dried dates,
    chopped

1 tbsp orange juice

1 tbsp demerara sugar

25 g/1 oz blanched almonds,
    chopped

2 tbsp apricot jam

method

1 Preheat the oven to 180°C/350°F/Gas Mark 4. Grease two 18-cm/7-inch sandwich cake tins and dust with flour. Break the chocolate into pieces, then place the chocolate, grenadine and syrup in the top of a double boiler or in a heatproof bowl set over a saucepan of barely simmering water. Stir over a low heat until the chocolate has melted and the mixture is smooth. Remove the pan from the heat and set aside to cool.

2 Beat the butter and caster sugar together in a bowl until pale and fluffy. Gradually beat in the eggs, then beat in the chocolate mixture. Sift the flour into another bowl and stir in the ground rice. Fold the 2 mixtures together.

3 Divide the cake batter between the prepared tins and level the surface. Bake in the preheated oven for 20–25 minutes, or until golden and firm to the touch. Turn out onto a wire rack to cool.

4 To make the filling, put all the ingredients into a saucepan and stir over a low heat for 4–5 minutes, or until fully blended. Remove from the heat, leave to cool, then use the filling to sandwich the cakes together. Dust the top of the cake with icing sugar and serve.

chocolate marshmallow cake

ingredients

SERVES 6

75 g/1³/₄ oz unsalted butter, plus extra for greasing

225 g/8 oz caster sugar

¹/₂ tsp vanilla extract

2 eggs, beaten lightly

85 g/3 oz plain chocolate, broken into pieces

150 ml/5 fl oz buttermilk

175 g/6 oz self-raising flour

¹/₂ tsp bicarbonate of soda

pinch of salt

frosting

175 g/6 oz white marshmallows

1 tbsp milk

2 egg whites

2 tbsp caster sugar

55 g/2 oz milk chocolate, grated, to decorate

method

1 Preheat the oven to 160°C/325°F/Gas Mark 3. Grease an 850-ml/1¹/₂-pint ovenproof bowl. Cream the butter, sugar and vanilla extract together in a bowl until pale and fluffy, then gradually beat in the eggs.

2 Melt the chocolate in a bowl over a saucepan of simmering water. Gradually stir in the buttermilk until well combined. Cool slightly.

3 Sift the flour, bicarbonate of soda and salt into a separate bowl. Add the chocolate and the flour mixtures alternately to the creamed mixture, a little at a time. Spoon the mixture into the prepared bowl and smooth the surface. Bake in the preheated oven for 50 minutes, until a skewer inserted into the centre of the cake comes out clean. Turn out onto a wire rack to cool.

4 Meanwhile, make the frosting. Heat the marshmallows and milk very gently in a small saucepan until the marshmallows have melted. Remove from the heat and cool. Whisk the egg whites until soft peaks form, then add the sugar and continue whisking, until stiff peaks form. Fold into the cooled marshmallow mixture and set aside for 10 minutes.

5 When the cake is cool, cover the top and sides with the marshmallow frosting. Top with grated milk chocolate.

family chocolate cake

ingredients

SERVES 8

125 g/4$\frac{1}{2}$ oz soft margarine,
   plus extra for greasing
125 g/4$\frac{1}{2}$ oz caster sugar
2 eggs
1 tbsp golden syrup
125 g/4$\frac{1}{2}$ oz self-raising flour,
   sifted
2 tbsp cocoa powder, sifted
a little milk or white chocolate,
   melted (optional)

filling and topping

4 tbsp icing sugar, sifted
25 g/1 oz butter
100 g/3$\frac{1}{2}$ oz white or milk
   cooking chocolate

method

1 Preheat the oven to 190°C/375°F/Gas Mark 5. Grease two 18-cm/7-inch shallow cake tins. Place all of the ingredients for the cake in a large mixing bowl and beat with a wooden spoon or electric mixer to form a smooth mixture.

2 Divide the mixture between the prepared tins and smooth the tops. Bake in the preheated oven for 20 minutes, or until springy to the touch. Cool for a few minutes in the tins, then transfer to a wire rack to cool completely.

3 To make the filling, beat the sugar and butter together in a bowl until light and fluffy. Melt the cooking chocolate and beat half into the filling mixture. Use to sandwich the cakes together.

4 Spread the remaining melted cooking chocolate over the top of the cake. Pipe circles of contrasting milk or white chocolate and feather into the cooking chocolate with a cocktail stick, if desired. Allow the cake to set before serving.

dark & white chocolate torte

ingredients

SERVES 6

butter, for greasing
4 eggs
100 g/3½ oz caster sugar
100 g/3½ oz plain flour

filling

300 ml/10 fl oz double cream
150 g/5½ oz plain chocolate,
    broken into small pieces

topping

75 g/2¾ oz white chocolate
1 tbsp butter
1 tbsp milk
4 tbsp icing sugar
chocolate caraque,
    to decorate

method

1 Preheat the oven to 180°C/350°F/Gas Mark 4. Grease and base-line a 20-cm/8-inch springform cake tin. Whisk the eggs and caster sugar in a large bowl with an electric whisk for 10 minutes, or until the mixture is very light and foamy and the whisk leaves a trail that lasts a few seconds when lifted.

2 Sift the flour and fold in with a metal spoon or spatula. Pour into the prepared tin and bake in the preheated oven for 35–40 minutes, or until springy to the touch. Leave to cool slightly in the tin, then transfer to a wire rack to cool completely.

3 For the filling, place the cream in a saucepan and bring to the boil, stirring. Add the chocolate and stir until melted. Remove from the heat, transfer to a bowl and leave to cool. When cool, beat with a wooden spoon until thick.

4 Slice the cold cake horizontally into two layers. Sandwich the layers together with the plain chocolate cream and place on a wire rack.

5 For the topping, melt the chocolate and butter together and stir until blended. Whisk in the milk and icing sugar. Continue whisking for a few minutes until the topping is cool. Pour it over the cake and spread with a spatula to coat the top and sides. Decorate with chocolate caraque. Allow the frosting to set before serving.

chocolate brandy torte

ingredients

SERVES 12

base

250 g/9 oz gingernut biscuits

75 g/2³/4 oz plain chocolate

100 g/3¹/2 oz butter, plus extra
   for greasing

filling

225 g/8 oz plain chocolate

250 g/9 oz mascarpone
   cheese

2 eggs, separated

3 tbsp brandy

300 ml/10 fl oz double cream

4 tbsp caster sugar

to decorate

100 ml/3¹/2 fl oz double cream

chocolate-covered coffee
   beans

method

1 Place the biscuits in a polythene bag and crush with a rolling pin. Transfer to a bowl. Grease a 23-cm/9-inch springform cake tin. Put the chocolate and butter into a small saucepan and heat gently until melted, then pour over the crushed biscuits. Mix well, then press into the base and sides of the prepared tin. Chill the base while preparing the filling.

2 To make the filling, place the chocolate in a heatproof bowl and set over a saucepan of simmering water, stirring, until melted. Remove from the heat and beat in the mascarpone cheese, egg yolks and brandy. Whip the cream until just holding its shape. Fold in the chocolate mixture.

3 Whisk the egg whites in a spotlessly clean, greasefree bowl until soft peaks form. Add the sugar, a little at a time, and whisk until thick and glossy. Fold into the chocolate mixture, in two batches, until just mixed.

4 Spoon the mixture into the prepared base and chill in the refrigerator for at least 2 hours. Carefully transfer to a serving plate. To decorate, whip the cream and pipe onto the torte, add the chocolate-covered coffee beans and serve.

chocolate & almond torte

ingredients

SERVES 10

225 g/8 oz plain chocolate,
   broken into pieces
3 tbsp water
150 g/5$\frac{1}{2}$ oz brown sugar
175 g/6 oz butter, softened,
   plus extra for greasing
25 g/1 oz ground almonds
3 tbsp self-raising flour
5 eggs, separated
100 g/3$\frac{1}{2}$ oz finely chopped
   blanched almonds
icing sugar, for dusting
fresh berries and double
   cream, to serve

method

1 Preheat the oven to 180°C/350°F/Gas Mark 4. Grease and base-line a 23-cm/9-inch loose-based cake tin. Melt the chocolate with the water in a saucepan set over a very low heat, stirring until smooth. Add the sugar and stir until dissolved, removing the pan from the heat to prevent it overheating.

2 Add the butter in small amounts until it has melted into the chocolate. Remove from the heat and lightly stir in the ground almonds and flour. Add the egg yolks one at a time, beating well after each addition.

3 Whisk the egg whites in a large mixing bowl, until they stand in soft peaks, then fold them into the chocolate mixture with a metal spoon. Stir in the chopped almonds. Pour the mixture into the prepared tin and smooth the surface.

4 Bake in the preheated oven for 40–45 minutes, until well risen and firm (the cake will crack on the surface during cooking).

5 Leave to cool in the tin for 30–40 minutes, then turn out onto a wire rack to cool completely. Dust with icing sugar and serve in slices with fresh berries and cream.

chocolate orange mousse cake

ingredients

SERVES 8

100 g/3½ oz caster sugar

100 g/3½ oz butter, plus extra
for greasing

2 eggs, lightly beaten

100 g/3½ oz plain flour

1 tsp baking powder

2 tbsp cocoa powder

finely pared strips of orange
rind, to decorate

mousse

200 g/7 oz plain chocolate

grated rind of 2 oranges

juice of 1 orange

4 eggs, separated

method

1 Preheat the oven to 180°C/350°F/Gas Mark 4. Grease and base-line a 23-cm/9-inch loose-based cake tin. Cream the sugar and butter together in a mixing bowl until pale and fluffy. Gradually add the eggs, beating well with a wooden spoon between each addition. Sift the flour, baking powder and cocoa powder together, fold half into the egg mixture, then fold in the remainder. Spoon the mixture into the prepared tin and level the surface with the back of a spoon. Bake in the preheated oven for 20 minutes or until risen and firm to the touch. Cool in the tin.

2 Meanwhile, melt the chocolate in a bowl placed over a saucepan of gently simmering water, making sure that the base of the bowl does not touch the water. Cool, then stir in the orange rind, orange juice and egg yolks.

3 Whisk the egg whites in a large bowl until stiff peaks form. Gently fold a large spoonful of the egg whites into the chocolate mixture, then fold in the remainder. Spoon the mixture on top of the sponge and level the top with the back of a spoon. Place in the refrigerator to set. Remove the sides of the tin if not already removed (though not the base), then decorate with the orange rind strips and serve.

sicilian cassata

ingredients

SERVES 8

150 g/5¹⁄₂ oz self-raising flour

2 tbsp cocoa powder

1 tsp baking powder

175 g/6 oz butter, softened, plus extra for greasing

175 g/6 oz golden caster sugar

3 eggs

icing sugar, for dusting

chocolate caraque, to decorate

filling

450 g/1 lb ricotta cheese

100 g/3¹⁄₂ oz plain chocolate, grated

115 g/4 oz golden caster sugar

3 tbsp Marsala

55 g/2 oz chopped candied peel

2 tbsp almonds, chopped

method

1 Preheat the oven to 190°C/375°F/Gas Mark 5. Grease and base-line an 18-cm/7-inch round cake tin. Sift the flour, cocoa and baking powder into a large bowl. Add the butter, sugar and eggs and beat together thoroughly until smooth and creamy. Pour the cake batter into the prepared tin and bake in the preheated oven for 30–40 minutes, or until well risen and firm to the touch. Leave to stand in the tin for 5 minutes, then turn out onto a wire rack to cool completely.

2 Wash and dry the cake tin and grease and line it again. To make the filling, rub the ricotta cheese through a sieve into a bowl. Add the grated chocolate, sugar and Marsala and beat together until the mixture is light and fluffy. Stir in the candied peel and almonds.

3 Cut the thin crust off the top of the cake and discard. Cut the cake horizontally into three layers. Place the first slice in the prepared tin and cover with half the ricotta mixture. Repeat the layers, finishing with a cake layer. Press down lightly, cover with a plate and a weight, and chill in the refrigerator for 8 hours, or overnight. To serve, turn out the cake onto a serving plate. Dust with icing sugar and decorate with chocolate caraque.

chocolate fudge gâteau

ingredients

SERVES 10

sunflower oil, for oiling

85 g/3 oz plain chocolate, melted and kept warm

225 g/8 oz butter, softened

225 g/8 oz light muscovado sugar

4 eggs, beaten

225 g/8 oz self-raising flour

55 g/2 oz ground almonds

1–2 tbsp cooled boiled water

115 g/4 oz soft vanilla fudge, chopped small

55 g/2 oz grated plain chocolate and cocoa-dusted chocolate truffles, to decorate

frosting

175 g/6 oz butter, softened

280 g/10 oz icing sugar, sifted

3–4 tbsp single cream

55 g/2 oz muscovado sugar

1 tbsp cocoa powder, sifted

method

1 Preheat the oven to 180°C/350°F/Gas Mark 4. Lightly oil and base-line two 20-cm/8-inch shallow cake tins. Cream the butter and sugar together until light and fluffy, then gradually add the eggs, beating well between each addition and adding a little flour after each addition. Stir in the melted chocolate and the remaining flour and mix lightly together.

2 Stir in the almonds with the water. Mix to form a soft dropping consistency. Stir in the fudge pieces, then divide between the tins and smooth the tops. Bake in the preheated oven for 35–40 minutes. Remove and leave to cool before turning out onto wire racks and discarding the lining paper. Leave until cold.

3 To make the frosting, beat the butter until soft and creamy, then gradually beat in the icing sugar, adding a little cream as the mixture becomes stiff. Add the muscovado sugar with the cocoa powder and stir lightly. Stir in enough of the remaining cream to give a soft, spreadable frosting.

4 Place the grated chocolate on a sheet of baking paper. Split the cakes in half horizontally and sandwich together with a third of the prepared frosting. Spread another third around the sides, then roll the cake in the grated chocolate. Place on a serving plate. Spread the top with the remaining frosting, piping rosettes around the outside edge. Decorate with truffles.

chocolate chestnut gâteau

ingredients

SERVES 8

sunflower oil, for oiling

225 g/8 oz butter, softened

225 g/8 oz caster sugar

4 eggs, beaten

225 g/8 oz self-raising flour

1–2 tbsp cooled boiled water

55 g/2 oz white chocolate,
    grated

a few marrons glacés,
    to decorate

chestnut frosting

115 g/4 oz canned or fresh
    sweetened chestnut purée

55 g/2 oz butter, softened

350 g/12 oz icing sugar, sifted

1–2 tbsp milk

1 tsp vanilla extract

55 g/2 oz plain chocolate,
    melted and kept warm

topping

55 g/2 oz chopped hazelnuts,
    toasted

55 g/2 oz plain chocolate

1 tbsp butter

2 tsp golden syrup

method

1 Preheat the oven to 180°C/350°F/Gas Mark 4. Lightly oil and base-line two 20-cm/8-inch shallow cake tins. Cream the butter and sugar until light and fluffy, then add the eggs a little at a time, beating well and adding a little flour after each addition. Stir in the remaining flour together with the water to give a smooth dropping consistency.

2 Stir in the grated chocolate, mix lightly and divide between the prepared tins. Smooth the tops and bake in the preheated oven for 25 minutes. Leave to cool before turning out and discarding the lining paper. Leave until cold, then split each cake in half horizontally.

3 Cream the chestnut purée and butter together until smooth, then gradually beat in the sifted icing sugar with a little milk to give a spreadable consistency. Stir in the vanilla extract and the melted chocolate. Set aside 2–3 tablespoons of the remaining icing, then use half the icing to sandwich the cakes together. Place the hazelnuts on a sheet of baking paper. Spread the remaining icing round the sides of the cake and roll in the nuts. Place on a serving plate. Place the reserved icing in a piping bag fitted with a star nozzle and pipe rosettes round the edge of the cake.

4 Place the topping ingredients in a heavy-based saucepan and heat gently, stirring, until the chocolate and butter have melted. Leave to cool until starting to thicken, then spoon over the top of the cake. Decorate with marrons glacés.

chocolate cherry gâteau

ingredients

SERVES 6

3 tbsp unsalted butter, melted,
    plus extra for greasing
900 g/2 lb fresh cherries,
    stoned and halved
150 g/5^1/$_2$ oz caster sugar
125 ml/4 fl oz cherry brandy
115 g/4 oz plain flour
25 g/1 oz cocoa powder
^{1}/$_2$ tsp baking powder
4 eggs
1 litre/1^3/$_4$ pints double cream
grated plain chocolate and
    whole fresh cherries,
    to decorate

method

1 Preheat the oven to 180°C/350°F/Gas Mark 4. Grease and line a 23-cm/9-inch round springform cake tin. Put the cherries into a saucepan, add 3 tablespoons of the sugar and the cherry brandy. Simmer for 5 minutes. Drain, reserving the syrup. In another bowl, sift together the flour, cocoa powder and baking powder.

2 Put the eggs in a heatproof bowl and beat in 55 g/2 oz of the sugar. Place the bowl over a saucepan of simmering water and beat for 6 minutes, until thickened. Remove from the heat, then gradually fold in the flour mixture and melted butter. Spoon into the cake tin and bake in the preheated oven for 40 minutes.

3 Remove from the oven and leave to cool. Turn out the cake and cut in half horizontally. Mix the cream with the remaining sugar. Spread the reserved syrup over the cut sides of the cake. Arrange the cherries over one half, top with a layer of cream and place the other half on top. Top with cream, sprinkle with grated chocolate and decorate with cherries.

white chocolate coffee gâteau

ingredients

SERVES 8–10

40 g/1½ oz unsalted butter,
  plus extra for greasing
85 g/3 oz white chocolate
125 g/4½ oz caster sugar
4 large eggs, beaten
2 tbsp very strong black coffee
1 tsp vanilla extract
125 g/4½ oz plain flour
white chocolate curls,
  to decorate

frosting
125 g/4½ oz crème fraîche
175 g/6 oz white chocolate,
  melted and kept warm
125 g/4½ oz icing sugar,
  sifted
1 tbsp coffee liqueur or very
  strong black coffee

method

1 Preheat the oven to 180°C/350°F/Gas Mark 4. Grease and base-line two 20-cm/8-inch sandwich cake tins. Place the butter and chocolate in a bowl set over a saucepan of hot, but not simmering, water and leave over a very low heat until just melted. Stir to mix lightly, then remove from the heat.

2 Place the caster sugar, eggs, coffee and vanilla extract in a large bowl set over a saucepan of hot water and whisk hard with an electric whisk until the mixture is pale and thick enough to leave a trail when the whisk is lifted. Remove from the heat, sift in the flour and fold in lightly and evenly. Quickly fold in the butter and chocolate mixture, then divide the mixture between the prepared tins.

3 Bake in the preheated oven for 25–30 minutes. Leave to cool in the tins for 2 minutes, then run a knife around the edges to loosen and turn out onto a wire rack to cool.

4 For the frosting, stir the crème fraîche into the chocolate, then add the icing sugar and coffee liqueur and mix until smooth. Chill for at least 30 minutes, stirring occasionally, until thick and glossy. Use one third of the frosting to sandwich the cakes together. Spread the remainder over the top and sides. Arrange the chocolate curls over the top of the cake and leave to set.

german chocolate & hazelnut gâteau

ingredients

SERVES 8

175 g/6 oz unsalted butter, softened, plus extra for greasing

150 g/5¹/2 oz self-raising flour, plus extra for dusting

150 g/5¹/2 oz brown sugar

1 tbsp cocoa powder

1 tsp allspice

3 eggs, beaten

125 g/4¹/2 oz ground hazelnuts

2 tbsp black coffee

icing sugar, for dusting

method

1 Preheat the oven to 180°C/350°F/Gas Mark 4. Grease and flour a 19-cm/7¹/2-inch kugelhopf tin. Place the butter and brown sugar in a large mixing bowl and beat together until light and fluffy. Sift the flour, cocoa powder and allspice into a separate bowl.

2 Beat the eggs into the creamed batter, one at a time, adding 1 tablespoon of the flour mixture with the second and third eggs. Fold in the remaining flour mixture, hazelnuts and coffee.

3 Turn into the prepared tin and bake in the preheated oven for 45–50 minutes, or until the cake springs back when lightly pressed. Leave to stand in the tin for 10 minutes, then turn out onto a wire rack to cool completely. Dust generously with icing sugar before serving.

muffins & cupcakes

Cupcakes are so called because they were originally baked in a small cup. Nowadays, we are more likely to use paper or foil cases. They are also sometimes called fairy cakes, clearly a reference to their size but perhaps also to their lightness. Muffins are like slightly larger cupcakes made with a thicker batter. They are usually less sweet and not quite as rich as cupcakes but because they contain baking powder, they rise much higher. Cupcakes are almost always iced but this is not so common with muffins. Note that traditional English muffins are quite different from the popular American version, as they are made from yeast dough and cooked on a griddle.

Both cupcakes and muffins are understandably well-liked by children and muffins, in particular, make a good addition to a school packed lunch. While chocolate is a favourite flavouring, those made with fresh or dried fruit are just as delicious and a healthier option. Of course, adults like cupcakes and muffins too and there are plenty of recipes to suit the more sophisticated palate, flavoured with edible flowers, coffee, lemon and even brandy and liqueurs. Muffins are a good choice for breakfast for all the family as they are tempting and

easy to eat, go well with tea, coffee and milk and, if you must, you can eat them on the move. If they're served still warm from the oven, they are irresistible. In fact, they make great snacks at any time of day, although try not to be too greedy as they are quite high in calories.

drizzled honey cupcakes

ingredients

MAKES 12

100 g/3½ oz self-raising flour
¼ tsp ground cinnamon
pinch of ground cloves
pinch of grated nutmeg
75 g/2¾ oz butter, softened
85 g/3 oz caster sugar
1 tbsp honey
finely grated rind of 1 orange
2 eggs, lightly beaten
85 g/3 oz walnut pieces,
    chopped

topping
15 g/½ oz walnut pieces,
    chopped
¼ tsp ground cinnamon
2 tbsp honey
juice of 1 orange

method

1 Preheat the oven to 190°C/375°F/Gas Mark 5. Put 12 double-layer paper cases on a baking sheet.

2 Sift the flour, cinnamon, cloves and nutmeg together into a bowl. Put the butter and sugar in a separate bowl and beat together until light and fluffy. Beat in the honey and orange rind, then gradually add the eggs, beating well after each addition. Using a metal spoon, fold in the flour mixture. Stir in the walnuts, then spoon the batter into the paper cases.

3 Bake the cupcakes in the preheated oven for 20 minutes, or until well risen and golden brown. Transfer to a wire rack and leave to cool.

4 To make the topping, mix together the walnuts and cinnamon. Put the honey and orange juice in a saucepan and heat gently, stirring, until combined.

5 When the cupcakes have almost cooled, prick the tops all over with a fork or skewer and then drizzle with the warm honey mixture. Sprinkle the walnut mixture over the top of each cupcake and serve warm or cold.

frosted peanut butter cupcakes

ingredients

MAKES 16

50 g/1³/₄ oz butter, softened,
    or soft
    margarine
125 g/4¹/₂ oz soft dark brown
    sugar
175 g/6 oz crunchy peanut
    butter
2 eggs, lightly beaten
1 tsp vanilla extract
250 g/9 oz plain flour
2 tsp baking powder
225 ml/8 fl oz milk

frosting
225 g/8 oz soft cream cheese
25 g/1 oz butter, softened
225 g/8 oz icing sugar

method

1 Preheat the oven to 180°C/350°F/Gas Mark 4. Put 16 paper cases in a muffin tin.

2 Put the butter, sugar and peanut butter in a bowl and beat together for 1–2 minutes, or until well mixed. Gradually add the eggs, beating well after each addition, then add the vanilla extract. Sift in the flour and baking powder and then, using a metal spoon, fold them into the mixture, alternating with the milk. Spoon the batter into the paper cases.

3 Bake the cupcakes in the preheated oven for 25 minutes, or until well risen and golden brown. Transfer to a wire rack and leave to cool.

4 To make the frosting, put the cream cheese and butter in a large bowl and, using an electric hand whisk, beat together until smooth. Sift the icing sugar into the mixture, then beat together until well mixed.

5 When the cupcakes are cold, spread the frosting on top of each cupcake, swirling it with a round-bladed knife. Store the cupcakes in the refrigerator until ready to serve.

rose petal cupcakes

ingredients

MAKES 12

100 g/3 $^1/_2$ oz butter, softened
60 g/2$^1/_4$ oz caster sugar
2 eggs, lightly beaten
1 tbsp milk
few drops extract of rose oil
$^1/_4$ tsp vanilla extract
185 g/6$^1/_2$ oz self-raising flour

frosting

75 g/2$^3/_4$ oz butter, softened
175 g/6 oz icing sugar
pink or purple food colouring
    (optional)
silver balls, to decorate

crystallized rose
    petals

12–24 rose petals
lightly beaten egg white,
    for brushing
caster sugar, for sprinkling

method

1 To make the crystallized rose petals, gently rinse the petals and dry well with kitchen paper. Using a pastry brush, paint both sides of a rose petal with egg white, then coat well with caster sugar. Place on a tray and repeat with the remaining petals. Cover the tray with foil and leave to dry overnight.

2 Preheat the oven to 200°C/400°F/Gas Mark 6. Put 12 double-layer paper cases on a baking sheet.

3 Put the butter and sugar in a bowl and beat together until light and fluffy. Gradually add the eggs, beating well after each addition. Stir in the milk, rose oil extract and vanilla extract, then, using a metal spoon, fold in the flour. Spoon the batter into the paper cases.

4 Bake the cupcakes in the preheated oven for 12–15 minutes, until well risen and golden brown. Transfer to a wire rack and leave to cool.

5 To make the frosting, put the butter in a large bowl and beat until fluffy. Sift in the icing sugar and mix well together. Add a few drops of pink or purple food colouring, if using, to complement the rose petals.

6 When the cupcakes are cold, spread the frosting on top of each cake. Top with 1–2 candied rose petals and sprinkle with silver balls to decorate.

sticky gingerbread cupcakes

ingredients

MAKES 16

40 g/1¹/₂ oz plain flour

2 tsp ground ginger

³/₄ tsp ground cinnamon

1 piece of stem ginger, finely
    chopped

³/₄ tsp bicarbonate of soda

4 tbsp milk

100 g/3¹/₂ oz butter, softened,
    or soft margarine

70 g/2¹/₂ oz soft dark brown
    sugar

2 tbsp treacle

2 eggs, lightly beaten

pieces of stem ginger,
    to decorate

frosting

75 g/2³/₄ oz butter, softened

175 g/6 oz icing sugar

2 tbsp ginger syrup from the
    stem ginger jar

method

1 Preheat the oven to 160°C/325°F/Gas Mark 3. Place 16 double-layer paper cases on a baking sheet.

2 Sift the flour, ground ginger and cinnamon together into a bowl. Add the chopped ginger and toss in the flour mixture until well coated. In a separate bowl, dissolve the bicarbonate of soda in the milk.

3 Put the butter and sugar in a bowl and beat together until fluffy. Beat in the treacle, then gradually add the eggs, beating well after each addition. Beat in the flour mixture, then gradually beat in the milk. Spoon the batter into the paper cases.

4 Bake the cupcakes in the preheated oven for 20 minutes, or until well risen and golden brown. Transfer to a wire rack and leave to cool.

5 To make the frosting, put the butter in a bowl and beat until fluffy. Sift in the icing sugar, add the ginger syrup and beat together until smooth and creamy. Finely chop the stem ginger.

6 When the cupcakes are cold, spread the frosting on top of each cupcake, then decorate with pieces of ginger.

fudge nut muffins

ingredients

MAKES 12

275 g/9¾ oz plain flour
4 tsp baking powder
85 g/3 oz caster sugar
6 tbsp crunchy peanut butter
1 large egg, beaten
55 g/2 oz butter, melted
175 ml/6 fl oz milk
150 g/5½ oz vanilla fudge,
    cut into small pieces
3 tbsp coarsely chopped
    unsalted peanuts

method

1 Preheat the oven to 200°C/400°F/Gas Mark 6. Line a 12-cup muffin tin with double paper muffin cases. Sift the flour and baking powder into a bowl. Stir in the caster sugar. Add the peanut butter and stir until the mixture resembles breadcrumbs.

2 Place the egg, butter and milk in a separate bowl and beat until blended, then stir into the dry ingredients until just blended. Lightly stir in the fudge pieces. Divide the batter evenly between the muffin cases.

3 Sprinkle the chopped peanuts on top and bake in the oven for 20–25 minutes until well risen and firm to the touch. Remove the muffins from the oven and leave to cool for 2 minutes, then place them on a wire rack to cool completely.

fig & almond muffins

ingredients

MAKES 12

275 g/9¾ oz plain flour

1 tsp bicarbonate of soda

½ tsp salt

200 g/7 oz demerara sugar

100 g/3½ oz chopped dried figs

150 g/5½ oz chopped almonds

2 tbsp sunflower oil or groundnut oil

225 ml/8 fl oz water

1 tsp almond extract

2 tbsp chopped almonds, to decorate

method

1 Preheat the oven to 190°C/375°F/Gas Mark 5. Line a 12-cup muffin tin with 12 paper muffin cases. Sift the flour, bicarbonate of soda and salt into a mixing bowl, then add the sugar and stir together.

2 In a separate bowl, mix the figs, almonds and oil together. Stir in the water and almond extract. Add the fruit and nut mixture to the flour mixture and gently stir together. Do not overstir – it is fine for it to be a little lumpy.

3 Divide the muffin batter evenly between the paper cups (they should be about two-thirds full), then sprinkle over the remaining chopped almonds to decorate. Transfer to the oven and bake for 25 minutes, or until risen and golden. Remove the muffins from the oven and serve warm, or place them on a wire rack and leave to cool.

banana & pecan nut cupcakes

ingredients

MAKES 12

90 g/3¼ oz plain flour

1¼ tsp baking powder

¼ tsp bicarbonate of soda

2 ripe bananas

100 g/3½ oz butter, softened,
   or soft margarine

100 g/3½ oz caster sugar

½ tsp vanilla extract

2 eggs, lightly beaten

60 ml/2 fl oz soured cream

60 g/2¼ oz pecan nuts,
   coarsely chopped

topping

100 g/3½ oz butter, softened

115 g/4 oz icing sugar

25 g/1 oz pecan nuts, finely
   chopped

method

1 Preheat the oven to 190°C/375°F/Gas Mark 5. Put 12 double-layer paper cases on a baking sheet.

2 Sift together the flour, baking powder and bicarbonate of soda. Peel the bananas, put them in a bowl and mash with a fork.

3 Put the butter, sugar and vanilla extract in a bowl and beat together until light and fluffy. Gradually add the eggs, beating well after each addition. Stir in the mashed bananas and soured cream. Using a metal spoon, fold in the sifted flour mixture and chopped nuts, then spoon the batter into the paper cases.

4 Bake the cupcakes in the preheated oven for 20 minutes, or until well risen and golden brown. Transfer to a wire rack and leave to cool.

5 To make the topping, put the butter in a bowl and beat until fluffy. Sift in the icing sugar and mix together well. Spread the frosting on top of each cupcake and sprinkle with the chopped pecan nuts before serving.

apple & cinnamon muffins

ingredients

MAKES 6

115 g/4 oz plain wholemeal
    flour
70 g/2^1/$_2$ oz plain white flour
1^1/$_2$ tsp baking powder
pinch of salt
1 tsp ground cinnamon
50 g/1^3/$_4$ oz golden caster
    sugar
2 small eating apples, peeled,
    cored and finely chopped
125 ml/4 fl oz milk
1 egg, beaten
55 g/2 oz butter, melted

topping

12 brown sugar lumps,
    coarsely crushed
^{1}/$_2$ tsp ground cinnamon

method

1 Preheat the oven to 200°C/400°F/Gas Mark 6. Place 6 paper muffin cases in a muffin tin.

2 Sift the flours, baking powder, salt and cinnamon together into a large bowl and stir in the sugar and chopped apples. Put the milk, egg and butter into a separate bowl and mix. Add the wet ingredients to the dry ingredients and gently stir until just combined.

3 Divide the batter evenly between the paper cases. To make the topping, mix the crushed sugar lumps and cinnamon together and sprinkle over the muffins. Bake in the oven for 20–25 minutes, or until risen and golden.

4 Remove the muffins from the oven and serve warm or place them on a wire rack and leave to cool.

warm molten-centred chocolate cupcakes

ingredients

MAKES 8

4 tbsp soft margarine
55 g/2 oz caster sugar
1 large egg
90 g/3¼ oz self-raising flour
1 tbsp cocoa powder
55 g/2 oz plain chocolate
icing sugar, for dusting

method

1 Preheat the oven to 190°C/375°F/Gas Mark 5. Put 8 double-layer paper cases on a baking sheet.

2 Put the margarine, sugar, egg, flour and cocoa powder into a large bowl and, using an electric hand whisk, beat together until just smooth.

3 Spoon half of the batter into the paper cases. Using a teaspoon, make an indentation in the centre of each cake. Break the chocolate into 8 equal squares and place a piece in each indentation, then spoon the remaining cake batter on top.

4 Bake the cupcakes in the preheated oven for 20 minutes, or until well risen and springy to the touch. Leave the cupcakes to stand for 2–3 minutes before serving warm, dusted with sifted icing sugar.

spiced chocolate muffins

ingredients

MAKES 12

100 g/3½ oz butter, softened

125 g/4½ oz caster sugar

100 g/3½ oz soft dark brown sugar

2 large eggs

150 ml/5 fl oz soured cream

5 tbsp milk

250 g/9 oz plain flour

1 tsp bicarbonate of soda

2 tbsp cocoa powder

1 tsp allspice

175 g/6 oz plain chocolate chips

method

1 Preheat the oven to 190°C/375°F/Gas Mark 5. Line a 12-cup muffin tin with paper cases.

2 Place the butter, caster sugar and brown sugar in a bowl and beat well. Beat in the eggs, soured cream and milk until thoroughly mixed. Sift the flour, bicarbonate of soda, cocoa powder and allspice into a separate bowl and stir into the mixture. Add the chocolate chips and mix well. Divide the batter evenly between the paper cases. Bake in the oven for 25–30 minutes.

3 Remove from the oven and leave to cool for 10 minutes. Place on a wire rack and allow to cool completely. Store in an airtight container until required.

devil's food cakes with chocolate frosting

ingredients

MAKES 18

3^1/$_2$ tbsp soft margarine
100 g/3^1/$_2$ oz soft dark brown
      sugar
2 large eggs
100 g/3^1/$_2$ oz plain flour
^{1}/$_2$ tsp bicarbonate of soda
25 g/1 oz cocoa powder
125 ml/4 fl oz soured cream
plain chocolate curls
      (optional), to decorate

frosting
125 g/4^1/$_2$ oz plain chocolate
2 tbsp caster sugar
150 ml/5 fl oz soured cream

method

1 Preheat the oven to 180ºC/350ºF/Gas Mark 4. Put put 18 double-layer paper cases on a baking sheet.

2 Put the margarine, sugar, eggs, flour, bicarbonate of soda and cocoa into a large bowl and, using an electric hand whisk, beat together until just smooth. Using a metal spoon, fold in the soured cream. Spoon the batter into the paper cases.

3 Bake the cupcakes in the preheated oven for 20 minutes, or until well risen and firm to the touch. Transfer to a wire rack to cool.

4 To make the frosting, break the chocolate into a heatproof bowl. Set the bowl over a saucepan of gently simmering water and heat until melted, stirring occasionally. Remove from the heat and leave to cool slightly, then whisk in the sugar and soured cream until combined. Spread the frosting over the tops of the cupcakes and allow to set in the refrigerator before serving. Decorate with chocolate curls, if using.

cranberry & cheese muffins

ingredients

MAKES 18

butter, for greasing
225 g/8 oz plain flour
2 tsp baking powder
1/2 tsp salt
55 g/2 oz caster sugar
55 g/2 oz butter, melted
2 large eggs, lightly beaten
175 ml/6 fl oz milk
115 g/4 oz fresh cranberries
25 g/1 oz freshly grated
    Parmesan cheese

method

1 Preheat the oven to 200°C/400°F/Gas Mark 6. Grease two 9-cup muffin tins with butter.

2 Sift the flour, baking powder and salt into a mixing bowl. Stir in the caster sugar.

3 In a separate bowl, combine the butter, beaten eggs and milk, then pour into the bowl of dry ingredients. Mix lightly together until all of the ingredients are evenly combined, then stir in the fresh cranberries.

4 Divide the mixture evenly between the prepared 18 cups in the muffin tins. Sprinkle the grated Parmesan cheese over the top. Transfer to the preheated oven and bake for 20 minutes or until the muffins are well risen and a golden brown colour.

5 Remove the muffins from the oven and leave them to cool slightly in the tins. Place the muffins on a wire rack to cool completely.

dried cherry cheesecake muffins

ingredients

MAKES 12

150 g/5^1/$_2$ oz butter, plus extra
    for greasing
200 g/7 oz cream cheese
150 g/5^1/$_2$ oz caster sugar
3 large eggs, lightly beaten
300 g/10^1/$_2$ oz self-raising flour
100 g/3^1/$_2$ oz dried cherries,
    chopped
icing sugar, for dusting

method

1 Preheat the oven to 180°C/350°F/Gas Mark 4. Grease a deep 12-cup muffin tin.

2 Melt the butter and cool slightly. In a large bowl, whisk the cream cheese and sugar together, add the eggs one at a time until well combined and then stir in the melted butter.

3 Mix the flour and cherries in a bowl, then stir gently into the mixture. Spoon into the prepared muffin tin, filling each hole to about two-thirds full, and bake in the preheated oven for 12–15 minutes, or until golden brown. Remove from the oven and leave to cool on a wire rack. Eat warm or cold, dusted lightly with icing sugar.

banana pecan muffins

ingredients

MAKES 8

150 g/5¹/₂ oz plain flour

1¹/₂ tsp baking powder

pinch of salt

70 g/2¹/₂ oz golden caster
      sugar

115 g/4 oz shelled pecan nuts,
      roughly chopped

2 large ripe bananas, mashed

5 tbsp milk

25 g/1 oz butter, melted

1 large egg, beaten

¹/₂ tsp vanilla extract

method

1 Preheat the oven to 190°C/375°F/Gas Mark 5. Place 8 paper muffin cases in a muffin tin. Sift the flour, baking powder and salt into a bowl, add the sugar and pecan nuts and stir to combine.

2 Place the mashed bananas, milk, butter, egg and vanilla extract in a separate bowl and mix together. Add the wet ingredients to the dry ingredients and gently stir until just combined.

3 Divide the mixture evenly between the paper cases and bake in the preheated oven for 20–25 minutes or until risen and golden. Remove the muffins from the oven and place them on a wire rack to cool.

nectarine & banana muffins

ingredients

MAKES 12

250 g/9 oz plain flour
1 tsp bicarbonate of soda
1/4 tsp salt
1/4 tsp allspice
100 g/3 1/2 oz caster sugar
55 g/2 oz shelled almonds,
    chopped
175 g/6 oz ripe nectarines,
    peeled and chopped
1 ripe banana, sliced
2 large eggs
75 ml/2 1/2 fl oz sunflower oil or
    groundnut oil
75 ml/2 1/2 fl oz thick natural
    yogurt or banana-flavoured
    yogurt
1 tsp almond extract

method

1 Preheat the oven to 200°C/400°F/Gas Mark 6. Line a 12-cup muffin tin with paper cases. Sift the flour, bicarbonate of soda, salt and allspice into a mixing bowl. Add the caster sugar and chopped almonds and stir together.

2 In a separate large bowl, mash the nectarine and banana together, then stir in the eggs, sunflower oil, yogurt and almond extract. Add the mashed fruit mixture to the flour mixture and then gently stir together until just combined. Do not overstir the mixture – it is fine for it to be a little lumpy.

3 Divide the muffin mixture evenly between the 12 paper cases (they should be about two-thirds full). Transfer to the preheated oven, and bake for 20 minutes or until risen and golden. Serve warm from the oven, or place them on a wire rack to cool.

tropical coconut muffins

ingredients

MAKES 12

sunflower or groundnut oil, for
    oiling
250 g/9 oz plain flour
1 tsp baking powder
1 tsp bicarbonate of soda
1/2 tsp allspice
115 g/4 oz butter
225 g/8 oz brown sugar
2 large eggs, beaten
2 tbsp thick natural yogurt,
    or banana- or pineapple-
    flavoured yogurt
1 tbsp rum
1 ripe banana, sliced
75 g/2 3/4 oz canned pineapple
    rings, drained and chopped
55 g/2 oz desiccated coconut

coconut topping
4 tbsp demerara sugar
1 tsp allspice
25 g/1 oz desiccated coconut

method

1 Preheat the oven to 200°C/400°F/Gas Mark 6. Oil a 12-cup muffin tin with sunflower oil or line it with 12 paper muffin cases. Sift the flour, baking powder, bicarbonate of soda and allspice into a mixing bowl.

2 In a separate large bowl, cream together the butter and brown sugar, then stir in the eggs, yogurt and rum. Add the banana, pineapple and desiccated coconut and mix together gently. Add the pineapple mixture to the flour mixture and then gently stir together until just combined. Do not overstir the mixture – it is fine for it to be a little lumpy.

3 Divide the muffin mixture evenly between the 12 cups in the muffin tin (they should be about two-thirds full). To make the topping, mix the sugar and allspice together and sprinkle over the muffins. Sprinkle over the desiccated coconut, then transfer to the preheated oven. Bake for 20 minutes or until risen and golden. Remove the muffins from the oven and serve warm, or place them on a wire rack to cool.

apple streusel cupcakes

ingredients

MAKES 14

1/2 tsp bicarbonate of soda
280-g/10-oz jar apple sauce
55 g/2 oz butter, softened, or
    soft margarine
85 g/3 oz demerara sugar
1 large egg, lightly beaten
175 g/6 oz self-raising flour
1/2 tsp ground cinnamon
1/2 tsp freshly ground nutmeg

topping
50 g/1 3/4 oz plain flour
50 g/1 3/4 oz demerara sugar
1/4 tsp ground cinnamon
1/4 tsp freshly grated nutmeg
40 g/1 1/2 oz butter

method

1 Preheat the oven to 180°C/350°F/Gas Mark 4. Put 14 paper cases in a muffin tin.

2 First make the topping. Put the flour, sugar, cinnamon and nutmeg in a bowl or in the bowl of a food processor. Cut the butter into small pieces, then either rub it in by hand or blend in the processor until the mixture resembles fine breadcrumbs. Set aside while you make the cakes.

3 To make the cupcakes, add the bicarbonate of soda to the apple sauce and stir until dissolved. Put the butter and sugar in a bowl and beat together until light and fluffy. Gradually beat in the egg. Sift in the flour, cinnamon and nutmeg and, using a large metal spoon, fold into the mixture, alternating with the apple sauce.

4 Spoon the mixture into the paper cases. Sprinkle a little topping over each cupcake to cover the tops and press down gently.

5 Bake the cupcakes in the preheated oven for 20 minutes or until well risen and golden brown. Leave the cakes for 2–3 minutes before serving warm or transfer to a wire rack to cool.

carrot & orange cupcakes with mascarpone frosting

ingredients

MAKES 12

100 g/3¹/₂ oz butter, softened, or soft margarine
115 g/4 oz brown sugar
juice and finely grated rind of 1 small orange
2 large eggs, lightly beaten
175 g/6 oz carrots, grated
25 g/1 oz walnut pieces, roughly chopped
125 g/4¹/₂ oz plain flour
1 tsp ground mixed spice
1¹/₂ tsp baking powder

frosting

280 g/10 oz mascarpone cheese
4 tbsp icing sugar
grated rind of 1 large orange

method

1 Preheat the oven to 180°C/350°F/Gas Mark 4. Put 12 paper muffin cases in a muffin tin.

2 Put the butter, sugar and orange rind in a bowl and beat together until light and fluffy. Gradually add the eggs, beating well after each addition. Squeeze any excess liquid from the carrots and add to the mixture with the walnuts and orange juice. Stir into the mixture until well mixed. Sift in the flour, mixed spice and baking powder and then, using a metal spoon, fold into the mixture. Spoon the mixture into the paper cases.

3 Bake the cupcakes in the preheated oven for 25 minutes, or until well risen, firm to the touch and golden brown. Transfer to a wire rack and leave to cool.

4 To make the frosting, put the mascarpone cheese, icing sugar and orange rind in a large bowl and beat together until well mixed.

5 When the cupcakes are cold, spread a little frosting on top of each, swirling it with a round-bladed knife. Store the cupcakes in the refrigerator until ready to serve.

shredded orange cupcakes

ingredients

MAKES 12

75 g/2³/₄ oz butter, softened,
    or soft margarine
85 g/3 oz caster sugar
1 large egg, lightly beaten
85 g/3 oz self-raising flour
25 g/1 oz ground almonds
grated rind and juice of
    1 small orange

orange topping

1 orange
55 g/2 oz caster sugar
15 g/¹/₂ oz toasted flaked
    almonds

method

1 Preheat the oven to 180°C/350°F/Gas Mark 4. Put 12 double-layer paper cases on a baking sheet.

2 Put the butter and sugar in a bowl and beat together until light and fluffy. Gradually beat in the egg. Add the flour, ground almonds and orange rind and, using a large metal spoon, fold into the mixture. Fold in the orange juice.

3 Spoon the mixture into the paper cases. Bake the cupcakes in the preheated oven for 20–25 minutes, or until well risen and golden brown.

4 Meanwhile, make the topping. Using a citrus zester, pare the rind from the orange, then squeeze the juice. Put the rind, juice and sugar in a saucepan and heat gently, stirring, until the sugar has dissolved, then simmer for 5 minutes.

5 When the cupcakes have cooked, prick them all over with a skewer. Spoon a little warm syrup and rind over each cupcake, then sprinkle the flaked almonds on top. Transfer to a wire rack and leave to cool.

cranberry cupcakes

ingredients

MAKES 14

70 g/2$\frac{1}{2}$ oz butter, softened,
    or soft margarine
100 g/3$\frac{1}{2}$ oz caster sugar
1 large egg
2 tbsp milk
100 g/3$\frac{1}{2}$ oz self-raising flour
1 tsp baking powder
75 g/2$\frac{3}{4}$ oz frozen cranberries

method

1 Preheat the oven to 180°C/350°F/Gas Mark 4. Place 14 double-layer paper cases on a baking sheet.

2 Put the butter and sugar in a bowl and beat together until light and fluffy. Gradually beat in the egg, then stir in the milk. Sift in the flour and baking powder and, using a large metal spoon, fold them into the mixture. Gently fold in the frozen cranberries. Spoon the mixture into the paper cases.

3 Bake the cupcakes in the preheated oven for 15–20 minutes or until well risen and golden brown. Transfer to a wire rack to cool.

coconut cherry cupcakes

ingredients

MAKES 12

100 g/3$\frac{1}{2}$ oz butter, softened,
    or soft margarine
115 g/4 oz caster sugar
2 tbsp milk
2 eggs, lightly beaten
85 g/3 oz self-raising flour
$\frac{1}{2}$ tsp baking powder
85 g/3 oz desiccated coconut
115 g/4 oz glacé cherries,
    quartered
12 whole fresh, glacé or
    maraschino cherries,
    to decorate

frosting
55 g/2 oz butter, softened
115 g/4 oz icing sugar
1 tbsp milk

method

1 Preheat the oven to 180°C/350°F/Gas Mark 4. Place 12 foil cases on a baking sheet.

2 Put the butter and sugar in a bowl and beat together until light and fluffy. Stir in the milk. Gradually add the eggs, beating well after each addition. Sift in the flour and baking powder and fold them in with the coconut. Gently fold in most of the quartered cherries, then spoon the mixture into the paper cases and sprinkle the remaining quartered cherries over the top.

3 Bake the cupcakes in a preheated oven for 20–25 minutes, or until well risen, golden brown and firm to the touch. Transfer to a wire rack to cool.

4 To make the frosting, put the butter in a bowl and beat until fluffy. Sift in the icing sugar and beat together until well mixed, gradually beating in the milk.

5 To decorate the cupcakes, using a piping bag fitted with a large star tip, pipe a little frosting on top of each cupcake, then add a cherry to decorate.

tropical pineapple cupcakes with citrus cream frosting

ingredients

MAKES 12

2 slices of canned pineapple in natural juice

75 g/2³/4 oz butter, softened, or soft margarine

85 g/3 oz caster sugar

1 large egg, lightly beaten

85 g/3 oz self-raising flour

1 tbsp juice from the canned pineapple

frosting

25 g/1 oz butter, softened

100 g/3¹/2 oz soft cream cheese

grated rind of 1 lemon or lime

100 g/3¹/2 oz icing sugar

1 tsp lemon juice or lime juice

method

1 Preheat the oven to 180°C/350°F/Gas Mark 4. Place 12 double-layer paper cases on a baking sheet.

2 Finely chop the pineapple slices. Put the butter and sugar in a bowl and beat together until light and fluffy. Gradually beat in the egg. Add the flour and, using a large metal spoon, fold into the mixture. Fold in the chopped pineapple and the pineapple juice. Spoon the mixture into the paper cases.

3 Bake the cupcakes in the preheated oven for 20 minutes, or until well risen and golden brown. Transfer to a wire rack to cool.

4 To make the frosting, put the butter and cream cheese in a large bowl and, using an electric hand whisk, beat together until smooth. Add the rind from the lemon or lime. Sift the icing sugar into the mixture, then beat together until well mixed. Gradually beat in the juice from the lemon or lime, adding enough to form a spreading consistency.

5 When the cupcakes are cold, spread a little frosting on top of each cake, or fill a piping bag fitted with a large star tip and pipe the frosting on top. Store the cupcakes in the refrigerator until ready to serve.

warm strawberry cupcakes baked in a teacup

ingredients

MAKES 6

100 g/3½ oz butter, softened, plus extra for greasing

4 tbsp strawberry jam

115 g/4 oz caster sugar

2 eggs, lightly beaten

1 tsp vanilla extract

115 g/4 oz self-raising flour

450 g/1 lb small whole fresh strawberries

icing sugar, for dusting

method

1 Preheat the oven to 180°C/350°F/Gas Mark 4. Grease six heavy, round teacups with butter. Spoon 2 teaspoons of the strawberry jam in the bottom of each teacup.

2 Put the butter and sugar in a bowl and beat together until light and fluffy. Gradually add the eggs, beating well after each addition, then add the vanilla extract. Sift in the flour and, using a large metal spoon, fold it into the mixture. Spoon the mixture into the teacups.

3 Stand the cups in a roasting tin, then pour in enough hot water to come one third of the way up the sides of the cups. Bake the cupcakes in the preheated oven for 40 minutes, or until well risen and golden brown and a skewer inserted in the centre comes out clean. If over-browning, cover the cupcakes with a sheet of foil. Leave the cupcakes to cool for 2–3 minutes, then carefully lift the cups from the tin and place them on saucers.

4 Place a few whole strawberries on each cake, then dust them with a little sifted icing sugar. Serve warm with the remaining strawberries.

double chocolate muffins

ingredients

MAKES 12

200 g/7 oz plain flour

25 g/1 oz cocoa powder, plus
extra for dusting

1 tbsp baking powder

1 tsp ground cinnamon

115 g/4 oz golden caster sugar

185 g/6^1/$_2$ oz white chocolate,
broken into pieces

2 large eggs

100 ml/3^1/$_2$ fl oz sunflower
or groundnut oil

200 ml/7 fl oz milk

method

1 Preheat the oven to 200°C/400°F/Gas Mark 6. Line a 12-cup muffin tin with paper muffin cases. Sift the flour, cocoa powder, baking powder and cinnamon into a large mixing bowl. Stir in the sugar and 125 g/4^1/$_2$ oz of the white chocolate.

2 Place the eggs and oil in a separate bowl and whisk until frothy, then gradually whisk in the milk. Stir into the dry ingredients until just blended. Divide the mixture evenly between the paper cases, filling each three-quarters full. Bake in the preheated oven for 20 minutes, or until well risen and springy to the touch. Remove the muffins from the oven, leave to cool in the tin for 2 minutes, then transfer to a wire rack to cool completely.

3 Place the remaining white chocolate in a heatproof bowl, set the bowl over a saucepan of barely simmering water and heat until melted. Spread over the top of the muffins. Leave to set, then dust the tops with a little cocoa powder and serve.

chocolate chip muffins

ingredients

MAKES 12

3 tbsp soft margarine

200 g/7 oz caster sugar

2 large eggs

150 ml/5 fl oz natural yogurt

5 tbsp milk

300 g/10½ oz plain flour

1 tsp bicarbonate of soda

115 g/4 oz plain chocolate
   chips

method

1 Preheat the oven to 200°C/400°F/Gas Mark 6. Line a 12-cup muffin tin with paper muffin cases. Place the margarine and sugar in a mixing bowl and beat with a wooden spoon until light and fluffy. Beat in the eggs, yogurt and milk until combined.

2 Sift the flour and bicarbonate of soda into the mixture. Stir until just blended.

3 Stir in the chocolate chips, then divide the mixture evenly between the paper cases and bake in the preheated oven for 25 minutes or until risen and golden. Remove the muffins from the oven and leave to cool in the tin for 5 minutes, then place them on a wire rack to cool completely.

chocolate orange muffins

ingredients

MAKES 9

sunflower or groundnut oil,
    for oiling
150 g/5½ oz self-raising white
    flour
150 g/5½ oz self-raising
    wholemeal flour
55 g/2 oz ground almonds
55 g/2 oz brown sugar
rind and juice of 1 orange
175 g/6 oz cream cheese
2 large eggs
55 g/2 oz plain chocolate
    chips

method

1 Preheat the oven to 190°C/375°F/Gas Mark 5. Thoroughly oil a 9-cup muffin tin.

2 Sift both flours into a mixing bowl and stir in the ground almonds and sugar.

3 Mix the orange rind and juice, cream cheese and eggs together in a separate bowl. Make a well in the centre of the dry ingredients and stir in the wet ingredients, then add the chocolate chips. Beat well to combine all the ingredients.

4 Divide the mixture between the cups, filling each no more than three-quarters full. Bake in the preheated oven for 20–25 minutes, or until well risen and golden brown.

5 Remove the muffins from the oven and cool slightly on a wire rack, but eat them as fresh as possible.

dark & white fudge cupcakes

ingredients

MAKES 20

200 ml/7 fl oz water
75 g/2¾ oz butter
85 g/3 oz caster sugar
1 tbsp golden syrup
3 tbsp milk
1 tsp vanilla extract
1 tsp bicarbonate of soda
225 g/8 oz plain flour
2 tbsp cocoa powder

topping
50 g/1¾ oz plain chocolate
4 tbsp water
50 g/1¾ oz butter
50 g/1¾ oz white chocolate
350 g/12 oz icing sugar

chocolate curls
100 g/3½ oz plain chocolate
100 g/3½ oz white chocolate

method

1 Preheat the oven to 180°C/350°F/Gas Mark 4. Place 20 double-layer paper cases on two baking sheets.

2 Put the water, butter, caster sugar and golden syrup into a saucepan. Heat gently, stirring, until the sugar has dissolved, then bring to the boil. Reduce the heat and cook gently for 5 minutes. Remove from the heat and cool.

3 Meanwhile, put the milk and vanilla extract into a bowl. Add the bicarbonate of soda and stir to dissolve. Sift the flour and cocoa powder into a separate bowl and add the syrup mixture. Stir in the milk and beat until smooth. Divide the mixture between the paper cases and bake the cupcakes in the preheated oven for 20 minutes or until well risen and firm to the touch. Transfer to a wire rack to cool.

4 To make the topping, break the plain chocolate into a small heatproof bowl, add half the water and half the butter and melt over a saucepan of gently simmering water. Stir until smooth and leave to stand over the water. Using another bowl, repeat with the white chocolate and remaining water and butter. Sift half the sugar into each bowl and beat until smooth and thick. Top the cupcakes with the frostings and leave to set. Decorate with chocolate curls made by shaving the chocolate with a vegetable peeler.

jumbo chocolate chip cupcakes

ingredients

MAKES 8

7 tbsp soft margarine

100 g/3^1/$_2$ oz caster sugar

2 large eggs

100 g/3^1/$_2$ oz self-raising flour

100 g/3^1/$_2$ oz plain chocolate
    chips

method

1 Preheat the oven to 190°C/375°F/Gas Mark 5. Put eight paper muffin cases in a muffin tin.

2 Put the margarine, sugar, eggs and flour in a large bowl and, using an electric hand whisk, beat together until just smooth. Fold in the chocolate chips. Spoon the mixture into the paper cases.

3 Bake the cupcakes in the preheated oven for 20–25 minutes or until well risen and golden brown. Transfer to a wire rack to cool.

mocha cupcakes with whipped cream

ingredients

MAKES 20

2 tbsp instant espresso
    coffee powder
75 g/2³/₄ oz butter
85 g/3 oz caster sugar
1 tbsp clear honey
200 ml/7 fl oz water
225 g/8 oz plain flour
2 tbsp cocoa powder
1 tsp bicarbonate of soda
3 tbsp milk
1 large egg, lightly beaten

topping

225 ml/8 fl oz whipping cream
sifted cocoa powder,
    for dusting

method

1 Preheat the oven to 180°C/350°F/Gas Mark 4. Place 20 double-layer paper cases on two baking sheets.

2 Put the coffee powder, butter, sugar, honey and water into a saucepan and heat gently, stirring, until the sugar has dissolved. Bring to the boil, then reduce the heat and simmer for 5 minutes. Pour into a large heatproof bowl and cool.

3 When the mixture has cooled, sift in the flour and cocoa. Dissolve the bicarbonate of soda in the milk, then add to the mixture with the egg and beat together until smooth. Spoon the mixture into the paper cases.

4 Bake the cupcakes in the preheated oven for 15–20 minutes, or until well risen and firm to the touch. Transfer to a wire rack to cool.

5 For the topping, whisk the cream in a bowl until it holds its shape. Just before serving, spoon a heaped teaspoonful of cream on top of each cake, then dust lightly with sifted cocoa. Store the cupcakes in the refrigerator until ready to serve.

chocolate cupcakes with cream cheese frosting

ingredients

MAKES 18

75 g/2³/₄ oz butter, softened, or soft margarine
100 g/3¹/₂ oz caster sugar
2 eggs, lightly beaten
2 tbsp milk
55 g/2 oz plain chocolate chips
225 g/8 oz self-raising flour
25 g/1 oz cocoa powder

frosting

225 g/8 oz white chocolate
150 g/5¹/₂ oz low-fat cream cheese

method

1 Preheat the oven to 200°C/400°F/Gas Mark 6. Place 18 double-layer paper cases on a baking sheet.

2 Put the butter and sugar into a bowl and beat together until light and fluffy. Gradually add the eggs, beating well after each addition.

3 Add the milk, then fold in the chocolate chips. Sift in the flour and cocoa powder, then fold into the mixture. Spoon the mixture into the paper cases and smooth the tops.

4 Bake the cupcakes in the preheated oven for 20 minutes, or until well risen and springy to the touch. Transfer to a wire rack to cool.

5 To make the frosting, break the chocolate into a small heatproof bowl and set the bowl over a saucepan of gently simmering water until melted. Cool slightly. Put the cream cheese into a bowl and beat until soft, then beat in the slightly cooled chocolate.

6 Spread a little of the frosting over the top of each cupcake, then chill in the refrigerator for 1 hour before serving.

tiny chocolate cupcakes with ganache frosting

ingredients

MAKES 20

50 g/1¾ oz butter, softened
55 g/2 oz caster sugar
1 large egg, lightly beaten
55 g/2 oz self-raising flour
2 tbsp cocoa powder
1 tbsp milk
20 chocolate-coated coffee
    beans, to decorate
    (optional)

frosting
100 g/3½ oz plain chocolate
100 ml/3½ fl oz double cream

method

1 Preheat the oven to 190°C/375°F/Gas Mark 5. Put 20 double-layer mini paper cases on two baking sheets.

2 Put the butter and sugar in a bowl and beat together until light and fluffy. Gradually beat in the egg. Sift in the flour and cocoa and then, using a metal spoon, fold them into the mixture. Stir in the milk.

3 Fill a piping bag fitted with a large plain tip with the mixture and pipe it into the paper cases, filling each one until half full.

4 Bake the cakes in the preheated oven for 10–15 minutes, or until well risen and firm to the touch. Transfer to a wire rack to cool.

5 To make the frosting, break the chocolate into a saucepan and add the cream. Heat gently, stirring, until the chocolate has melted. Pour into a large heatproof bowl and, using an electric hand whisk, beat the mixture for 10 minutes or until thick, glossy and cool.

6 Fill a piping bag fitted with a large star tip with the frosting and pipe a swirl on top of each cupcake. Alternatively, spoon over the frosting. Chill in the refrigerator for 1 hour before serving. Serve decorated with a chocolate-coated coffee bean, if using.

frosted lavender muffins

ingredients

MAKES 12

1 large cooking apple, peeled, cored and thinly sliced
3 tbsp water
150 g/5¹/₂ oz plain flour
1 tsp baking powder
1 tsp bicarbonate of soda
pinch of salt
50 g/1³/₄ oz butter
4 tbsp caster sugar
1 large egg, beaten
¹/₂ tsp vanilla extract
1 tbsp dried lavender flowers, stripped from their stalks

lavender icing

100 g/3¹/₂ oz icing sugar
1 tbsp dried lavender flowers
1 tbsp liquid glucose
1–2 tbsp milk

method

1 The day before you make the muffins, place the icing sugar in a bowl, then add the dried lavender flowers. Cover with clingfilm and leave overnight until ready for use.

2 To make the muffins, place the sliced apple and water in a saucepan and bring to the boil, then cover and simmer for 15–20 minutes, stirring occasionally, until the water has been absorbed. Remove from the heat and cool. Process in a food processor until smooth.

3 Preheat the oven to 200°C/400°F/Gas Mark 6. Line a 12-cup muffin tin with 12 paper cases. Sift the flour, baking powder, bicarbonate of soda and salt into a mixing bowl. In a separate bowl, cream together the butter and caster sugar, then stir in the beaten egg, vanilla extract, apple purée and dried lavender flowers. Stir the egg mixture into the flour mixture until just combined. Do not overstir the mixture – it is fine for it to be a little lumpy.

4 Divide the muffin mixture between the paper cases (they should be about two-thirds full). Transfer to the preheated oven and bake for 20 minutes or until risen and golden. Cool completely on a wire rack.

5 To finish making the icing, sift the sugar/lavender mixture into a bowl and discard the flowers. Stir in the liquid glucose and enough milk to make the icing easy to spread. Spread each muffin with icing and serve.

irish coffee muffins

ingredients

MAKES 12

280 g/10 oz plain flour
1 tbsp baking powder
pinch of salt
85 g/3 oz butter
55 g/2 oz demerara sugar
1 large egg, beaten
125 ml/4 fl oz double cream
1 tsp almond extract
2 tbsp strong coffee
2 tbsp coffee-flavoured liqueur
4 tbsp Irish whiskey
whipped double cream,
    to serve (optional)

method

1 Preheat the oven to 200°C/400°F/Gas Mark 6. Line a 12-cup muffin tin with 12 foil cases. Sift the flour, baking powder and salt into a large mixing bowl.

2 In a separate large bowl, cream the butter and sugar together, then stir in the beaten egg. Pour in the double cream, almond extract, coffee, liqueur and whiskey and stir together. Add the whiskey mixture to the flour mixture and then gently stir together until just combined. Do not overstir the mixture – it is fine for it to be a little lumpy.

3 Divide the muffin mixture evenly between the 12 cups in the muffin tin (they should be about two-thirds full). Transfer to the preheated oven and bake for 20 minutes or until risen and golden. Remove the muffins from the oven and serve warm, or place them on a wire rack to cool. If liked, fill the muffins with whipped double cream, to serve.

mocha muffins

ingredients

MAKES 12

225 g/8 oz plain flour

1 tbsp baking powder

2 tbsp cocoa powder

pinch of salt

115 g/4 oz butter, melted

150 g/5½ oz demerara sugar

1 large egg, beaten

125 ml/4 fl oz milk

1 tsp almond extract

2 tbsp strong coffee

1 tbsp instant coffee powder

55 g/2 oz plain chocolate
    chips

25 g/1 oz raisins

cocoa topping

3 tbsp demerara sugar

1 tbsp cocoa powder

1 tsp allspice

method

1 Preheat the oven to 190°C/375°F/Gas Mark 5. Line a 12-cup muffin tin with 12 paper muffin cases. Sift the flour, baking powder, cocoa powder and salt into a large mixing bowl.

2 In a separate large bowl, cream the butter and sugar together, then stir in the beaten egg. Pour in the milk, almond extract and coffee, then add the coffee powder, chocolate chips and raisins and gently mix together.

3 Add the raisin mixture to the flour mixture and stir together until just combined. Do not overstir the mixture – it is fine for it to be a little lumpy.

4 Divide the muffin mixture evenly between the 12 cups in the muffin tin (they should be about two-thirds full). To make the topping, place the sugar in a bowl, add the cocoa and allspice and mix together well. Sprinkle the topping over the muffins, then transfer to the preheated oven and bake for 20 minutes, or until risen and golden. Remove the muffins from the oven and serve warm, or place them on a wire rack and leave to cool.

triple chocolate muffins

ingredients

MAKES 12

225 g/8 oz plain flour

25 g/1 oz cocoa powder

2 tsp baking powder

1/2 tsp bicarbonate of soda

100 g/3 1/2 oz plain chocolate
chips

100 g/3 1/2 oz white chocolate
chips

2 large eggs, beaten

300 ml/10 fl oz soured cream

85 g/3 oz brown sugar

85 g/3 oz butter, melted

method

1 Preheat the oven to 200°C/400°F/Gas Mark 6. Line a 12-cup muffin tin with foil cases. Sift the flour, cocoa, baking powder and bicarbonate of soda into a large bowl, add the plain chocolate chips and white chocolate chips and stir.

2 Place the eggs, soured cream, sugar and melted butter in a separate mixing bowl and mix well. Add the wet ingredients to the dry ingredients and stir gently until just combined.

3 Divide the mixture between the foil cases and bake in the preheated oven for 20 minutes, or until well risen and firm to the touch. Remove from the oven and serve warm, or place on a wire rack to cool.

rice muffins with amaretto

ingredients

MAKES 9

butter, for greasing

150 g/5^1/$_2$ oz plain flour

1 tbsp baking powder

^{1}/$_2$ tsp bicarbonate of soda

^{1}/$_2$ tsp salt

1 large egg

4 tbsp honey

125 ml/4 fl oz milk

2 tbsp sunflower or groundnut
   oil

^{1}/$_2$ tsp almond extract

55 g/2 oz cooked risotto rice

2–3 amaretti biscuits, roughly
   crushed

amaretto butter

1 tbsp clear honey

1–2 tbsp amaretto

100 g/3^1/$_2$ oz mascarpone
   cheese

method

1 Preheat the oven to 200°C/400°F/Gas Mark 6. Grease nine cups of a 12-cup muffin tin. Sift the flour, baking powder, bicarbonate of soda and salt into a large bowl and stir. Make a well in the centre.

2 In a separate bowl, beat the egg, honey, milk, oil and almond extract with an electric whisk for about 2 minutes or until light and frothy. Gradually beat in the rice. Pour into the well in the dry ingredients and, using a fork, stir lightly until just combined.

3 Divide the mixture evenly between the nine cups in the muffin tin. Sprinkle each muffin with biscuit crumbs and bake in the preheated oven for 15 minutes, or until risen and golden. The tops should spring back when pressed. Remove from the oven and cool in the tin for about 1 minute. Carefully remove the muffins and cool slightly.

4 To make the amaretto butter, place the honey, amaretto and mascarpone cheese in a small bowl and beat together. Spoon into a small serving bowl and serve with the warm muffins.

brandied cherry muffins

ingredients

MAKES 12

1 tbsp sunflower or groundnut
   oil, for oiling (if using)
225 g/8 oz plain flour
1 tbsp baking powder
pinch of salt
40 g/1^1/$_2$ oz butter
2 tbsp caster sugar
1 large egg, beaten
200 ml/7 fl oz milk
2 tsp cherry brandy
300 g/10^1/$_2$ oz drained canned
   cherries, chopped

method

1 Preheat the oven to 200°C/400°F/Gas Mark 6. Line a 12-cup muffin pan with 12 paper muffin cases. Sift the flour, baking powder and salt into a large mixing bowl.

2 In a separate large bowl, cream the butter and caster sugar together, then stir in the beaten egg. Pour in the milk and cherry brandy, then add the chopped cherries and gently stir together. Add the cherry mixture to the flour mixture, then gently stir together until just combined. Do not overstir the mixture – it is fine for it to be a little lumpy.

3 Divide the muffin mixture between the 12 paper cases (they should be about two-thirds full). Transfer to the preheated oven and bake for 20–25 minutes, or until risen and golden. Remove from the oven and serve warm, or place them on a wire rack to cool.

apricot muffins with cointreau

ingredients

MAKES 12

125 g/4¹/₂ oz self-raising flour

2 tsp baking powder

175 g/6 oz butter

125 g/4¹/₂ oz caster sugar

2 large eggs, beaten

125 ml/4 fl oz milk

4 tbsp single cream

1 tbsp orange-flavoured
   liqueur, such as Cointreau

85 g/3 oz ready-to-eat dried
   apricots, chopped

85 g/3 oz ready-to-eat dried
   dates, stoned and chopped

cinnamon topping

3 tbsp demerara sugar

1 tsp ground cinnamon

1 tbsp freshly grated orange
   rind

method

1 Preheat the oven to 190°C/375°F/Gas Mark 5. Line a 12-cup muffin tin with 12 double-layer paper muffin cases.

2 Sift the flour and baking powder into a large mixing bowl.

3 In a separate large bowl, cream together the butter and caster sugar, then stir in the beaten eggs. Pour in the milk, cream and orange-flavoured liqueur, then add the chopped apricots and dates and gently mix together. Add the fruit mixture to the flour mixture and then gently stir together until just combined. Do not overstir the mixture – it is fine for it to be a little lumpy.

4 Divide the muffin mixture evenly between the 12 paper liners (they should be about two-thirds full). To make the topping, place the sugar in a small bowl, then mix in the cinnamon and orange rind. Sprinkle the topping over the muffins, then transfer to the oven and bake in the preheated oven for 20 minutes or until risen and golden. Remove the muffins from the oven and serve warm, or place them on a wire rack to cool.

marshmallow muffins

ingredients

MAKES 12

70 g/2^1/$_2$ oz butter

280 g/10 oz plain flour

6 tbsp cocoa powder

3 tsp baking powder

85 g/3 oz caster sugar

100 g/3^1/$_2$ oz milk chocolate
    chips

55 g/2 oz multi-coloured mini
    marshmallows

1 large egg, beaten

300 ml/10 fl oz milk

method

1 Preheat the oven to 190°C/375°F/Gas Mark 5. Line a 12-cup muffin tin with paper muffin cases. Melt the butter in a saucepan.

2 Sift the flour, cocoa powder and baking powder together into a large bowl. Stir in the sugar, chocolate chips and marshmallows until thoroughly mixed.

3 Whisk the egg, milk and melted butter together in a separate bowl, then gently stir into the flour to form a stiff mixture. Divide the mixture evenly between the muffin cases.

4 Bake in the preheated oven for 20–25 minutes, or until well risen and golden brown. Remove from the oven and cool in the tin for about 5 minutes, then place on a wire rack to cool completely.

lime & poppy seed muffins

ingredients

MAKES 12

225 g/8 oz plain flour

1 tsp baking powder

1/2 tsp salt

225 g/8 oz caster sugar

1 large egg

1 large egg white

175 ml/6 fl oz sunflower or
    groundnut oil

150 ml/5 fl oz milk

1 tbsp lime juice

1 tbsp grated lime rind

2 tsp poppy seeds

2 tsp grated lime rind and
    1–2 tsp poppy seeds,
    to decorate

method

1 Preheat the oven to 190°C/375°F/Gas Mark 5. Line a 12-cup muffin tin with 12 paper muffin cases.

2 Sift the flour, baking powder and salt into a mixing bowl. Then add the caster sugar and stir together.

3 In a separate bowl, whisk the egg, egg white, oil and milk together, then stir in the lime juice and grated lime rind. Add the egg mixture to the flour mixture, then add the poppy seeds and gently stir. Do not overstir the mixture – it is fine for it to be a little lumpy.

4 Divide the muffin mixture evenly between the 12 paper cases (they should be about two-thirds full). Sprinkle over the grated lime rind and poppy seeds to decorate, then bake in the preheated oven, for 25 minutes, or until risen and golden. Serve the muffins warm, or place them on a wire rack and leave to cool.

doughnut muffins

ingredients

MAKES 12

175 g/6 oz butter, softened,
    plus extra for greasing
200 g/7 oz caster sugar
2 large eggs, lightly beaten
375 g/13 oz plain flour
3/4 tbsp baking powder
1/4 tsp bicarbonate of soda
pinch of salt
1/2 tsp freshly grated nutmeg
250 ml/9 fl oz milk

topping

100 g/3½ oz caster sugar
1 tsp ground cinnamon
25 g/1 oz butter, melted

method

1 Preheat the oven to 180°C/350°F/Gas Mark 4. Grease a deep 12-cup muffin tin. In a large bowl, beat the butter and sugar together until light and creamy. Add the eggs, a little at a time, beating well between additions.

2 Sift the flour, baking powder, bicarbonate of soda, salt and nutmeg together. Add half to the creamed mixture with half of the milk.

3 Gently fold the ingredients together before incorporating the remaining flour and milk. Spoon the mixture into the prepared muffin tin, filling each hole to about two-thirds full.

4 Bake in the preheated oven for 15–20 minutes, or until the muffins are lightly brown and firm to the touch.

5 For the topping, mix the sugar and cinnamon together. While the muffins are still warm from the oven, brush lightly with melted butter, and sprinkle over the cinnamon and sugar mixture. Eat warm or cold.

marbled chocolate cupcakes

ingredients

MAKES 21

175 g/6 oz soft margarine

175 g/6 oz caster sugar

3 eggs

175 g/6 oz self-raising flour

2 tbsp milk

55 g/2 oz plain chocolate, melted

method

1 Preheat the oven to 180°C/350°F/Gas Mark 4. Put 21 paper baking cases in a muffin tin, or place 21 double-layer paper cases on a baking sheet.

2 Put the margarine, sugar, eggs, flour and milk in a large bowl and, using an electric hand whisk, beat together until just smooth.

3 Divide the mixture between two bowls. Add the melted chocolate to one bowl and stir together until well mixed. Using a teaspoon, and alternating the chocolate mixture with the plain mixture, put 4 half-teaspoons into each paper case.

4 Bake the cupcakes in the preheated oven for 20 minutes, or until well risen and springy to the touch. Transfer to a wire rack to cool.

banana & date muffins

ingredients

MAKES 12

225 g/8 oz plain flour

2 tsp baking powder

1/4 tsp salt

1/2 tsp allspice

5 tbsp caster sugar

2 large egg whites

2 ripe bananas, sliced

55 g/2 oz ready-to-eat dried
    dates, stoned and chopped

4 tbsp skimmed milk

5 tbsp maple syrup

method

1 Preheat the oven to 200°C/400°F/Gas Mark 6. Line a 12-cup muffin tin with 12 paper muffin cases. Sift the flour, baking powder, salt and allspice into a mixing bowl. Add the caster sugar and mix together.

2 In a separate bowl, whisk the egg whites together. Mash the sliced bananas in a separate bowl, then add them to the egg whites. Add the dates, then pour in the milk and maple syrup and stir together gently to mix. Add the banana and date mixture to the flour mixture and then gently stir together until just combined. Do not overstir the mixture – it is fine for it to be a little lumpy.

3 Divide the muffin mixture evenly between the 12 paper cases (they should be about two-thirds full).

4 Bake in the preheated oven for 25 minutes, or until risen and golden. Remove the muffins from the oven and serve warm, or place them on a wire rack to cool.

apple & raspberry muffins

ingredients

MAKES 12

3 large baking apples, peeled
   and cored
450 ml/16 fl oz water
1 1/2 tsp allspice
300 g/10 1/2 oz plain
   wholemeal flour
1 tbsp baking powder
1/4 tsp salt
3 tbsp caster sugar
85 g/3 oz fresh raspberries

method

1 Thinly slice 2 apples and place them in a saucepan with 6 tablespoons of the water. Bring to the boil, then reduce the heat. Stir in 1/2 teaspoon of the allspice, cover the pan and simmer, stirring occasionally, for 15–20 minutes, or until the water has been absorbed. Remove from the heat and cool. Blend in a food processor until smooth. Stir in the remaining water and mix well.

2 Preheat the oven to 200°C/400°F/Gas Mark 6. Line a 12-cup muffin tin with 12 paper muffin cases. Sift the flour, baking powder, salt and remaining allspice into a mixing bowl. Then stir in the sugar.

3 Chop the remaining apple and add to the flour mixture. Add the raspberries, then combine gently with the flour mixture until lightly coated. Finally, gently stir in the cooled apple/water mixture. Do not overstir the mixture – it is fine for it to be a little lumpy.

4 Divide the muffin mixture evenly between the 12 paper cases (they should be about two-thirds full).

5 Bake in the preheated oven for 25 minutes, or until risen and golden. Remove the muffins from the oven and serve warm, or place them on a wire rack to cool.

dairy-free berry muffins

ingredients

MAKES 12

1 large cooking apple, peeled, cored and thinly sliced

3 tbsp water

1 tsp allspice

225 g/8 oz plain white flour or wholemeal flour

1 tbsp baking powder

1/4 tsp salt

40 g/1 1/2 oz wheatgerm

25 g/1 oz fresh raspberries

25 g/1 oz fresh strawberries, hulled and chopped

6 tbsp maple syrup

2 tbsp sunflower or groundnut oil

175 ml/6 fl oz apple juice

method

1 Place the sliced apple and the water in a saucepan and bring to the boil. Reduce the heat and stir in half of the allspice, then cover the pan and simmer, stirring occasionally, for 15–20 minutes, or until the water has been absorbed. Remove the pan from the heat and cool. Transfer the apple mixture to a food processor and blend until smooth.

2 Preheat the oven to 190°C/375°F/Gas Mark 5. Line a 12-cup muffin tin with 12 paper muffin cases.

3 Sift the flour, baking powder, salt and the remaining allspice into a mixing bowl, then stir in the wheatgerm.

4 In a separate bowl, mix the raspberries, strawberries, maple syrup, oil, puréed apple and apple juice together. Add the fruit mixture to the flour mixture and gently stir until just combined. Do not overstir the mixture – it is fine for it to be a little lumpy.

5 Divide the muffin mixture evenly between the 12 paper cases (they should be about two-thirds full). Transfer to the preheated oven and bake for 25 minutes, or until risen and golden. Remove from the oven and serve warm, or place them on a wire rack to cool.

blueberry muffins

ingredients

MAKES 12

225 g/8 oz plain flour
1 tsp bicarbonate of soda
1/4 tsp salt
1 tsp allspice
115 g/4 oz caster sugar
3 large egg whites
3 tbsp low-fat margarine
150 ml/5 fl oz thick low-fat
   natural or blueberry-
   flavoured yogurt
1 tsp vanilla extract
85 g/3 oz fresh blueberries

method

1 Preheat the oven to 190°C/375°F/Gas Mark 5. Line a 12-cup muffin tin with 12 paper muffin cases.

2 Sift the flour, bicarbonate of soda, salt and half of the allspice into a large mixing bowl. Add 6 tablespoons of the caster sugar and mix together.

3 In a separate bowl, whisk the egg whites together. Add the margarine, yogurt and vanilla extract and mix together well, then stir in the fresh blueberries until thoroughly mixed. Add the fruit mixture to the flour mixture, then gently stir until just combined. Do not overstir the mixture – it is fine for it to be a little lumpy.

4 Divide the muffin mixture evenly between the 12 paper cups (they should be about two-thirds full). Mix the remaining sugar with the remaining allspice, then sprinkle the mixture over the muffins. Transfer to the preheated oven and bake for 25 minutes, or until risen and golden. Remove the muffins from the oven and serve warm, or place them on a wire rack to cool.

fruity muffins

ingredients

MAKES 10

280 g/10 oz self-raising
    wholemeal flour
2 tsp baking powder
2 tbsp brown sugar
85 g/3 oz ready-to-eat dried
    apricots, finely chopped
1 banana, mashed with 1 tbsp
    orange juice
1 tsp finely grated orange rind
300 ml/10 fl oz skimmed milk
1 large egg, beaten
3 tbsp sunflower or
    groundnut oil
2 tbsp rolled oats
honey, fruit spread or maple
    syrup, to serve

method

1 Preheat the oven to 200°C/400°F/Gas Mark 6. Line ten cups of a 12-cup muffin tin with paper muffin cases. Sift the flour and baking powder into a mixing bowl, adding any husks that remain in the sieve. Stir in the sugar and chopped apricots.

2 Make a well in the centre and add the mashed banana, orange rind, milk, beaten egg and oil. Mix together well to form a thick mixture and divide the mixture evenly between the muffin cases.

3 Sprinkle with a few rolled oats and bake in the preheated oven for 25–30 minutes, or until well risen and firm to the touch or until a cocktail stick inserted into the centre comes out clean.

4 Remove the muffins from the oven and place them on a wire rack to cool slightly. Serve the muffins while still warm with a little honey.

honey & lemon muffins

ingredients

MAKES 12

50 g/1³/₄ oz caster sugar

2 tbsp unsalted butter, melted and cooled slightly

150 ml/5 fl oz buttermilk

2 eggs, beaten

4 tbsp flower honey

finely grated rind of 1 lemon and juice of ¹/₂ lemon

225 g/8 oz plain flour

150 g/5¹/₂ oz oat bran

1¹/₂ tbsp baking powder

method

1 Preheat the oven to 180°C/350°F/Gas Mark 4. Line a 12-cup muffin tin with paper muffin cases. Put the sugar into a jug and add the butter, buttermilk, eggs, half the honey and lemon rind. Mix briefly to combine.

2 Sift the flour into a large mixing bowl, add the oat bran and baking powder, and stir to combine. Make a well in the centre of the flour mixture and add the buttermilk mixture. Quickly mix together – do not overmix; the mixture should be slightly lumpy.

3 Spoon the mixture into the paper muffin cases and bake in the preheated oven for 25 minutes. Turn out onto a wire rack.

4 Mix the lemon juice with the remaining honey in a small bowl or jug and drizzle over the muffins while they are still hot. Leave the muffins to stand for 10 minutes before serving.

easter cupcakes

ingredients

MAKES 12

100 g/3¹/₂ oz butter, softened,
    or soft margarine
115 g/4 oz caster sugar
2 eggs, lightly beaten
85 g/3 oz self-raising flour
25 g/1 oz cocoa powder

topping

75 g/2³/₄ oz butter, softened
175 g/6 oz icing sugar
1 tbsp milk
2–3 drops of vanilla extract
36 mini sugar-coated
    chocolate eggs, to decorate

method

1 Preheat the oven to 180°C/350°F/Gas Mark 4. Line a 12-hole muffin tin with 12 paper cases.

2 Put the butter and sugar in a bowl and beat together until light and fluffy. Gradually add the eggs, beating well after each addition. Sift in the flour and cocoa and, using a large metal spoon, fold into the mixture. Spoon the mixture into the paper cases.

3 Bake the cupcakes in the preheated oven for 15–20 minutes, or until well risen and firm to the touch. Transfer to a wire rack to cool.

4 To make the buttercream topping, put the butter in a bowl and beat until fluffy. Sift in the icing sugar and beat together until well mixed, adding the milk and vanilla extract.

5 When the cupcakes are cold, put the topping in a piping bag fitted with a large star tip and pipe a circle around the edge of each cupcake to form a nest. Place 3 chocolate eggs in the centre of each nest, to decorate.

halloween cupcakes

ingredients

MAKES 12

8 tbsp soft margarine
115 g/4 oz caster sugar
2 eggs
115 g/4 oz self-raising flour

topping

200 g/7 oz orange ready-to-roll
    coloured fondant icing
icing sugar, for dusting
55 g/2 oz black ready-to-roll
    coloured fondant icing
black cake writing icing
silver cake writing icing

method

1 Preheat the oven to 180°C/350°F/Gas Mark 4. Line a 12-hole muffin tin with 12 paper cases.

2 Put the margarine, sugar, eggs and flour in a bowl and, using an electric hand whisk, beat together until smooth. Spoon the mixture into the cases.

3 Bake the cupcakes in the preheated oven for 15–20 minutes, or until well risen, golden brown and firm to the touch. Transfer to a wire rack to cool.

4 Knead the orange icing until pliable, then roll out on a work surface dusted with icing sugar. Using the palm of your hand, lightly rub icing sugar into the icing to prevent it spotting. Using a 5.5-cm/2¼-inch plain round cutter, cut out 12 circles, re-rolling the icing as necessary. Place a circle on top of each cupcake.

5 Roll out the black icing on a work surface lightly dusted with icing sugar. Using the palm of your hand, lightly rub icing sugar into the icing to prevent it spotting. Using a 3-cm/1¼-inch plain round cutter, cut out 12 circles and place them on the centre of the cupcakes. Using black writing icing, pipe eight legs on each spider and, using silver writing icing, draw two eyes and a mouth.

christmas cupcakes

ingredients

MAKES 16

60 g/2¼ oz butter, softened
200 g/7 oz caster sugar
4–6 drops almond extract
4 eggs, lightly beaten
150 g/5½ oz self-raising flour
175 g/6 oz ground almonds

topping

450 g/1 lb white ready-to-roll
    fondant icing
55 g/2 oz green ready-to-roll
    coloured fondant icing
25 g/1 oz red ready-to-roll
    coloured fondant icing
icing sugar, for dusting

method

1 Preheat the oven to 180°C/350°F/Gas Mark 4. Put 16 paper muffin cases in a muffin tin.

2 Put the butter, sugar and almond extract in a bowl and beat together until light and fluffy. Gradually add the eggs, beating well after each addition. Add the flour and, using a large metal spoon, fold it into the mixture, then fold in the ground almonds. Spoon the mixture into the paper cases to half-fill them.

3 Bake the cakes in the preheated oven for 20 minutes, or until well risen and firm to the touch. Transfer to a wire rack to cool.

4 When the cakes are cold, knead the white icing until pliable, then roll out on a work surface lightly dusted with icing sugar. Using a 7-cm/2¾-inch plain round cutter, cut out 16 circles, re-rolling the icing as necessary. Place a circle on top of each cupcake.

5 Roll out the green icing on a work surface lightly dusted with icing sugar. Using the palm of your hand, rub icing sugar into the icing to prevent it spotting. Using a holly leaf-shaped cutter, cut out 32 leaves, rerolling the icing as necessary. Brush each leaf with a little cooled boiled water and place two leaves on top of each cake. Roll the red icing between the palms of your hands to form 48 berries and place in the centre of the leaves.

valentine heart cupcakes

ingredients

MAKES 6

75 g/2³/₄ oz butter, softened,
   or soft margarine
85 g/3 oz caster sugar
¹/₂ tsp vanilla extract
2 eggs, lightly beaten
70 g/2¹/₂ oz plain flour
1 tbsp cocoa powder
1 tsp baking powder

marzipan hearts
35 g/1¹/₄ oz marzipan
red food colouring (liquid
   or paste)
icing sugar, for dusting

topping
55 g/2 oz butter, softened
115 g/4 oz icing sugar
25 g/1 oz plain chocolate,
   melted
6 chocolate flower decorations

method

1 Line a tray with greaseproof paper and dust with icing sugar. To make the hearts, knead the marzipan until pliable, then add a few drops of red colouring and knead until evenly coloured red. Roll out the marzipan to a thickness of 5 mm/¹/₄ inch on a work surface dusted with icing sugar. Using a small heart-shaped cutter, cut out 6 hearts. Place on the prepared tray and set aside to dry for 3–4 hours.

2 Preheat the oven to 180°C/350°F/Gas Mark 4. Put six paper muffin cases in a muffin tin.

3 Put the butter, sugar and vanilla extract in a bowl and beat together until light and fluffy. Gradually add the eggs, beating well after each addition. Sift in the flour, cocoa and baking powder and, using a large metal spoon, fold into the mixture. Spoon the mixture into the paper cases. Bake the cupcakes in the preheated oven for 20–25 minutes, or until well risen and firm to the touch. Transfer to a wire rack to cool.

4 To make the topping, put the butter in a large bowl and beat until fluffy. Sift in the icing sugar and beat together until smooth. Add the melted chocolate and beat together until well mixed. When the cakes are cold, spread a little frosting on top of each cake and decorate with a chocolate flower.

cupcake wedding cake

ingredients

MAKES 48

450 g/1 lb butter, softened
450 g/1 lb caster sugar
2 tsp vanilla extract
8 large eggs, lightly beaten
450 g/1 lb self-raising flour
150 ml/5 fl oz milk

topping

550 g/1 lb 4 oz icing sugar
48 ready-made sugar roses,
    or 48 small fresh rosebuds
    gently rinsed and left to dry
    on kitchen paper

to assemble the
    cake

1 x 50-cm/20-inch,
    1 x 40-cm/16-inch,
    1 x 30-cm/12-inch and
    1 x 20-cm/8-inch
    sandblasted glass discs
    with polished edges, or
    4 silver cake boards
13 white or Perspex cake
    pillars
1 small bouquet of fresh
    flowers in a small vase

method

1 Preheat the oven to 180°C/350°F/Gas Mark 4. Put 48 paper baking cases in a muffin tin.

2 Put the butter, sugar and vanilla extract in a bowl and beat together until light and fluffy. Gradually add the eggs, beating well after each addition. Add the flour and, using a large metal spoon, fold into the mixture with the milk. Spoon the mixture into the paper cases.

3 Bake the cupcakes in the preheated oven for 15–20 minutes, or until well risen and firm to the touch. Transfer to a wire rack to cool.

4 To make the topping, sift the icing sugar into a large bowl. Add 3–4 tablespoons of hot water and stir until the mixture is smooth and thick enough to coat the back of a wooden spoon. Spoon a little on top of each cupcake. Store in an airtight container for up to one day.

5 On the day of serving, carefully place a sugar rose or rosebud on top of each cupcake. To arrange the cupcakes, place the largest disc or board on a table where the finished display is to be. Stand 5 pillars on the disc and arrange some of the cupcakes on the base. Continue with the remaining bases, pillars (using only 4 pillars to support each remaining tier), and cupcakes to make 4 tiers, standing the bouquet of flowers in the centre of the top tier.

christening cupcakes

ingredients

MAKES 24

400 g/14 oz butter, softened
400 g/14 oz caster sugar
finely grated rind of 2 lemons
8 eggs, lightly beaten
400 g/14 oz self-raising flour

topping
350 g/12 oz icing sugar
red or blue food colouring
    (liquid or paste)
24 sugared almonds

method

1 Preheat the oven to 180°C/350°F/Gas Mark 4. Put 24 paper muffin cases in muffin tins.

2 Put the butter, sugar and lemon rind in a bowl and beat together until light and fluffy. Gradually add the eggs, beating well after each addition. Add the flour and, using a large metal spoon, fold into the mixture. Spoon the mixture into the paper cases to half-fill them.

3 Bake the cupcakes in the preheated oven for 20–25 minutes, or until well risen and firm to the touch. Transfer to a wire rack to cool.

4 When the cakes are cold, make the topping. Sift the icing sugar into a bowl. Add 6–8 teaspoons of hot water and stir until the mixture is smooth and thick enough to coat the back of a wooden spoon. Dip a skewer into the red or blue food colouring, then stir it into the icing until it is evenly coloured pale pink or pale blue.

5 Spoon a little icing on top of each cupcake. Top each with a sugared almond and allow to set for about 30 minutes before serving.

birthday party cupcakes

ingredients

MAKES 24

225 g/8 oz soft margarine
225 g/8 oz caster sugar
4 eggs
225 g/8 oz self-raising flour

topping

175 g/6 oz butter, softened
350 g/12 oz icing sugar
a variety of edible sugar flower
    shapes, cake decorating
    sprinkles, silver balls and
    sugar strands
tubes of different-coloured
    writing frosting
24 birthday cake candles
    (optional)

method

1 Preheat the oven to 180°C/350°F/Gas Mark 4. Put 24 paper baking cases in muffin tins.

2 Put the margarine, sugar, eggs and flour in a large bowl and, using an electric hand whisk, beat together until just smooth. Spoon the mixture into the paper cases.

3 Bake the cupcakes in the preheated oven for 15–20 minutes, or until well risen and firm to the touch. Transfer to a wire rack to cool.

4 To make the frosting, put the butter in a bowl and beat until fluffy. Sift in the icing sugar and beat together until smooth and creamy. When the cupcakes are cold, spread a little frosting on top of each cupcake, then decorate to your choice and, if using, place a candle in the top of each.

gold & silver anniversary cupcakes

ingredients

MAKES 24

225 g/8 oz butter, softened
225 g/8 oz caster sugar
1 tsp vanilla extract
4 large eggs, lightly beaten
225 g/8 oz self-raising flour
5 tbsp milk

topping
175 g/6 oz unsalted butter
350 g/12 oz icing sugar
silver or gold balls

method

1 Preheat the oven to 180°C/350°F/Gas Mark 4. Put 24 silver or gold foil cake cases on baking sheets.

2 Put the butter, sugar and vanilla extract in a bowl and beat together until light and fluffy. Gradually add the eggs, beating well after each addition. Add the flour and, using a large metal spoon, fold into the mixture with the milk. Spoon the mixture into the paper cases.

3 Bake the cupcakes in the preheated oven for 15–20 minutes, or until well risen and firm to the touch. Transfer to a wire rack to cool.

4 To make the topping, put the butter in a large bowl and beat until fluffy. Sift in the icing sugar and beat together until well mixed. Put the topping in a piping bag fitted with a medium star-shaped tip.

5 When the cupcakes are cold, pipe icing on top of each. Sprinkle over the silver or gold balls before serving.

feather-iced coffee cupcakes

ingredients

MAKES 16

1 tbsp instant coffee granules

1 tbsp boiling water

100 g/3^1/$_2$ oz butter, softened,
    or soft margarine

115 g/4 oz brown sugar

2 eggs

115 g/4 oz self-raising flour

^{1}/$_2$ tsp baking powder

2 tbsp soured cream

icing

225 g/8 oz icing sugar

4 tsp warm water

1 tsp instant coffee granules

2 tsp boiling water

method

1 Preheat the oven to 190°C/375°F/Gas Mark 5. Line a 16-cup muffin tin with paper cases.

2 Put the coffee granules in a cup or small bowl, add the boiling water and stir until dissolved. Set aside to cool slightly.

3 Put the butter, sugar and eggs in a bowl. Sift in the flour and baking powder, then beat the ingredients together until smooth. Add the dissolved coffee and the soured cream and beat together until well mixed. Spoon the mixture into the paper cases. Bake in the preheated oven for 20 minutes, or until well risen and golden brown. Transfer to a wire rack to cool.

4 To make the icing, sift 140 g/5 oz of the icing sugar into a bowl, then gradually mix in the warm water to make a coating consistency that will cover the back of a wooden spoon. Dissolve the coffee granules in the boiling water. Sift the remaining icing sugar into a bowl, then stir in the dissolved coffee granules. Spoon the icing into a piping bag fitted with a fine nozzle. When the cupcakes are cold, coat the tops with the white icing, then quickly pipe the coffee icing in parallel lines on top. Using a skewer, draw it across the piped lines in both directions. Leave to set before serving.

small bites

Brownies, squares, slices, bars, tartlets, flapjacks and all kinds of little cakes are quick and easy to make – and even quicker and easier to eat. These tasty sweet snacks run the gamut of textures and flavours – rich gooey chocolate, light zesty citrus, chewy crunchy nuts, moist crumbly spices and fragrant succulent berries. There is certainly something for everyone from after-school snacks to a coffee morning with the neighbours.

Many of these recipes are so simple and have such speedy results that they are a great way to introduce children to cooking and to occupy a rainy afternoon – real quality time. They also make the perfect contribution to the cake stall at fund-raisers, especially as many of them can be cooked in advance and frozen. A batch of home-made brownies can be rustled up in no time, yet will make visitors feel welcome and right at home and they make fabulous picnic or lunch-box treats. Pretty little iced cakes, fruit tartlets, shortcake and éclairs require slightly more effort and time but it's well spent and they may even tempt you to re-introduce the old-fashioned custom of afternoon tea – you don't have to have a silver teapot and a butler to make this a truly delightful occasion.

As these small bites usually bake quickly, it is important to keep an eye on them. Even a few minutes too long can result in unattractive crusty edges. If using a fan oven, reduce the oven temperature slightly and don't switch the fan on until halfway through the cooking time.

chocolate brownies

ingredients

MAKES 12

butter, for greasing

55 g/2 oz unsweetened stoned dates, chopped

55 g/2 oz ready-to-eat dried prunes, chopped

6 tbsp unsweetened apple juice

4 eggs, beaten

300 g/10$\frac{1}{2}$ oz brown sugar

1 tsp vanilla extract

4 tbsp low-fat drinking chocolate powder, plus extra for dusting

2 tbsp cocoa powder

175 g/6 oz plain flour

55 g/2 oz plain chocolate chips

icing

125 g/4$\frac{1}{2}$ oz icing sugar

1–2 tsp water

1 tsp vanilla extract

method

1 Preheat the oven to 180°C/350°F/Gas Mark 4. Grease an 18 x 28-cm/7 x 11-inch cake tin and line with baking paper. Place the dates and prunes in a small saucepan and add the apple juice. Bring to the boil, cover and simmer for 10 minutes, or until soft. Beat to form a smooth paste, then cool.

2 Place the cooled fruit in a mixing bowl and stir in the eggs, sugar and vanilla extract. Sift in the drinking chocolate, cocoa and flour, and fold in along with the chocolate chips until well incorporated.

3 Spoon the mixture into the prepared tin and smooth over the top. Bake in the preheated oven for 25–30 minutes, until firm to the touch or until a skewer inserted into the centre comes out clean. Cut into 12 bars and leave to cool in the tin for 10 minutes. Transfer to a wire rack to cool completely.

4 To make the icing, sift the sugar into a bowl and mix with enough water and the vanilla extract to form a soft, but not too runny, icing. Drizzle the icing over the chocolate brownies and leave to set. Dust with the extra chocolate powder before serving.

super mocha brownies

ingredients

MAKES 12

150 g/5¹/₂ oz plain chocolate
100 g/3¹/₂ oz margarine, plus
   extra for greasing
1 tsp strong instant coffee
1 tsp vanilla extract
100 g/3¹/₂ oz ground almonds
175 g/6 oz caster sugar
4 eggs, separated
icing sugar, to decorate
   (optional)

method

1 Preheat the oven to 180°C/350°F/Gas Mark 4. Grease and base-line a 20-cm/8-inch square cake tin.

2 Melt the chocolate and margarine in a heatproof bowl placed over a saucepan of gently simmering water, making sure that the base of the bowl does not touch the water. Stir very occasionally, until the chocolate and margarine have melted and are smooth.

3 Carefully remove the bowl from the heat. Cool slightly, then stir in the coffee and the vanilla extract. Add the almonds and sugar and mix well until combined. Lightly beat the egg yolks in a separate bowl, then stir into the chocolate mixture.

4 Whisk the egg whites in a large bowl until they form stiff peaks. Gently fold a large spoonful of the egg whites into the chocolate mixture, then fold in the remainder until completely incorporated.

5 Spoon the mixture into the prepared tin and bake in the preheated oven for 35–40 minutes or until risen and firm on top but still slightly gooey in the centre. Leave to cool in the tin, then turn out, remove the lining paper and cut into 12 pieces. Dust with icing sugar before serving, if using.

pecan brownies

ingredients

MAKES 20

70 g/2¹/₂ oz plain chocolate
140 g/5 oz plain flour
³/₄ tsp bicarbonate of soda
¹/₄ tsp baking powder
40 g/1¹/₂ oz pecan nuts
225 g/8 oz unsalted butter,
    plus extra for greasing
55 g/2 oz demerara sugar
¹/₂ tsp almond extract
1 egg
1 tsp milk

method

1 Preheat the oven to 180°C/350°F/Gas Mark 4. Grease a large baking dish and line it with baking paper. Put the chocolate in a heatproof bowl set over a saucepan of gently simmering water and heat until it is melted. Meanwhile, sift together the flour, bicarbonate of soda and baking powder into a large bowl.

2 Finely chop the pecan nuts and set aside. In a separate bowl, beat together the butter and sugar, then mix in the almond extract and the egg. Remove the chocolate from the heat and stir into the butter mixture. Add the flour mixture, milk and chopped nuts to the bowl and stir until well combined.

3 Spoon the mixture into the prepared baking dish and smooth it. Transfer to the preheated oven and cook for 30 minutes, or until firm to the touch (it should still be a little soft in the centre). Remove from the oven and leave to cool completely. Cut into 20 squares and serve.

no-bake chocolate squares

ingredients

MAKES 16

275 g/9¾ oz plain chocolate
175 g/6 oz butter
4 tbsp golden syrup
2 tbsp dark rum (optional)
175 g/6 oz plain biscuits
25 g/1 oz toasted rice cereal
50 g/1¾ oz chopped walnuts
    or pecan nuts
100 g/3½ oz glacé cherries,
    roughly chopped
25 g/1 oz white chocolate,
    to decorate

method

1 Line an 18-cm/7-inch square cake tin with baking paper. Place the plain chocolate in a large bowl with the butter, golden syrup and rum, if using, and set over a saucepan of gently simmering water, stirring constantly, until melted and blended.

2 Break the biscuits into small pieces and stir into the chocolate mixture with the rice cereal, nuts and cherries.

3 Pour the mixture into the tin and level the top, pressing down well with the back of a spoon. Chill in the refrigerator for 2 hours.

4 To decorate, melt the white chocolate and drizzle it over the top of the cake in a random pattern. Leave to set. To serve, carefully turn out of the tin and remove the baking paper. Cut into 16 squares and serve.

chocolate peanut butter squares

ingredients

MAKES 20

300 g/10½ oz milk chocolate
350 g/12 oz plain flour
1 tsp baking powder
225 g/8 oz butter
350 g/12 oz soft light brown
    sugar
175 g/6 oz rolled oats
70 g/2½ oz chopped mixed
    nuts
1 egg, beaten
400 g/14 oz canned
    condensed milk
70 g/2½ oz crunchy peanut
    butter

method

1 Preheat the oven to 180°C/350°F/Gas Mark 4.

2 Finely chop the chocolate. Sift the flour and baking powder into a large bowl. Add the butter to the flour mixture and rub in using your fingertips until the mixture resembles breadcrumbs. Stir in the sugar, rolled oats and nuts.

3 Put a quarter of the mixture into a bowl and stir in the chopped chocolate. Set aside.

4 Stir the egg into the remaining mixture, then press into the base of a 30 x 20-cm/12 x 8-inch baking tin. Bake in the preheated oven for 15 minutes. Meanwhile, mix the condensed milk and peanut butter together. Pour the mixture over the base and spread evenly, then sprinkle the reserved chocolate mixture on top and press down lightly.

5 Return to the oven and bake for a further 20 minutes, until golden brown. Leave to cool in the tin, then cut into squares.

chocolate caramel shortbread

ingredients

MAKES 12

115 g/4 oz butter, plus extra
    for greasing
175 g/6 oz plain flour
55 g/2 oz golden caster sugar

filling and topping

175 g/6 oz butter
115 g/4 oz golden caster sugar
3 tbsp golden syrup
400 g/14 oz canned
    condensed milk
200 g/7 oz plain chocolate,
    broken into pieces

method

1 Preheat the oven to 180°C/350°F/Gas Mark 4. Grease and base-line a 23-cm/9-inch shallow square cake tin.

2 Place the butter, flour and sugar in a food processor and process until it begins to bind together. Press the mixture into the prepared tin and smooth the top. Bake in the preheated oven for 20–25 minutes, or until golden.

3 Meanwhile, make the filling. Place the butter, sugar, golden syrup and condensed milk in a saucepan and heat gently until the sugar has dissolved. Bring to the boil and simmer for 6–8 minutes, stirring constantly, until the mixture becomes very thick. Pour over the shortbread base and leave to chill in the refrigerator until firm.

4 To make the topping, melt the chocolate and leave to cool, then spread over the caramel. Chill in the refrigerator until set. Cut the shortbread into 12 pieces with a sharp knife and serve.

chocolate peppermint slices

ingredients

MAKES 16

4 tbsp unsalted butter, plus
    extra for greasing
55 g/2 oz caster sugar
100 g/3½ oz plain flour
225 g/8 oz icing sugar
1–2 tbsp warm water
½ tsp peppermint extract
175 g/6 oz plain chocolate,
    broken into pieces

method

1 Preheat the oven to 180°C/350°F/Gas Mark 4. Grease and line a 20 x 30-cm/8 x 12-inch Swiss roll tin. Beat the butter and sugar together until pale and fluffy. Stir in the flour until the mixture binds together.

2 Knead the mixture to form a smooth dough, then press into the prepared tin. Prick the surface all over with a fork. Bake in the preheated oven for 10–15 minutes, or until lightly browned and just firm to the touch. Remove from the oven and cool in the tin.

3 Sift the icing sugar into a bowl. Gradually add the water, then the peppermint extract. Spread the frosting over the base, then leave to set.

4 Melt the chocolate in a heatproof bowl set over a saucepan of gently simmering water, then remove from the heat and spread over the frosting. Leave to set, then cut into slices.

chocolate butterfly cakes

ingredients

MAKES 12

8 tbsp soft margarine

100 g/3½ oz caster sugar

150 g/5½ oz self-raising flour

2 large eggs

2 tbsp cocoa powder

25 g/1 oz plain chocolate,
    melted

icing sugar, for dusting

filling

75 g/2¾ oz butter, softened

175 g/6 oz icing sugar

25 g/1 oz plain chocolate,
    melted

method

1 Preheat the oven to 180°C/350°F/Gas Mark 4. Put 12 foil baking cases in a 12-cup muffin tin.

2 Put the margarine, sugar, flour, eggs and cocoa in a large bowl and, using an electric hand whisk, beat together until just smooth. Beat in the melted chocolate. Spoon the mixture into the foil cases, filling them three-quarters full.

3 Bake the cupcakes in the preheated oven for 15 minutes, or until springy to the touch. Transfer to a wire rack to cool completely.

4 To make the filling, put the butter in a bowl and beat until fluffy. Sift in the icing sugar and beat together until smooth. Add the melted chocolate and beat until well mixed.

5 When the cupcakes are cold, use a serrated knife to cut a circle from the top of each cake and then cut each circle in half. Spread or pipe a little of the buttercream into the centre of each cupcake and press the two semicircular halves into it at an angle to resemble butterfly wings. Dust with a little sifted icing sugar before serving.

chocolate tartlets

ingredients

MAKES 4

275 g/10 oz ready-made sweet
    pastry
150 g/5^1/$_2$ oz plain chocolate,
    broken into pieces
50 g/1^3/$_4$ oz butter
100 ml/3^1/$_2$ fl oz whipping
    cream
1 large egg
25 g/1 oz caster sugar
cocoa powder and chocolate
    curls, to decorate
crème fraîche, to serve

method

1 Preheat the oven to 200°C/400°F/Gas Mark 6. Roll out the pastry and use to line four 12-cm/4^1/$_2$-inch loose-based fluted tart tins with removable bases. Line the pastry cases with greaseproof paper, then fill with baking beans. Place on a baking sheet and bake in the preheated oven for 5 minutes, or until the pastry rims look set. Remove the paper and beans and return the pastry cases to the oven for 5 minutes or until the bases look dry. Remove from the oven, then set aside on the baking sheet. Reduce the oven temperature to 180°C/350°F/Gas Mark 4.

2 Meanwhile, place the chocolate in a bowl set over a saucepan of simmering water so that the bowl does not touch the water. Add the butter and cream and heat until the chocolate and butter melt. Remove from the heat.

3 Beat the egg and sugar together until light and fluffy. Stir the melted chocolate mixture until smooth, then stir it into the egg mixture. Carefully pour the filling into the pastry cases, then bake for 15 minutes or until the filling is set and the pastry is golden brown. If the pastry looks as though it is becoming too brown, cover it with foil.

4 Transfer the tartlets to a wire rack to cool completely. Dust with cocoa powder, decorate with chocolate curls and serve with the crème fraîche.

chocolate temptations

ingredients

MAKES 24

350 g/12¹/₂ oz plain chocolate

175 g/6 oz unsalted butter,
plus extra for greasing

1 tsp strong coffee

2 eggs

115 g/4 oz soft light brown
sugar

175 g/6 oz plain flour

¹/₄ tsp baking powder

pinch of salt

2 tsp almond extract

55 g/2 oz chopped Brazil nuts

55 g/2 oz chopped hazelnuts

40 g/1¹/₂ oz white chocolate

method

1 Preheat the oven to 180°C/350°F/Gas Mark 4. Grease two large baking sheets. Place 225 g/8 oz of the plain chocolate with the butter and coffee in a heatproof bowl set over a saucepan of gently simmering water and heat until the chocolate is almost melted.

2 Meanwhile, beat the eggs in a bowl until fluffy. Gradually whisk in the sugar until thick. Remove the chocolate from the heat and stir until smooth. Add to the egg mixture and stir until combined.

3 Sift the flour, baking powder and salt into a bowl, then stir into the chocolate mixture. Chop 85 g/3 oz of the remaining plain chocolate into pieces and stir into the mixture. Stir in the almond extract and chopped nuts.

4 Put 24 tablespoonfuls of the mixture onto the baking sheets, then transfer to the preheated oven and bake for 16 minutes. Remove from the oven and transfer to a wire rack to cool.

5 To decorate, melt the remaining plain chocolate and white chocolate in turn, then spoon into a piping bag and pipe thin lines onto the biscuits.

chocolate fudge brownies

ingredients

MAKES 16

200 g/7 oz low-fat soft cheese

1/2 tsp vanilla extract

2 eggs

225 g/8 oz caster sugar

75 g/2³/4 oz butter, plus extra
    for greasing

3 tbsp cocoa powder

100 g/3¹/2 oz self-raising flour,
    sifted

50 g/1³/4 oz chopped pecan
    nuts

frosting

55 g/2 oz butter

1 tbsp milk

75 g/2³/4 oz icing sugar

2 tbsp cocoa powder

pecan nuts, to decorate
    (optional)

method

1 Preheat the oven to 180°C/350°F/Gas Mark 4. Lightly grease and base-line a 20-cm/8-inch square shallow cake tin.

2 Beat together the cheese, vanilla extract and 5 teaspoons of caster sugar until smooth, then set aside.

3 Beat the eggs and remaining caster sugar together until light and fluffy. Place the butter and cocoa in a small saucepan and heat gently, stirring, until the butter melts and the mixture combines, then stir it into the egg mixture. Fold in the flour and nuts.

4 Pour half of the mixture into the tin and smooth the top. Carefully spread the soft cheese over it, then cover it with the remaining mixture. Bake in the preheated oven for 40–45 minutes. Leave to cool in the tin.

5 To make the frosting, melt the butter in the milk. Stir in the icing sugar and cocoa. Spread the icing over the brownies and decorate with pecan nuts, if using. Leave the frosting to set, then cut into squares to serve.

chocolate crispy bites

ingredients

MAKES 16

white layer

50 g/1³/₄ oz butter, plus extra
    for greasing
1 tbsp golden syrup
150 g/5¹/₂ oz white chocolate
50 g/1³/₄ oz toasted rice cereal

dark layer

50 g/1³/₄ oz butter
2 tbsp golden syrup
125 g/4¹/₂ oz plain chocolate,
    broken into small pieces
75 g/2³/₄ oz toasted rice cereal

method

1 Grease a 20-cm/8-inch square cake tin and line with baking paper.

2 To make the white chocolate layer, melt the butter, golden syrup and chocolate in a bowl set over a saucepan of gently simmering water.

3 Remove from the heat and stir in the rice cereal until it is well combined.

4 Press into the prepared tin and smooth the surface.

5 To make the plain chocolate layer, melt the butter, golden syrup and plain chocolate in a bowl set over a saucepan of gently simmering water.

6 Remove from the heat and stir in the rice cereal. Pour the plain chocolate over the hardened white chocolate layer, leave to cool, then leave to chill until hardened.

7 Turn out of the cake tin and cut into small squares, using a sharp knife.

chocolate parfait slices

ingredients

MAKES 4

3 large egg whites

140 g/5 oz caster sugar

400 ml/14 fl oz whipping
cream, whipped

140 g/5 oz white chocolate,
grated

350 g/12 oz ready-rolled
puff pastry

method

1 To make the parfait, beat the egg whites and the sugar together in a heatproof bowl, then set the bowl over a saucepan of gently simmering water. Using an electric whisk, beat the whites over the heat until you have a light and fluffy meringue. This will take up to 10 minutes. Remove from the heat, add the chocolate and keep whisking to cool. Fold in the whipping cream.

2 Spoon the parfait into a shallow rectangular freezerproof container and freeze for 5–6 hours.

3 Meanwhile, preheat the oven to 180°C/350°F/ Gas Mark 4 and line a baking sheet with baking paper. Cut the pastry into regular-sized rectangles to accommodate a slice of the parfait. Place the pastry rectangles on the baking sheet and top with another baking sheet, which will keep the pastry flat but crisp. Bake in the oven for 15 minutes, transfer to a wire rack and leave to cool.

4 About 20 minutes before you are ready to serve, remove the parfait from the freezer. When it has softened, cut the parfait into slices and put each slice between two pieces of pastry to make a 'sandwich'.

panforte di siena

ingredients

SERVES 12–16

butter, for greasing

55 g/2 oz glacé cherries, quartered

115 g/4 oz mixed candied orange and lemon peel, finely chopped

2 tbsp stem ginger, roughly chopped

115 g/4 oz flaked almonds

115 g/4 oz hazelnuts, toasted and coarsely ground

55 g/2 oz plain flour

25 g/1 oz cocoa powder

1 tsp ground cinnamon

1/4 tsp ground cloves

1/4 tsp ground nutmeg

1/4 tsp ground coriander

115 g/4 oz honey

115 g/4 oz golden caster sugar

1 tsp orange-flower water

icing sugar, for dusting

method

1 Preheat the oven to 160°C/325°F/Gas Mark 3. Thoroughly grease and line the base of a 20-cm/8-inch loose-based cake or tart tin. Place the cherries, peel, ginger, almonds and hazelnuts in a bowl. Sift in the flour, cocoa powder, cinnamon, cloves, nutmeg and coriander and mix. Set aside.

2 Place the honey, sugar and orange-flower water in a saucepan and heat gently until the sugar has dissolved. Bring the mixture to the boil and boil steadily until a temperature of 116°C/241°F has been reached on a sugar thermometer, or a small amount of the mixture forms a soft ball when dropped into cold water.

3 Quickly remove the pan from the heat and stir in the dry ingredients. Mix thoroughly and turn into the prepared tin. Spread evenly and bake in the preheated oven for 30 minutes. Leave to cool in the tin, then turn out and carefully peel away the lining paper. Dust icing sugar lightly over the top and cut into wedges to serve.

refrigerator cake

ingredients

MAKES 12

55 g/2 oz raisins

2 tbsp brandy

115 g/4 oz plain chocolate,
   broken into pieces

115 g/4 oz milk chocolate,
   broken into pieces

55 g/2 oz butter, plus extra
   for greasing

2 tbsp golden syrup

175 g/6 oz digestive biscuits,
   roughly broken

55 g/2 oz flaked almonds,
   lightly toasted

25 g/1 oz glacé cherries,
   chopped

topping

100 g/3^{1}/$_{2}$ oz plain chocolate,
   broken into pieces

20 g/^{3}/$_{4}$ oz butter

method

1 Grease and base-line an 18-cm/7-inch shallow square cake tin. Place the raisins and brandy in a bowl and soak for 30 minutes. Put the chocolate, butter and golden syrup in a saucepan and heat gently until melted.

2 Stir in the biscuits, almonds, cherries, raisins and brandy. Turn into the prepared tin and leave to cool, then cover and chill in the refrigerator for 1 hour.

3 To make the topping, place the chocolate and butter in a small heatproof bowl and melt over a saucepan of gently simmering water. Stir, then pour the chocolate mixture over the biscuit base. Chill in the refrigerator for 8 hours, or overnight. Cut into bars or squares to serve.

malted chocolate wedges

ingredients

MAKES 16

85 g/3 oz butter, plus extra
  for greasing
2 tbsp golden syrup
2 tbsp malted chocolate drink
225 g/8 oz malted milk
  biscuits
75 g/2³/4 oz milk or plain
  chocolate, broken into
  pieces
2 tbsp icing sugar
2 tbsp milk

method

1 Grease and base-line a shallow 18-cm/7-inch round cake tin or flan tin.

2 Place the butter, golden syrup and malted chocolate drink in a small saucepan and heat gently, stirring constantly, until the butter has melted and the mixture is well combined.

3 Crush the biscuits in a polythene bag with a rolling pin, or process them in a food processor. Stir the biscuit crumbs into the chocolate mixture and mix well.

4 Press the mixture into the prepared tin, then chill in the refrigerator until firm.

5 Place the chocolate pieces in a small heatproof bowl with the sugar and the milk. Place the bowl over a saucepan of gently simmering water and stir until the chocolate melts and the mixture is combined.

6 Spread the chocolate icing over the biscuit base and let the icing set in the tin. Using a sharp knife, cut into wedges to serve.

white chocolate brownies

ingredients

MAKES 9

8 squares white chocolate

115 g/4 oz unsalted butter,
  plus extra for greasing

85 g/3 oz walnut pieces

2 eggs

100 g/3^1/$_2$ oz soft light brown
  sugar

100 g/3^1/$_2$ oz self-raising flour

method

1 Preheat the oven to 180°C/350°F/Gas Mark 4. Lightly grease an 18-cm/7-inch square cake tin.

2 Coarsely chop 6 squares of white chocolate and all the walnuts. Put the remaining chocolate and the butter in a heatproof bowl set over a saucepan of gently simmering water. When melted, stir together, then leave to cool slightly.

3 Whisk the eggs and sugar together, then beat in the cooled chocolate mixture until well mixed. Fold in the flour, the chopped chocolate and the walnuts. Turn the mixture into the prepared tin and smooth the surface.

4 Transfer the tin to the preheated oven and bake for 30 minutes, or until just set. The mixture should still be a little soft in the centre. Remove from the oven and leave to cool in the tin, then cut into 9 squares before serving.

white chocolate tarts

ingredients

MAKES 12

225 g/8 oz plain flour, plus
    extra for dusting

2 tbsp golden caster sugar

150 g/5$\frac{1}{2}$ oz chilled butter,
    diced

2 egg yolks

2 tbsp cold water

plain chocolate curls,
    to decorate

cocoa powder, for dusting

filling

1 vanilla pod

400 ml/14 fl oz double cream

350 g/12 oz white chocolate,
    broken into pieces

method

1 Place the flour and sugar in a bowl. Add the butter and rub it in until the mixture resembles fine breadcrumbs. Place the egg yolks and water in a separate bowl and mix together. Stir into the dry ingredients and mix to form a dough. Knead for 1 minute, or until smooth. Wrap in clingfilm and chill for 20 minutes.

2 Preheat the oven to 200°C/400°F/Gas Mark 6. Roll out the dough on a floured work surface and use to line 12 tartlet tins. Prick the bases, cover and chill for 15 minutes. Line the cases with foil and baking beans and bake in the preheated oven for 10 minutes. Remove the beans and foil and cook for a further 5 minutes. Set aside to cool.

3 To make the filling, split the vanilla pod lengthways and scrape out the black seeds with a knife. Place the seeds in a saucepan with the cream and heat until almost boiling. Place the chocolate in a heatproof bowl and pour over the hot cream. Keep stirring until smooth. Whisk the mixture with an electric whisk until thickened and the whisk leaves a trail when lifted. Chill in the refrigerator for 30 minutes, then whisk until soft peaks form. Divide the filling between the pastry shells and chill for 30 minutes. Decorate with chocolate curls and dust with cocoa.

mocha brownies

ingredients

MAKES 16

55 g/2 oz butter, plus extra
for greasing
115 g/4 oz plain chocolate,
broken into pieces
175 g/6 oz brown sugar
2 eggs
1 tbsp instant coffee powder,
dissolved in 1 tbsp hot
water, cooled
85 g/3 oz plain flour
1/2 tsp baking powder
55 g/2 oz pecan nuts, roughly
chopped

method

1 Preheat the oven to 180°C/350°F/Gas Mark 4. Grease and base-line a 20-cm/8-inch square cake tin. Place the butter and chocolate in a heavy-based saucepan over low heat, until melted. Stir and set aside to cool.

2 Place the sugar and eggs in a large bowl and cream together until light and fluffy. Fold in the chocolate mixture and cooled coffee and mix thoroughly. Sift in the flour and baking powder and lightly fold into the mixture, then carefully fold in the pecan nuts.

3 Pour the mixture into the prepared tin and bake in the preheated oven for 25–30 minutes, or until firm and a skewer inserted into the centre comes out clean.

4 Cool in the tin for a few minutes, then run a knife round the edge of the cake to loosen it. Turn the cake out onto a wire rack and peel off the lining paper. Cool completely and cut into squares.

mocha brownies with soured cream frosting

ingredients

MAKES 9

55 g/2 oz butter, plus extra
for greasing
115 g/4 oz plain chocolate,
broken into pieces
175 g/6 oz soft dark brown
sugar
2 eggs
2 tbsp strong coffee, cooled
85 g/3 oz plain flour
1/2 tsp baking powder
pinch of salt
55 g/2 oz shelled walnuts,
chopped

frosting
115 g/4 oz plain chocolate,
broken into pieces
150 ml/5 fl oz soured cream

method

1 Preheat the oven to 180°C/350°F/Gas Mark 4. Grease and base-line a 20-cm/8-inch square cake tin.

2 Place the butter and chocolate in a small heatproof bowl and set over a saucepan of gently simmering water until melted. Stir until smooth. Remove from the heat and cool.

3 Beat the sugar and eggs together until pale and thick. Fold in the chocolate mixture and coffee. Mix well. Sift the flour, baking powder and salt into the cake mixture and fold in. Fold in the walnuts. Pour the cake mixture into the tin and bake in the preheated oven for 20–25 minutes, or until set. Leave to cool in the tin.

4 To make the frosting, melt the chocolate. Stir in the soured cream and beat until evenly blended. Spoon over the brownies and make a swirling pattern with a spatula. Leave to set in a cool place. Cut into squares, then remove from the tin and serve.

cappuccino squares

ingredients

MAKES 15

225 g/8 oz self-raising flour

1 tsp baking powder

1 tsp cocoa powder, plus extra
for dusting

225 g/8 oz butter, softened,
plus extra for greasing

225 g/8 oz golden caster sugar

4 eggs, beaten

3 tbsp instant coffee powder,
dissolved in 2 tbsp hot
water

frosting

115 g/4 oz white chocolate,
broken into pieces

55 g/2 oz butter, softened

3 tbsp milk

175 g/6 oz icing sugar

method

1 Preheat the oven to 180°C/350°F/Gas Mark 4.
Grease and base-line a shallow 28 x 18-cm/
11 x 7-inch tin.

2 Sift the flour, baking powder and cocoa
powder into a bowl and add the butter, sugar,
eggs and coffee. Beat well, by hand or with an
electric whisk, until smooth, then spoon into the
tin and smooth the top.

3 Bake in the preheated oven for 35–40
minutes, or until risen and firm. Leave to cool
in the tin for 10 minutes, then turn out onto
a wire rack, peel off the lining paper and cool
completely.

4 To make the frosting, place the chocolate,
butter and milk in a bowl set over a saucepan
of simmering water and stir until the chocolate
has melted.

5 Remove the bowl from the pan and sift in the
icing sugar. Beat until smooth, then spread over
the cake. Dust the top of the cake with sifted
cocoa, then cut into squares.

chocolate coconut layers

ingredients

MAKES 9

225 g/8 oz chocolate digestive biscuits

85 g/3 oz unsalted butter or margarine, plus extra for greasing

200 ml/7 fl oz condensed milk

1 egg, beaten

1 tsp vanilla extract

2 tbsp caster sugar

40 g/1$\frac{1}{2}$ oz self-raising flour, sifted

115 g/4 oz desiccated coconut

50 g/1$\frac{3}{4}$ oz plain chocolate (optional)

method

1 Preheat the oven to 190°C/375°F/Gas Mark 5. Line a shallow 20-cm/8-inch square cake tin with baking paper. Crush the biscuits in a polythene bag with a rolling pin or process them in a food processor. Melt the butter in a saucepan and stir in the biscuit crumbs thoroughly. Remove from the heat and press the mixture into the prepared tin.

2 In a separate bowl, beat together the condensed milk, egg, vanilla extract and sugar until smooth. Stir in the flour and coconut. Pour over the biscuit layer and use a spatula to smooth the top.

3 Bake in the preheated oven for 30 minutes, or until the coconut topping has become firm and just golden. Remove from the oven and leave to cool in the tin for about 5 minutes, then cut into squares. Leave to cool completely in the tin.

4 Carefully remove the squares from the tin and place them on a chopping board. Melt the chocolate, if using, and drizzle it over the squares to decorate them. Allow the chocolate to set before serving.

chocolate chip & walnut slices

ingredients

MAKES 18

115 g/4 oz walnut pieces

225 g/8 oz butter, plus extra for greasing

175 g/6 oz caster sugar

a few drops vanilla extract

225 g/8 oz plain flour

200 g/7 oz plain chocolate chips

method

1 Preheat the oven to 180°C/350°F/Gas Mark 4. Grease a 20 x 30-cm/8 x 12-inch Swiss roll tin. Coarsely chop the walnut pieces to about the same size as the chocolate chips.

2 Beat the butter and sugar together until pale and fluffy. Add the vanilla extract, then stir in the flour. Stir in the walnuts and chocolate chips. Press the mixture into the prepared tin.

3 Bake in the preheated oven for 20–25 minutes, until golden brown. Leave to cool in the tin, then cut into slices.

coconut bars

ingredients

MAKES 10

125 g/4½ oz unsalted butter,
    plus extra for greasing
225 g/8 oz golden caster sugar
2 eggs, beaten
finely grated rind of 1 orange
3 tbsp orange juice
150 ml/5 fl oz soured cream
140 g/5 oz self-raising flour
85 g/3 oz desiccated coconut
toasted desiccated coconut,
    to decorate

frosting
1 egg white
200 g/7 oz icing sugar
85 g/3 oz desiccated coconut
about 1 tbsp orange juice

method

1 Preheat the oven to 180°C/350°F/Gas Mark 4. Grease and base-line a 23-cm/9-inch square cake tin.

2 Cream together the butter and caster sugar until pale and fluffy, then gradually beat in the eggs. Stir in the orange rind, orange juice and soured cream. Fold in the flour and desiccated coconut evenly using a metal spoon.

3 Spoon the mixture into the prepared cake tin and level the surface. Bake in the preheated oven for 35–40 minutes, or until risen and firm to the touch.

4 Leave to cool for 10 minutes in the tin, then turn out and finish cooling on a wire rack.

5 For the frosting, lightly beat the egg white, just enough to break it up, and stir in the icing sugar and desiccated coconut, adding enough orange juice to mix to a thick paste. Spread over the top of the cake, sprinkle with toasted shredded coconut, then leave to set before slicing into bars.

coconut flapjacks

ingredients

MAKES 16

200 g/7 oz unsalted butter,
  plus extra for greasing
200 g/7 oz demerara sugar
2 tbsp golden syrup
275 g/9³/₄ oz porridge oats
100 g/3¹/₂ oz desiccated
  coconut
75 g/2³/₄ oz glacé cherries,
  chopped

method

1 Preheat the oven to 160°C/325°F/Gas Mark 3. Grease a 30 x 23-cm/12 x 9-inch baking tray.

2 Put the butter, sugar and syrup in a large saucepan and set over a low heat until just melted. Stir in the oats, coconut and cherries and mix until evenly combined.

3 Spread the mixture evenly on to the baking tray and press down with the back of a spatula or palette knife to make a smooth surface.

4 Bake in the preheated oven for 30 minutes. Remove from the oven and leave to cool on the baking tray for 10 minutes. Using a sharp knife, cut the flapjack into rectangles. Carefully transfer the pieces of flapjack to a wire rack and leave to cool completely.

chocolate éclairs

ingredients

MAKES 10

dough

150 ml/5 fl oz water

70 g/2¹/₂ oz butter, cut into
    small pieces, plus extra for
    greasing

100 g/3¹/₂ oz plain flour, sifted

2 eggs

pastry cream

2 eggs, lightly beaten

4 tbsp caster sugar

2 tbsp cornflour

300 ml/10 fl oz milk

¹/₄ tsp vanilla extract

icing

25 g/1 oz butter

1 tbsp milk

1 tbsp cocoa powder

55 g/2 oz icing sugar

white chocolate, broken
    into pieces

method

1 Preheat the oven to 200°C/400°F/Gas Mark 6. Lightly grease a baking sheet. Place the water in a saucepan, add the butter and heat gently until it melts. Bring to a rolling boil, remove the saucepan from the heat and add the flour all at once, beating well until the mixture leaves the sides of the pan and forms a ball. Cool slightly, then gradually beat in the eggs to form a smooth, glossy mixture. Spoon into a large piping bag fitted with a 1-cm/¹/₂-inch plain nozzle.

2 Sprinkle the baking sheet with a little water. Pipe éclairs 7.5 cm/3 inches long, spaced well apart. Bake in the preheated oven for 30–35 minutes, or until crisp and golden. Make a small slit in the side of each éclair to let the steam escape. Cool on a wire rack.

3 Meanwhile, make the pastry cream. Whisk the eggs and sugar until thick and creamy, then fold in the cornflour. Heat the milk until almost boiling and pour over the eggs, whisking. Transfer to the pan and cook over a low heat, stirring until thick. Remove the pan from the heat and stir in the vanilla extract. Cover and leave to cool.

4 For the icing, melt the butter with the milk in a saucepan, remove from the heat and stir in the cocoa and sugar. Split the éclairs lengthways, pipe in the pastry cream and spread the icing over the tops of the éclairs. Melt the white chocolate in a heatproof bowl set over a saucepan of gently simmering water, swirl it over the chocolate icing, and leave to set.

carrot bars

ingredients

MAKES 14–16

corn oil, for oiling

175 g/6 oz unsalted butter

85 g/3 oz brown sugar

2 eggs, beaten

55 g/2 oz self-raising
  wholemeal flour, sifted

1 tsp baking powder, sifted

1 tsp ground cinnamon, sifted

115 g/4 oz ground almonds

115 g/4 oz carrot, coarsely
  grated

85 g/3 oz sultanas

85 g/3 oz ready-to-eat dried
  apricots, finely chopped

55 g/2 oz toasted chopped
  hazelnuts

1 tbsp flaked almonds

method

1 Preheat the oven to 180°C/350°F/Gas Mark 4. Lightly oil and base-line a shallow 25 x 20-cm/ 10 x 8-inch baking tin.

2 Cream the butter and sugar together in a mixing bowl until light and fluffy, then gradually beat in the eggs, adding a little flour after each addition.

3 Add all the remaining ingredients, except the flaked almonds. Spoon the mixture into the prepared tin and smooth the top. Sprinkle with the flaked almonds.

4 Bake in the preheated oven for 35–45 minutes, or until the mixture is cooked and a skewer inserted into the centre comes out clean.

5 Remove from the oven and cool in the tin. Remove from the tin, discard the lining paper and cut into bars.

mincemeat crumble bars

ingredients

MAKES 12

400 g/14 oz ready-made
   mincemeat
icing sugar, for dusting

bottom layer

140 g/5 oz butter, plus extra
   for greasing
85 g/3 oz golden caster sugar
150 g/5½ oz plain flour
85 g/3 oz cornflour

topping

115 g/4 oz self-raising flour
75 g/2¾ oz butter, cut into
   pieces
85 g/3 oz golden caster sugar
25 g/1 oz flaked almonds

method

1 Preheat the oven to 200°C/400°F/Gas Mark 6. Grease a shallow 28 x 20-cm/11 x 8-inch cake tin. To make the bottom layer, beat the butter and sugar together in a bowl until light and fluffy. Sift in the flour and cornflour and, with your hands, bring the mixture together to form a ball. Push the dough into the cake tin, pressing it out and into the corners, then chill in the refrigerator for 20 minutes. Bake in the preheated oven for 12–15 minutes, or until puffed and golden.

2 To make the topping, place the flour, butter and sugar in a bowl and rub together into coarse crumbs. Stir in the flaked almonds.

3 Spread the mincemeat over the bottom layer and scatter the crumbs on top. Bake in the oven for a further 20 minutes or until golden brown. Cool slightly, then cut into 12 pieces and cool completely. Dust with sifted icing sugar, then serve.

cinnamon squares

ingredients

MAKES 16

225 g/8 oz butter, softened,
  plus extra for greasing
225 g/8 oz caster sugar
3 eggs, lightly beaten
225 g/8 oz self-raising flour
1/2 tsp bicarbonate of soda
1 tbsp ground cinnamon
150 ml/5 fl oz soured cream
55 g/2 oz sunflower seeds

method

1 Preheat the oven to 180°C/350°F/Gas Mark 4. Grease and base-line a 23-cm/9-inch square cake tin.

2 In a large mixing bowl, cream together the butter and caster sugar until the mixture is light and fluffy.

3 Gradually add the eggs to the mixture, beating thoroughly after each addition.

4 Sift the flour, bicarbonate of soda and cinnamon together into the creamed mixture and fold in evenly using a metal spoon.

5 Spoon in the soured cream and sunflower seeds and mix gently until well combined.

6 Spoon the mixture into the prepared tin and smooth the surface with the back of a spoon or a knife. Bake in the preheated oven for about 45 minutes, until the mixture is firm to the touch. Loosen the edges with a round-bladed knife, then turn out onto a wire rack to cool completely. Slice into squares before serving.

ginger-topped bars

ingredients

MAKES 16

210 g/7$\frac{1}{2}$ oz plain flour

1 tsp ground ginger

100 g/3$\frac{1}{2}$ oz golden caster
  sugar

175 g/6 oz unsalted butter,
  plus extra for greasing

ginger topping

1 tbsp golden syrup

4 tbsp unsalted butter

2 tbsp icing sugar

1 tsp ground ginger

white frosting
  (optional)

140 g/5 oz icing sugar

1 tbsp milk

method

1 Preheat the oven to 180°C/350°F/Gas Mark 4. Grease a 28 x 18-cm/11 x 7-inch rectangular cake tin. Sift the flour and ginger into a bowl and stir in the sugar. Rub in the butter until the mixture resembles a dough.

2 Press the mixture into the prepared tin and smooth the top with a spatula. Bake in the preheated oven for 40 minutes, or until very lightly browned.

3 To make the ginger topping, place the syrup and butter in a small saucepan over a low heat and stir until melted. Stir in the icing sugar and ginger. Remove the cake tin from the oven and pour over the topping while hot. Leave to cool slightly in the tin, then cut into 16 bars. Transfer to wire racks to cool completely.

4 To make the frosting, if using, mix the icing sugar with the milk until smooth. Pour it into a piping bag with a thin tip, and pipe thin parallel lines lengthways on top of each bar. Drag a cocktail stick or the tip of a knife crossways through the lines, alternately towards you and then away from you, about 1 cm/$\frac{1}{2}$ inch apart, to create a wavy effect.

gingerbread squares

ingredients

MAKES 24

55 g/2 oz eating apple, cored and cooked

175 g/6 oz unsalted butter, plus extra for greasing

55 g/2 oz soft light brown sugar

5 tbsp treacle

1 egg white

1 tsp almond extract

185 g/6 1/2 oz plain flour

1/4 tsp bicarbonate of soda

1/4 tsp baking powder

pinch of salt

1/2 tsp allspice

1/2 tsp ground ginger

method

1 Preheat the oven to 180°C/350°F/Gas Mark 4. Grease a large cake tin and line it with baking paper. Chop the apple and set aside. Put the butter, sugar, treacle, egg white and almond extract in a food processor and process until the mixture is smooth.

2 Sift together the flour, bicarbonate of soda, baking powder, salt, allspice and ginger in another bowl. Add to the creamed mixture and beat together well until combined. Stir the apple into the mixture, then pour the mixture into the cake tin.

3 Transfer to the preheated oven and bake for 10 minutes, or until golden brown. Remove from the oven and cut into 24 pieces. Transfer to a wire rack and leave to cool completely before serving.

ginger chocolate chip squares

ingredients

MAKES 15

4 pieces stem ginger in syrup
225 g/8 oz plain flour
1$\frac{1}{2}$ tsp ground ginger
1 tsp ground cinnamon
$\frac{1}{4}$ tsp ground cloves
$\frac{1}{4}$ tsp grated nutmeg
115 g/4 oz soft light brown
   sugar
115 g/4 oz butter
115 g/4 oz golden syrup
100 g/3$\frac{1}{2}$ oz plain chocolate
   chips

method

1 Preheat the oven to 150°C/300°F/Gas Mark 2. Finely chop the stem ginger. Sift the flour, ground ginger, cinnamon, cloves and nutmeg into a large bowl. Stir in the chopped stem ginger and sugar.

2 Put the butter and the syrup into a saucepan and heat gently until melted. Bring to the boil, then pour the mixture into the flour mixture, stirring all the time. Beat until the mixture is cool enough to handle.

3 Add the chocolate chips to the mixture. Press evenly into a 20 x 30-cm/8 x 12-inch Swiss roll tin.

4 Transfer to the oven and bake for 30 minutes. Cut into squares, then leave to cool in the tin.

buttermilk scones

ingredients

MAKES 8

300 g/10½ oz self-raising
    flour, plus extra for dusting
1 tsp baking powder
pinch of salt
55 g/2 oz cold butter, cut
    into pieces, plus extra for
    greasing
40 g/1½ oz golden caster
    sugar
300 ml/10 fl oz buttermilk
2 tbsp milk
whipped cream and
    strawberry jam, to serve

method

1 Preheat the oven to 220°C/425°F/Gas Mark 7. Grease a baking sheet. Sift the flour, baking powder and salt into a bowl. Add the butter and rub in until the mixture resembles fine breadcrumbs. Add the sugar and buttermilk and quickly mix together.

2 Turn the mixture out onto a floured work surface and knead lightly. Roll out to 2.5 cm/ 1 inch thick. Using a 6-cm/2½-inch plain or fluted cutter, stamp out the scones and place on the prepared baking sheet. Gather the trimmings, re-roll and stamp out more scones until all the dough is used up.

3 Brush the tops of the scones with milk. Bake in the preheated oven for 12–15 minutes, or until well risen and golden. Transfer to a wire rack to cool. Split and serve with whipped cream and strawberry jam.

rock drops

ingredients

MAKES 8

200 g/7 oz plain flour

2 tsp baking powder

100 g/3^1/$_2$ oz butter, cut into
   small pieces, plus extra
   for greasing

75 g/2^3/$_4$ oz golden caster
   sugar

100 g/3^1/$_2$ oz sultanas

25 g/1 oz glacé cherries,
   finely chopped

1 egg, beaten

2 tbsp milk

method

1 Preheat the oven to 200°C/400°F/Gas Mark 6. Lightly grease a large baking sheet.

2 Sift the flour and baking powder into a mixing bowl. Rub in the butter with your fingertips until the mixture resembles fine breadcrumbs. Stir in the sugar, sultanas and chopped glacé cherries, mixing well. Add the beaten egg and the milk to the mixture and mix to form a soft dough.

3 Spoon eight mounds of the mixture onto the prepared baking sheet, spacing them well apart, as they will spread while cooking. Bake in the preheated oven for 15–20 minutes, or until firm to the touch.

4 Remove the rock drops from the baking sheet. Either serve immediately or transfer to a wire rack to cool before serving.

strawberry & chocolate slices

ingredients

MAKES 16

225 g/8 oz plain flour
1 tsp baking powder
100 g/3½ oz caster sugar
85 g/3 oz soft light
    brown sugar
225 g/8 oz unsalted butter
150 g/5½ oz porridge oats
225 g/8 oz strawberry jam
100 g/3½ oz plain chocolate
    chips
25 g/1 oz almonds, chopped

method

1 Preheat the oven to 190°C/375°F/Gas Mark 5. Line a 30 x 20-cm/12 x 8-inch deep-sided Swiss roll tin with baking paper. Sift the flour and baking powder into a large bowl.

2 Add the caster sugar and brown sugar to the flour and mix well. Add the butter and rub in until the mixture resembles breadcrumbs. Stir in the oats.

3 Press three-quarters of the mixture into the base of the prepared cake tin. Bake in the preheated oven for 10 minutes.

4 Spread the jam over the cooked base, then sprinkle over the chocolate chips. Mix the remaining flour mixture with the almonds. Sprinkle evenly over the chocolate chips and press down gently.

5 Return to the oven and bake for a further 20–25 minutes until golden brown. Remove from the oven, leave to cool in the tin, then cut into slices.

summer fruit tartlets

ingredients

MAKES 12

pastry

200 g/7 oz plain flour, plus
    extra for dusting
85 g/3 oz icing sugar
55 g/2 oz ground almonds
115 g/4 oz butter
1 egg yolk
1 tbsp milk

filling

225 g/8 oz cream cheese
sifted icing sugar, to taste, plus
    extra for dusting
350 g/12 oz fresh summer
    fruits, such as redcurrants,
    blueberries, raspberries
    and small strawberries

method

1 Preheat the oven to 200°C/400°F/Gas Mark 6. To make the pastry, sift the flour and icing sugar into a bowl. Stir in the ground almonds. Add the butter and rub in until the mixture resembles breadcrumbs. Add the egg yolk and milk and work in with a spatula, then mix with your fingers until the dough binds together. Wrap the dough in clingfilm and chill in the refrigerator for 30 minutes.

2 On a floured work surface, roll out the pastry and use to line 12 deep tartlet or individual brioche tins. Prick the bases. Press a piece of foil into each tartlet, covering the edges, and bake in the preheated oven for 10–15 minutes or until light golden brown. Remove the foil and bake for a further 2–3 minutes. Transfer to a wire rack to cool.

3 To make the filling, place the cream cheese and icing sugar in a bowl and mix together. Place a spoonful of filling in each tartlet case and arrange the fruit on top. Dust with sifted icing sugar and serve.

strawberry tartlets

ingredients

SERVES 4

pastry

125 g/4¹/₂ oz plain flour

2 tbsp icing sugar

70 g/2¹/₂ oz unsalted butter,
    at room temperature

1 egg yolk

1–2 tbsp water

filling

1 vanilla pod, split

200 ml/7 fl oz milk

2 egg yolks

40 g/1¹/₂ oz caster sugar

1 tbsp plain flour

1 tbsp cornflour

125 ml/4 fl oz double cream,
    softly whipped

350 g/12 oz strawberries,
    hulled

4 tbsp redcurrant jelly, melted

method

1 To make the pastry, sift the flour and icing sugar into a bowl. Chop the butter into small pieces and add to the flour with the egg yolk, mixing with your fingertips and adding a little water, if necessary, to mix to a soft dough. Cover and place in the refrigerator to rest for 15 minutes.

2 Preheat the oven to 200°C/400°F/Gas Mark 6. Roll out the pastry and use to line four 9-cm/3¹/₂-inch tartlet tins. Prick the bases with a fork, line with baking paper and fill with baking beans, then bake blind in the preheated oven for 10 minutes. Remove the paper and beans and bake for a further 5 minutes, until golden brown. Remove from the oven and cool.

3 For the filling, place the vanilla pod in a saucepan with the milk and leave on a low heat to infuse, without boiling, for 10 minutes. Whisk the egg yolks, sugar, flour and cornflour together in a mixing bowl until smooth. Strain the milk into the bowl and whisk until smooth.

4 Pour the mixture back into the pan and stir over a moderate heat until boiling. Cook, stirring constantly, for about 2 minutes, until thickened and smooth. Remove from the heat and fold in the whipped cream. Spoon the mixture into the pastry cases.

5 When the filling has set slightly, top with strawberries, sliced if large, then spoon over a little redcurrant jelly to glaze.

raspberry éclairs

ingredients

MAKES 8

choux pastry

55 g/2 oz butter

150 ml/5 fl oz water

70 g/2½ oz plain flour, sifted

2 eggs, beaten

filling

300 ml/10 fl oz double cream

1 tbsp icing sugar

175 g/6 oz fresh raspberries

icing

115 g/4 oz icing sugar

2 tsp lemon juice

pink food colouring (optional)

method

1 Preheat the oven to 200°C/400°F/Gas Mark 6. To make the choux pastry, place the butter and water in a large, heavy-based saucepan and bring to the boil. Add the flour, all at once, and beat thoroughly until the mixture leaves the sides of the pan. Cool slightly, then vigorously beat in the eggs, 1 at a time.

2 Spoon the mixture into a piping bag fitted with a 1-cm/½-inch nozzle and make eight 7.5-cm/3-inch lengths on several dampened baking sheets. Bake in the preheated oven for 30 minutes or until crisp and golden. Remove from the oven and make a small hole in each éclair with the tip of a knife to let out the steam, then return to the oven for a further 5 minutes, to dry out the insides. Transfer to a wire rack and leave to cool.

3 To make the filling, place the cream and icing sugar in a bowl and whisk until thick. Split the éclairs and fill with the cream and raspberries. To make the icing, sift the icing sugar into a bowl and stir in the lemon juice and enough water to make a smooth paste. Add the pink food colouring, if using. Drizzle the icing generously over the éclairs and allow to set before serving.

cherry & sultana rock cakes

ingredients

MAKES 10

250 g/9 oz self-raising flour

1 tsp ground allspice

75 g/2³/4 oz butter, plus extra
     for greasing

85 g/3 oz golden caster sugar

55 g/2 oz glacé cherries,
     quartered

55 g/2 oz sultanas

1 egg

2 tbsp milk

demerara sugar, for sprinkling

method

1 Preheat the oven to 200°C/400°F/Gas Mark 6. Grease a baking sheet. Sift the flour and allspice into a bowl. Add the butter and rub it in until the mixture resembles breadcrumbs. Stir in the caster sugar, cherries and sultanas.

2 Break the egg into a bowl and whisk in the milk. Pour most of the egg mixture into the dry ingredients and mix with a fork to make a stiff, coarse dough, adding the rest of the egg and milk, if necessary.

3 Using two forks, pile the mixture into ten rocky heaps onto the prepared baking sheet. Sprinkle with demerara sugar. Bake in the preheated oven for 10–15 minutes, or until golden and firm to the touch. Cool on the baking sheet for 2 minutes, then transfer to a wire rack to cool completely.

orange & raisin brioches

ingredients

MAKES 12

210 g/7¹/₂ oz strong white
    flour, plus extra for dusting
¹/₂ tsp salt
2 tsp easy-blend dried yeast
1 tbsp golden caster sugar
115 g/4 oz raisins
grated rind of 1 orange
2 tbsp lukewarm water
55 g/2 oz butter, melted, plus
    extra for greasing
2 eggs, beaten
vegetable oil, for brushing
1 beaten egg, for glazing
butter, to serve

method

1 Preheat the oven to 220°C/425°F/Gas Mark 7. Grease 12 individual brioche moulds. Sift the flour and salt into a warmed bowl and stir in the yeast, sugar, raisins and orange rind. Make a well in the centre. In a separate bowl, mix together the water, eggs and melted butter and pour into the dry ingredients. Beat vigorously to make a soft dough. Turn out onto a lightly floured work surface and knead for 5 minutes, or until smooth and elastic. Brush a clean bowl with oil. Place the dough in the bowl, cover with clingfilm, and leave to stand in a warm place for 1 hour, or until doubled in size.

2 Turn out onto a floured work surface, knead lightly for 1 minute, then roll into a rope shape. Cut into 12 equal pieces. Shape three quarters of each piece into a ball and place in a mould. With a floured finger, press a hole in the centre of each ball. Shape the remaining pieces of dough into little plugs and press into the holes, flattening the top slightly.

3 Place the moulds on a baking sheet, cover lightly with oiled clingfilm, and leave to stand in a warm place for 1 hour, until the dough comes almost to the top.

4 Brush the brioches with beaten egg and bake in the preheated oven for 15 minutes, or until golden brown. Serve warm with butter.

lemon drizzle bars

ingredients

MAKES 12

2 eggs
175 g/6 oz caster sugar
150 g/5½ oz soft margarine,
    plus extra for greasing
finely grated rind of 1 lemon
175 g/6 oz self-raising flour
125 ml/4 fl oz milk
icing sugar, for dusting

syrup
140 g/5 oz icing sugar
50 ml/2 fl oz fresh lemon juice

method

1 Preheat the oven to 180°C/350°F/Gas Mark 4. Grease an 18-cm/7-inch square cake tin and line with non-stick baking paper.

2 Place the eggs, caster sugar and margarine in a mixing bowl and beat hard until smooth and fluffy. Stir in the lemon rind, then fold in the flour lightly and evenly. Stir in the milk, mixing evenly, then spoon into the prepared cake tin, smoothing level.

3 Bake in the preheated oven for 45–50 minutes, or until golden brown and firm to the touch. Remove from the oven and stand the tin on a wire rack.

4 To make the syrup, place the icing sugar and lemon juice in a small saucepan and heat gently, stirring until the sugar dissolves. Do not boil.

5 Prick the warm cake all over with a skewer, and spoon the hot syrup evenly over the top, allowing it to be absorbed.

6 Leave to cool completely in the tin, then turn out the cake, cut into 12 pieces and dust with a little icing sugar before serving.

lemon butterfly cakes

ingredients

MAKES 12

115 g/4 oz self-raising flour
1/2 tsp baking powder
100 g/3 1/2 oz soft margarine
100 g/3 1/2 oz caster sugar
2 eggs, lightly beaten
finely grated rind of 1/2 lemon
2 tbsp milk
icing sugar, for dusting

lemon filling

75 g/2 3/4 oz butter, softened
175 g/6 oz icing sugar
1 tbsp lemon juice

method

1 Preheat the oven to 190°C/375°F/Gas Mark 5. Put 12 double-layer paper cases on a baking sheet.

2 Sift the flour and baking powder into a large bowl. Add the margarine, sugar, eggs, lemon rind and milk and, using an electric hand whisk, beat together until smooth. Spoon the batter into the paper cases.

3 Bake the cupcakes in the preheated oven for 15–20 minutes, or until well risen and golden brown. Transfer to a wire rack and leave to cool.

4 To make the filling, put the butter in a bowl and beat until fluffy. Sift in the icing sugar, add the lemon juice and beat together until smooth and creamy.

5 When the cupcakes are cold, use a serrated knife to cut a circle from the top of each cupcake and then cut each circle in half. Spread or pipe a little of the filling into the centre of each cupcake, then press the two semicircular halves into it at an angle to resemble butterfly wings. Dust with sifted icing sugar before serving.

apple shortcakes

ingredients

MAKES 4

150 g/5¹/2 oz plain flour, plus
  extra for dusting

¹/2 tsp salt

1 tsp baking powder

1 tbsp caster sugar

25 g/1 oz butter, cut into
  small pieces, plus extra for
  greasing

50 ml/2 fl oz milk

icing sugar, for dusting

filling

3 dessert apples, peeled,
  cored and sliced

100 g/3¹/2 oz caster sugar

1 tbsp lemon juice

1 tsp ground cinnamon

300 ml/10 fl oz water

150 ml/5 fl oz double cream,
  lightly whipped

method

1 Preheat the oven to 220°C/425°F/Gas Mark 7. Lightly grease a baking sheet. Sift the flour, salt and baking powder into a large bowl. Stir in the sugar, then add the butter and rub it in with your fingertips until the mixture resembles fine breadcrumbs. Pour in the milk and mix to a soft dough.

2 On a lightly floured work surface, lightly knead the dough, then roll out to 1 cm/1/2 inch thick. Stamp out four rounds, using a 5-cm/2-inch cutter. Transfer to the prepared baking sheet.

3 Bake in the preheated oven for 15 minutes, until the shortcakes are well risen and lightly browned. Set aside to cool.

4 To make the filling, place the apple, sugar, lemon juice and cinnamon in a saucepan. Add the water, bring to the boil and simmer, uncovered, for 5–10 minutes or until the apples are tender. Cool slightly, then remove the apples from the pan.

5 To serve, split the shortcakes in half. Place each bottom half on an individual serving plate and spoon on a quarter of the apple slices, then the cream. Place the other half of the shortcake on top. Serve dusted with icing sugar.

apricot slices

ingredients

MAKES 12

pastry

350 g/10½ oz plain
   wholemeal flour
50 g/1¾ oz finely ground
   mixed nuts
100 g/3½ oz margarine, cut
   into small pieces, plus
   extra for greasing
4 tbsp water
milk, for glazing

filling

175 g/6 oz ready-to-eat dried
   apricots
grated rind of 1 orange
350 ml/12 fl oz apple juice
1 tsp ground cinnamon
55 g/2 oz raisins

method

1 Preheat the oven to 200°C/400°F/Gas Mark 6. Lightly grease a 23-cm/9-inch square cake tin. To make the dough, place the flour and nuts in a mixing bowl and rub in the margarine with your fingers until the mixture resembles breadcrumbs. Stir in the water and bring together to form a dough. Wrap and leave to chill for 30 minutes.

2 To make the filling, place the apricots, orange rind and apple juice in a saucepan and bring to the boil. Simmer for 30 minutes until the apricots are mushy. Cool slightly, then process in a food processor or blender to a purée. Alternatively, press the mixture through a fine sieve. Stir in the cinnamon and raisins.

3 Divide the dough in half, roll out 1 half and use to line the base of the tin. Spread the apricot purée over the top and brush the edges of the dough with water. Roll out the rest of the dough to fit over the top of the apricot purée. Press down and seal the edges.

4 Prick the top of the dough with a fork and brush with milk. Bake in the preheated oven for 20–25 minutes, until the pastry is golden. Leave to cool slightly before cutting into 12 slices. Serve either warm or cold.

chocolate & apricot squares

ingredients

MAKES 12

125 g/4¹/₂ oz butter, plus extra
   for greasing
175 g/6 oz white chocolate,
   chopped
4 eggs
100 g/3¹/₂ oz caster sugar
250 g/9 oz plain flour, sifted
1 tsp baking powder
pinch of salt
100 g/3¹/₂ oz ready-to-eat
   dried apricots, chopped

method

1 Preheat the oven to 180°C/350°F/Gas Mark 4. Lightly grease and base-line a 20-cm/8-inch square cake tin.

2 Melt the butter and chocolate in a heatproof bowl set over a saucepan of gently simmering water. Stir frequently with a wooden spoon until the mixture is smooth and glossy. Leave the mixture to cool slightly.

3 Beat the eggs and caster sugar into the butter and chocolate mixture until well combined.

4 Fold in the flour, baking powder, salt and chopped dried apricots and mix thoroughly.

5 Pour the mixture into the prepared tin and bake in the preheated oven for 25–30 minutes.

6 The centre of the cake may not be completely firm, but it will set as it cools. Leave in the tin to cool.

7 When the cake is completely cold, turn it out carefully and slice into small squares.

macadamia nut caramel bars

ingredients

MAKES 16

base

115 g/4 oz macadamia nuts

280 g/10 oz plain flour

175 g/6 oz soft light brown sugar

115 g/4 oz butter

topping

115 g/4 oz butter

100 g/3½ oz soft light brown sugar

200 g/7 oz milk chocolate chips

method

1 Preheat the oven to 180°C/350°F/Gas Mark 4. Coarsely chop the macadamia nuts. To make the base, beat together the flour, sugar and butter until the mixture resembles fine breadcrumbs. Press into the base of a 30 x 20-cm/12 x 8-inch Swiss roll tin. Sprinkle over the chopped nuts.

2 To make the topping, put the butter and sugar in a saucepan and, stirring constantly, slowly bring the mixture to the boil. Boil for 1 minute, stirring constantly, then carefully pour the mixture over the macadamia nuts.

3 Bake in the preheated oven for about 20 minutes, until the caramel topping is bubbling. Remove from the oven and immediately sprinkle the chocolate chips evenly on top. Leave for 2–3 minutes, until the chocolate chips start to melt, then, using the blade of a knife, swirl the chocolate over the top. Leave to cool in the tin, then cut into bars.

hazelnut squares

ingredients

MAKES 16

150 g/5$\frac{1}{2}$ oz plain flour

pinch of salt

1 tsp baking powder

75 g/2$\frac{3}{4}$ oz butter, cut into
    small pieces, plus extra
    for greasing

150 g/5$\frac{1}{2}$ oz soft brown sugar

1 egg, beaten lightly

4 tbsp milk

150 g/5$\frac{1}{2}$ oz hazelnuts,
    halved

demerara sugar, for sprinkling
    (optional)

method

1 Preheat the oven to 180°C/350°F/Gas Mark 4. Grease and line a 23-cm/9-inch square cake tin.

2 Sift the flour, salt and baking powder into a large bowl.

3 Rub in the butter with your fingertips until the mixture resembles fine breadcrumbs. Stir in the soft brown sugar.

4 Add the beaten egg, milk and nuts to the mixture and stir well until thoroughly combined.

5 Spoon the mixture into the prepared cake tin, spreading it out evenly, and smooth the surface. Sprinkle with demerara sugar, if using.

6 Bake in the preheated oven for about 25 minutes, or until the mixture is firm to the touch when pressed gently with a finger.

7 Leave to cool for 10 minutes in the tin, then loosen the edges with a round-bladed knife and turn out on to a wire rack. Cut into squares and leave to cool completely before serving.

hazelnut chocolate crunch

ingredients

MAKES 12

200 g/7 oz rolled oats

40 g/1$\frac{1}{2}$ oz hazelnuts, lightly
toasted and chopped

50 g/1$\frac{3}{4}$ oz plain flour

115 g/4 oz unsalted butter,
plus extra for greasing

85 g/3 oz soft light brown
sugar

2 tbsp golden syrup

55 g/2 oz plain chocolate
chips

method

1 Preheat the oven to 180°C/350°F/Gas Mark 4. Grease a 23-cm/9-inch shallow, square baking tin.

2 Mix the oats, nuts and flour in a large bowl. Place the butter, sugar and syrup in a large saucepan and heat gently until the sugar has dissolved. Pour in the dry ingredients and mix well. Stir in the chocolate chips.

3 Turn the mixture into the prepared tin and bake in the preheated oven for 20–25 minutes, or until golden brown and firm to the touch. Using a knife, mark into 12 rectangles and leave to cool in the tin. Cut the hazelnut chocolate crunch bars with a sharp knife before carefully removing them from the tin.

nutty flapjacks

ingredients

MAKES 16

200 g/7 oz rolled oats
115 g/4 oz chopped hazelnuts
55 g/2 oz plain flour
115 g/4 oz butter, plus
    extra for greasing
2 tbsp golden syrup
85 g/3 oz light muscovado
    sugar

method

1 Preheat the oven to 180°C/350°F/Gas Mark 4. Grease a 23-cm/9-inch square cake tin.

2 Place the rolled oats, hazelnuts and flour in a large mixing bowl and stir together.

3 Place the butter, golden syrup and sugar in a saucepan over a low heat and stir until melted. Pour onto the dry ingredients and mix well. Spoon the mixture into the prepared cake tin and smooth the surface with the back of a spoon.

4 Bake in the preheated oven for 20–25 minutes, or until golden and firm to the touch. Mark into 16 pieces and leave to cool in the tin. When completely cold, cut with a sharp knife and remove from the tin.

bakewell slices

ingredients

MAKES 12

pastry

175 g/6 oz plain flour
125 g/4½ oz butter
25 g/1 oz caster sugar
1 egg yolk
about 1 tbsp cold water

filling

115 g/4 oz unsalted butter
115 g/4 oz caster sugar
115 g/4 oz ground almonds
3 eggs, beaten
½ tsp almond extract
4 tbsp raspberry jam
2 tbsp flaked almonds

method

1 For the pastry, sift the flour into a bowl and rub in the butter with your fingertips until the mixture resembles fine breadcrumbs. Stir in the sugar, then mix the egg yolk with the water and stir in to make a firm dough, adding a little more water if necessary. Wrap in clingfilm and chill in the refrigerator for about 15 minutes, until firm enough to roll out.

2 Preheat the oven to 200°C/400°F/Gas Mark 6. Roll out the dough and use to line a 23-cm/ 9-inch square tart tin or shallow cake tin. Prick the base and chill for 15 minutes.

3 Meanwhile, to make the filling, cream together the butter and sugar until pale and fluffy, then beat in the ground almonds, eggs and almond extract.

4 Spread the jam over the pastry base, then top with the almond mixture, spreading evenly. Sprinkle with the flaked almonds.

5 Bake in the preheated oven for 10 minutes, then reduce the heat to 180°C/350°F/Gas Mark 4 and bake for a further 25–30 minutes, or until the filling is golden brown and firm to the touch. Leave to cool in the tin, then cut into bars.

maple pecan tartlets

ingredients

MAKES 12

pastry

150 g/5½ oz plain flour,
    plus extra for dusting
85 g/3 oz butter
55 g/2 oz golden caster sugar
2 egg yolks

filling

2 tbsp maple syrup
150 ml/5 fl oz double cream
115 g/4 oz golden caster sugar
pinch of cream of tartar
6 tbsp water
175 g/6 oz pecan nuts
12 pecan nut halves,
    to decorate

method

1 Preheat the oven to 200°C/400°F/Gas Mark 6. Sift the flour into a large bowl, then cut the butter into pieces and rub it into the flour using your fingertips until the mixture resembles breadcrumbs. Stir in the sugar, then stir in the egg yolks to make a smooth dough. Wrap in clingfilm and chill for 30 minutes.

2 On a floured work surface, roll out the pastry thinly, cut out circles and use to line 12 tartlet tins. Prick the bases and press a piece of foil into each pastry case. Bake in the preheated oven, for 10–15 minutes, or until light golden. Remove the foil and bake for a further 2–3 minutes. Leave to cool on a wire rack.

3 To make the filling, mix together half the maple syrup and half the cream in a bowl. Place the sugar, cream of tartar and water in a saucepan over a low heat and stir until the sugar dissolves. Bring to the boil and boil until light golden. Remove from the heat and stir in the maple syrup and cream mixture.

4 Return to the heat and cook until a little of the mixture forms a soft ball when dropped into cold water. Stir in the remaining cream and stand until warm. Brush the remaining maple syrup over the edges of the tarts. Place the pecan nuts in the pastry cases, spoon in the toffee and top with a pecan nut half. Cool before serving.

almond slices

ingredients

MAKES 8

3 eggs

60 g/2¼ oz ground almonds

140 g/5 oz milk powder

200 g/7 oz granulated sugar

½ tsp saffron threads

115 g/4 oz unsalted butter

1 tbsp flaked almonds,
    to decorate

method

1 Preheat the oven to 160°C/325°F/Gas Mark 3. Lightly beat the eggs together in a mixing bowl and set aside.

2 Place the ground almonds, milk powder, sugar and saffron in a large mixing bowl and stir to mix well.

3 Melt the butter in a small saucepan over a low heat. Pour the melted butter over the dry ingredients and mix well with a wooden spoon until thoroughly combined.

4 Add the beaten eggs to the mixture and stir to blend well.

5 Spread the mixture evenly in a shallow 20-cm/8-inch square ovenproof dish and bake in the preheated oven for 45 minutes, or until a cocktail stick inserted into the centre comes out clean.

6 Remove from the oven and cut into slices. Decorate the slices with flaked almonds and transfer to serving plates. Serve hot or cold.

moist walnut cupcakes

ingredients

MAKES 12

85 g/3 oz walnuts
55 g/2 oz butter, softened
100 g/3^1/$_2$ oz caster sugar
grated rind of ^{1}/$_2$ lemon
75 g/2^3/$_4$ oz self-raising flour
2 eggs
12 walnut halves, to decorate

frosting

50 g/2 oz butter, softened
85 g/3 oz icing sugar
grated rind of ^{1}/$_2$ lemon
1 tsp lemon juice

method

1 Preheat the oven to 190ºC/375ºF/Gas Mark 5. Put 12 double-layer paper cases on a baking sheet.

2 Put the walnuts in a food processor and, using a pulsating action, blend until finely ground, being careful not to overgrind, which will turn them to oil. Add the butter, cut into small pieces, along with the sugar, lemon rind, flour and eggs, then blend until evenly mixed. Spoon the batter into the paper cases.

3 Bake the cupcakes in the preheated oven for 20 minutes, or until well risen and golden brown. Transfer to a wire rack and leave to cool.

4 To make the frosting, put the butter in a bowl and beat until fluffy. Sift in the icing sugar, add the lemon rind and juice and mix well together.

5 When the cupcakes are cold, spread the frosting on top of each cupcake and top with a walnut half to decorate.

walnut & cinnamon blondies

ingredients

MAKES 8

115 g/4 oz unsalted butter, plus extra for greasing
250 g/9 oz soft light brown sugar
1 egg
1 egg yolk
150 g/5 oz self-raising flour
1 tsp ground cinnamon
85 g/3 oz walnuts, coarsely chopped

method

1 Preheat the oven to 180°C/350°F/Gas Mark 4. Grease and line an 18-cm/7-inch square cake tin.

2 Place the butter and sugar in a saucepan over a low heat and stir until the sugar has dissolved. Cook, stirring, for a further minute. The mixture will bubble slightly, but do not allow it to boil. Leave to cool for 10 minutes.

3 Stir the egg and egg yolk into the mixture. Sift in the flour and cinnamon, then add the nuts and stir until just blended. Pour the cake mixture into the prepared tin and bake in the preheated oven for 20–25 minutes, or until springy in the middle and a cocktail stick inserted into the centre comes out clean.

4 Leave to cool in the tin for a few minutes, then run a knife around the edge of the tin to loosen. Turn out onto a wire rack and peel off the paper. Leave to cool completely. When cold, cut into squares.

chocolate chip shortbread

ingredients

MAKES 18

115 g/4 oz butter, diced, plus extra for greasing
115 g/4 oz plain flour
55 g/2 oz cornflour
55 g/2 oz golden caster sugar
40 g/1½ oz plain chocolate chips

method

1 Preheat the oven to 160°C/325°F/Gas Mark 3. Grease a 23-cm/9-inch loose-bottom fluted flan tin. Sift the flour and cornflour into a large bowl. Stir in the sugar, then add the butter and rub it in until the mixture starts to bind together.

2 Turn into the prepared flan tin and press evenly over the bottom. Prick the surface with a fork. Sprinkle with the chocolate chips and press lightly into the surface.

3 Bake in the preheated oven for 35–40 minutes, or until cooked but not browned. Mark into 8 portions with a sharp knife. Leave to cool in the tin for 10 minutes, then transfer to a wire rack to cool completely.

fruit & nut squares

ingredients

MAKES 9

115 g/4 oz unsalted butter,
    plus extra for greasing
2 tbsp clear honey
1 egg, beaten
150 g/5^1/$_2$ oz ground almonds
85 g/3 oz ready-to-eat dried
    apricots, finely chopped
55 g/2 oz dried cherries
40 g/1^1/$_2$ oz toasted hazelnuts
2 tbsp sesame seeds
85 g/3 oz rolled oats

method

1 Preheat the oven to 180°C/350°F/Gas Mark 4. Lightly grease an 18-cm/7-inch shallow, square cake tin with butter. Beat the remaining butter with the honey in a bowl until creamy, then beat in the egg with the almonds.

2 Add the remaining ingredients and mix together well. Press into the prepared tin, ensuring that the mixture is firmly packed. Smooth the top.

3 Transfer to the preheated oven and bake for 20–25 minutes, or until firm to the touch and golden brown.

4 Remove from the oven and leave to stand for 10 minutes before marking into squares.

5 Leave to stand until cold before removing from the tin. Cut into squares, store in an airtight container and eat within 2–3 days.

toffee apple cakes

ingredients

MAKES 12

2 eating apples

1 tbsp lemon juice

250 g/9 oz plain flour

2 tsp baking powder

1½ tsp ground cinnamon

70 g/2½ oz light muscovado
   sugar

55 g/2 oz butter, plus extra
   for greasing

100 ml/3½ fl oz milk

100 ml/3½ fl oz apple juice

1 egg, beaten

topping

2 tbsp single cream

40 g/1½ oz light muscovado
   sugar

15 g/½ oz unsalted butter

method

1 Preheat the oven to 200°C/400°F/Gas Mark 6. Grease a 12-cup muffin tin.

2 Core and coarsely grate one of the apples. Slice the remaining apple into 5-mm/¼-inch thick wedges and toss in the lemon juice. Sift together the flour, baking powder and cinnamon, then stir in the sugar and grated apple.

3 Melt the butter and mix with the milk, apple juice and egg. Stir the liquid mixture into the dry ingredients, mixing lightly until just combined.

4 Spoon the mixture into the prepared muffin tin. Arrange two apple slices on top of each.

5 Bake in the preheated oven for 20–25 minutes or until risen, firm and golden brown. Run a knife round the edge of each cake to loosen, then turn out onto a wire rack to cool.

6 For the topping, place all the ingredients in a small saucepan and heat, stirring, until the sugar has dissolved. Increase the heat and boil rapidly for 2 minutes, or until slightly thickened and syrupy. Cool slightly, then drizzle over the cakes and leave to set.

cookies

Keeping the cookie jar topped up has never been easier with this fabulous collection of scrumptious recipes for all the family. As well as all the kids' favourites such as chocolate chip and classics such as Florentines, there are fragrant herb-flavoured biscuits to serve with cold desserts, creamy sandwich cookies and novelty shapes for parties and festivals. There are even cookies you can hang on the Christmas tree.

Making cookies is probably even easier and quicker than any other type of baking, and they not only taste more delicious than the ones you can buy, they also cost less. Like all home-baking, cookies are a special treat and can be served with tea, coffee, milk and fruit juice or, Italian-style, with a glass of wine. They're popular at children's parties, delicious with ice cream at the end of a family supper and the perfect self-indulgent treat on a well-deserved coffee break.

Most of the equipment required is the same as for other types of baking. It is worth buying good-quality, non-stick baking sheets that disperse the heat evenly and won't wobble when you take them out of the oven. A couple of wire cooling racks are useful as cookies take up quite a lot of room and it is important that the air can circulate

properly so that the cookies end up beautifully crisp. Most cooks already have plain and/or fluted round cookie cutters, but it's great fun to use some of the other shapes available – shooting stars, diamonds, hearts, flowers and even Father Christmas.

chocolate chip oaties

ingredients

MAKES 20

115 g/4 oz unsalted butter,
  softened, plus extra
  for greasing
100 g/3¹/₂ oz muscovado
  sugar
1 egg
55 g/2 oz rolled oats
1 tbsp milk
1 tsp vanilla extract
140 g/5 oz plain flour
1 tbsp cocoa powder
¹/₂ tsp baking powder
6 squares plain chocolate,
  broken into pieces
6 squares milk chocolate,
  broken into pieces

method

1 Preheat the oven to 180°C/350°F/Gas Mark 4. Grease two large baking sheets. Place the butter and sugar in a bowl and beat with a wooden spoon until light and fluffy.

2 Beat in the egg, then add the oats, milk and vanilla extract. Beat together until well blended, then sift the flour, cocoa powder and baking powder into the mixture and stir. Stir in the chocolate pieces.

3 Place dessertspoonfuls of the mixture on the prepared baking sheets and flatten slightly with a fork. Bake in the preheated oven for 15 minutes, or until slightly risen and firm. Remove from the oven and leave to cool on the sheets for 2 minutes, then transfer to wire racks to cool completely.

double chocolate chip cookies

ingredients

MAKES 24

115 g/4 oz unsalted butter, softened, plus extra for greasing
55 g/2 oz granulated sugar
55 g/2 oz soft light brown sugar
1 egg, beaten
1/2 tsp vanilla extract
115 g/4 oz plain flour
2 tbsp cocoa powder
1/2 tsp bicarbonate of soda
115 g/4 oz milk chocolate chips
55 g/2 oz walnuts, coarsely chopped

method

1 Preheat the oven to 180°C/350°F/Gas Mark 4. Grease three baking sheets.

2 Place the butter, granulated sugar, and light brown sugar in a bowl and beat until light and fluffy. Gradually beat in the egg and vanilla extract.

3 Sift the flour, cocoa and bicarbonate of soda into the mixture and stir in carefully. Stir in the chocolate chips and walnuts. Drop dessert-spoonfuls of the mixture onto the baking sheets, spaced well apart to allow for spreading.

4 Bake in the preheated oven for 10–15 minutes, or until the mixture has spread and the cookies are beginning to feel firm. Remove from the oven and leave to cool on the sheets for 2 minutes, before transferring to wire racks.

chocolate viennese fingers

ingredients

MAKES ABOUT 30

115 g/4 oz butter, softened,
    plus extra for greasing
55 g/2 oz golden icing sugar,
    sifted
125 g/4$^{1}/_{2}$ oz plain flour
1 tbsp cocoa powder
100 g/3$^{1}/_{2}$ oz plain chocolate,
    melted and cooled

method

1 Preheat the oven to 180°C/350°F/Gas Mark 4. Grease two baking sheets. Beat the butter and sugar together until light and fluffy. Sift the flour and cocoa powder into the bowl and work the mixture until it is a smooth, piping consistency.

2 Spoon into a large piping bag fitted with a 2.5-cm/1-inch fluted tip. Pipe 6-cm/2$^{1}/_{2}$-inch lengths of the mixture onto the prepared baking sheets, allowing room for expansion during cooking. Bake in the preheated oven for 15 minutes, or until firm.

3 Leave to cool on the sheets for 2 minutes, then transfer to a wire rack to cool completely. Dip the ends of the biscuits into the melted chocolate and allow to set before serving.

cookie & cream sandwiches

ingredients

MAKES 12

125 g/4¹/₂ oz unsalted butter, softened

125 g/4¹/₂ oz golden icing sugar

125 g/4¹/₂ oz plain flour

55 g/2 oz cocoa powder

¹/₂ tsp ground cinnamon

filling

125 g/4¹/₂ oz plain chocolate, broken into pieces

4 tbsp double cream

method

1 Preheat the oven to 160°C/325°F/Gas Mark 3. Place the butter and sugar in a large bowl and beat together until light and fluffy. Sift the flour, cocoa powder and ground cinnamon into the bowl and mix until a smooth dough forms.

2 Place the dough between two sheets of non-stick baking paper and roll out to 3 mm/¹/₈ inch thick. Stamp out 6-cm/2¹/₂-inch circles and place on a baking sheet lined with non-stick baking paper. Bake in the preheated oven for 15 minutes, until firm to the touch. Leave to cool for 2 minutes, then transfer to wire racks to cool completely.

3 To make the filling, place the chocolate and cream in a saucepan and heat gently until the chocolate has melted. Stir until smooth. Leave to cool, then chill in the refrigerator for 2 hours, or until firm. Sandwich the cookies together in pairs with a spoonful of chocolate cream and serve.

chocolate-dipped cookies

ingredients

MAKES 20

75 g/2³/₄ oz unsalted butter,
    plus extra for greasing
85 g/3 oz demerara sugar
1 egg
25 g/1 oz wheat germ
115 g/4 oz wholemeal
    self-raising flour
6 tbsp white self-raising flour,
    sifted
125 g/4¹/₂ oz plain chocolate,
    broken into pieces

method

1 Preheat the oven to 180°C/350°F/Gas Mark 4. Grease two baking sheets.

2 Beat the butter and sugar together in a bowl until fluffy. Add the egg and beat well. Stir in the wheat germ and flours. Bring the mixture together with your hands.

3 Roll rounded teaspoonfuls of the mixture into balls and place on the prepared baking sheets, spaced well apart. Flatten the cookies slightly with a fork, then bake in the preheated oven for 15–20 minutes, or until golden.

4 Remove from the oven and leave to cool on the sheets for a few minutes before transferring to a wire rack to cool completely.

5 Melt the chocolate in a heatproof bowl set over a saucepan of gently simmering water, then dip each cookie in the chocolate to cover the base and a little way up the sides. Let the excess chocolate drip back into the bowl. Place the cookies on a sheet of baking paper and leave to set in a cool place before serving.

button cookies

ingredients

MAKES 18–20

55 g/2 oz plain chocolate, broken into pieces
150 g/5 oz plain flour
1 tsp baking powder
1 egg
150 g/5 oz caster sugar
4 tbsp corn oil, plus extra for oiling
1/2 tsp vanilla extract
2 tbsp icing sugar
30 milk chocolate buttons
30 white chocolate buttons

method

1 Preheat the oven to 190°C/375°F/Gas Mark 5. Oil two large baking sheets. Melt the plain chocolate in a heatproof bowl set over a saucepan of gently simmering water. Remove from the heat and leave to cool. Sift the flour and baking powder together.

2 In a large bowl, whisk the egg, sugar, oil and vanilla extract together. Whisk in the cooled, melted chocolate until well blended, then gradually stir in the flour. Cover the bowl with clingfilm and chill in the refrigerator for at least 3 hours.

3 Shape tablespoonfuls of the mixture into log shapes using your hands, each measuring about 5 cm/2 inches. Roll the logs generously in the icing sugar, then place on the prepared baking sheets, allowing room for the cookies to spread during cooking.

4 Bake the cookies in the preheated oven for 15 minutes, or until firm. Remove from the oven, and place 3 chocolate buttons down the centre of each cookie, alternating the colours. Transfer to a wire rack and leave to cool.

chocolate dominoes

ingredients

MAKES 28

225 g/8 oz butter, softened
140 g/5 oz caster sugar
1 egg yolk, lightly beaten
2 tsp vanilla extract
250 g/9 oz plain flour
25 g/1 oz cocoa powder
pinch of salt
25 g/1 oz desiccated coconut
50 g/1¾ oz white chocolate
    chips

method

1 Put the butter and sugar into a bowl and mix well with a wooden spoon, then beat in the egg yolk and vanilla extract. Sift the flour, cocoa powder and a pinch of salt together into the mixture, add the coconut and stir until thoroughly combined. Halve the dough, shape into balls, wrap in clingfilm and chill in the refrigerator for 30–60 minutes.

2 Preheat the oven to 190°C/375°F/Gas Mark 5. Line two baking trays with baking paper.

3 Unwrap the dough and roll out between two sheets of baking paper. Stamp out biscuits with a 9-cm/3½-inch plain square cutter, then cut them in half to make rectangles. Put them on the prepared baking trays and, using a knife, make a line across the centre of each without cutting through. Arrange the chocolate chips on top of the biscuits to give the appearance of dominoes, pressing them in gently.

4 Bake in the preheated oven for 10–15 minutes, until golden brown. Leave to cool on the baking trays for 5–10 minutes, then, using a palette knife, carefully transfer to wire racks to cool completely.

chocolate fudge squares

ingredients

MAKES ABOUT 30

225 g/8 oz butter, softened
140 g/5 oz golden caster sugar
1 egg yolk, lightly beaten
2 tsp vanilla extract
225 g/8 oz plain flour
55 g/2 oz cocoa powder
salt

chocolate fudge topping

8 chocolate-coated fudge
    fingers, broken into pieces
4 tbsp double cream

method

1 Put the butter and sugar into a bowl and mix well with a wooden spoon, then beat in the egg yolk and vanilla extract. Sift the flour, cocoa powder and a pinch of salt together into the mixture and stir until thoroughly combined. Halve the dough, shape into balls, wrap in clingfilm and allow to chill in the refrigerator for 30–60 minutes.

2 Preheat the oven to 190°C/375°F/Gas Mark 5. Line two baking sheets with baking paper.

3 Unwrap the dough and roll out between two sheets of baking paper to about 3 mm/$1/8$ inch thick. Stamp out cookies with a 6-cm/$21/2$-inch square cutter and put them on the prepared baking sheets, spaced well apart.

4 Bake for 10–15 minutes, until golden brown. Leave to cool on the baking sheets for 5–10 minutes, then using a palette knife, carefully transfer the cookies to wire racks to cool completely.

5 For the chocolate fudge topping, put the fudge fingers into a heatproof bowl and melt over a saucepan of gently simmering water. Remove the bowl from the heat and gradually whisk in the cream. Leave to cool, then chill until spreadable. Spread the fudge topping over the cookies before serving.

chocolate, date & pecan nut pinwheels

ingredients

MAKES ABOUT 10

225 g/8 oz butter, softened
200 g/7 oz caster sugar
1 egg yolk, lightly beaten
225 g/8 oz plain flour
55 g/2 oz cocoa powder
100 g/3$1/2$ oz pecan nuts,
    finely ground
280 g/10 oz dried dates,
    coarsely chopped
finely grated rind of 1 orange
175 ml/6 fl oz orange
    flower water
salt

method

1 Put the butter and 140 g/5 oz of the sugar into a bowl, mix well with a wooden spoon, then beat in the egg yolk. Sift together the flour, cocoa powder and a pinch of salt into the mixture, add the nuts and stir until thoroughly combined. Halve the dough, shape into balls, wrap in clingfilm and chill for 30–60 minutes.

2 Meanwhile, put the dates, orange rind, orange flower water and remaining sugar into a saucepan and cook over a low heat, stirring constantly, until the sugar has dissolved. Bring to the boil, then reduce the heat and simmer, stirring occasionally, for 5 minutes. Remove from the heat, pour the mixture into a bowl and leave to cool, then chill in the refrigerator.

3 Unwrap the dough and roll out between two pieces of baking paper to rectangles about 5 mm/$1/4$ inch thick. Spread the date filling evenly over the rectangles. Roll up the dough from a short side like a Swiss roll, wrap in the baking paper and chill for a further 30 minutes.

4 Meanwhile, preheat the oven to 190°C/375°F/ Gas Mark 5. Line two baking sheets with baking paper. Unwrap the rolls and cut into 1-cm/$1/2$- inch slices. Put them on the baking sheets and bake for 15–20 minutes, until golden brown. Leave to cool on the sheets for 5–10 minutes, then transfer to wire racks to cool completely.

chocolate sprinkle cookies

ingredients

MAKES ABOUT 30

225 g/8 oz butter, softened

140 g/5 oz caster sugar

1 egg yolk, lightly beaten

2 tsp vanilla extract

225 g/8 oz plain flour, plus
    extra for dusting

55 g/2 oz cocoa powder

200 g/7 oz white chocolate,
    broken into pieces

85 g/3 oz chocolate vermicelli

salt

method

1 Put the butter and sugar into a bowl and mix well with a wooden spoon, then beat in the egg yolk and vanilla extract. Sift the flour, cocoa powder and a pinch of salt together into the mixture and stir until thoroughly combined. Halve the dough, roll each piece into a ball, wrap in clingfilm and chill in the refrigerator for 30–60 minutes to firm up.

2 Preheat the oven to 190°C/375°F/Gas Mark 5. Line two baking sheets with baking paper.

3 Unwrap the dough and roll out between two pieces of baking paper to 5 mm/1/4 inch thick. Stamp out 30 cookies with a 6-cm/21/2-inch fluted round cutter. Put them on the prepared baking sheets spaced well apart.

4 Bake in the preheated oven for 10–12 minutes. Leave to cool on the baking sheets for 5–10 minutes, then, using a palette knife, carefully transfer the cookies to wire racks to cool completely.

5 Put the pieces of white chocolate into a heatproof bowl and melt over a saucepan of gently simmering water, then immediately remove from the heat. Spread the melted chocolate over the cookies, leave to cool slightly and then sprinkle with the chocolate vermicelli. Leave to cool and set.

chocolate spread & hazelnut drops

ingredients

MAKES ABOUT 30

225 g/8 oz butter, softened
140 g/5 oz caster sugar
1 egg yolk, lightly beaten
2 tsp vanilla extract
225 g/8 oz plain flour
55 g/2 oz cocoa powder
55 g/2 oz ground hazelnuts
4 tbsp chocolate and hazelnut
   spread
salt

method

1 Preheat the oven to 190°C/375°F/Gas Mark 5. Line two baking sheets with baking paper.

2 Put the butter and sugar into a bowl and mix well with a wooden spoon, then beat in the egg yolk and vanilla extract. Sift the flour, cocoa powder and a pinch of salt together into the mixture, add the ground hazelnuts and stir until thoroughly combined.

3 Scoop out tablespoons of the mixture and shape into balls with your hands, then put them on the prepared baking sheets, spaced well apart. Use the dampened handle of a wooden spoon to make a hollow in the centre of each drop.

4 Bake in the preheated oven for 12–15 minutes. Leave to cool on the baking sheets for 5–10 minutes, then using a palette knife, carefully transfer the drops to wire racks to cool completely. When they are cold fill the hollows in the centre with chocolate and hazelnut spread.

chocolate buttons

ingredients

MAKES ABOUT 30

2 sachets instant chocolate or
 fudge chocolate drink
1 tbsp hot water
225 g/8 oz butter, softened
140 g/5 oz caster sugar, plus
 extra for sprinkling
1 egg yolk, lightly beaten
280 g/10 oz plain flour
salt

method

1 Empty the chocolate drink sachets into a bowl and stir in the hot water to make a paste. Put the butter and sugar into a bowl and mix well with a wooden spoon, then beat in the egg yolk and chocolate paste. Sift the flour and a pinch of salt together into the mixture and stir until thoroughly combined. Halve the dough, shape into rounds, wrap in clingfilm and chill in the refrigerator for 30–60 minutes.

2 Preheat the oven to 190°C/375°F/Gas Mark 5. Line two baking sheets with baking paper.

3 Unwrap the dough and roll out between two sheets of baking paper to 3 mm/1/8 inch thick. Stamp out rounds with a plain 5-cm/ 2-inch cutter. Using a 3-cm/11/4-inch cap from a soft drink or mineral water bottle, make an indentation in the centre of each button. Using a wooden cocktail stick, make four holes in the centre of each button, then put them on the prepared baking sheets spaced well apart. Sprinkle with caster sugar.

4 Bake in the preheated oven for 10–15 minutes, until firm. Leave to cool on the baking sheets for 5–10 minutes, then, using a palette knife, transfer to wire racks to cool completely.

mocha walnut cookies

ingredients

MAKES ABOUT 16

115 g/4 oz unsalted butter, softened, plus extra for greasing

115 g/4 oz soft light brown sugar

115 g/4 oz granulated sugar

1 tsp vanilla extract

1 tbsp instant coffee granules, dissolved in 1 tbsp hot water

1 egg

175 g/6 oz plain flour

$1/2$ tsp baking powder

$1/4$ tsp bicarbonate of soda

55 g/2 oz milk chocolate chips

85 g/3 oz shelled walnuts, coarsely chopped

method

1 Preheat the oven to 180°C/350°F/Gas Mark 4. Grease two large baking sheets. Place the butter, brown sugar and granulated sugar in a large bowl and beat together thoroughly until light and fluffy. Place the vanilla extract, coffee and egg in a separate large bowl and whisk together.

2 Gradually add the coffee mixture to the butter and sugar, beating until fluffy. Sift the flour, baking powder and bicarbonate of soda into the mixture and fold in carefully. Fold in the chocolate chips and walnuts.

3 Drop dessertspoonfuls of the mixture onto the baking sheets, spacing well apart to allow room for spreading. Bake in the preheated oven for 10–15 minutes, or until crisp on the outside but still soft inside. Remove from the oven. Cool on the baking sheets for 2 minutes, then transfer to wire racks to cool completely.

chocolate & coffee wholemeal cookies

ingredients

MAKES 24

85 g/3 oz unsalted butter or margarine, plus extra for greasing

225 g/8 oz soft light brown sugar

1 egg

70 g/2 1/2 oz plain flour

1 tsp bicarbonate of soda

pinch of salt

55 g/2 oz wholemeal flour

1 tbsp bran

225 g/8 oz plain chocolate chips

200 g/7 oz rolled oats

1 tbsp strong coffee

85 g/3 oz hazelnuts, toasted and coarsely chopped

method

1 Preheat the oven to 190°C/375°F/Gas Mark 5. Grease two large baking sheets. Beat the butter and sugar together in a bowl. Add the egg and beat well, using a hand whisk if preferred.

2 Sift the plain flour, bicarbonate of soda and salt together into a separate bowl, then add in the wholemeal flour and bran. Mix in the egg mixture, then stir in the chocolate chips, oats, coffee and hazelnuts. Mix well.

3 Put 24 rounded tablespoonfuls of the mixture onto the baking sheets, leaving room for the cookies to spread during cooking. Transfer the cookie sheets to the preheated oven and bake for 16–18 minutes, or until the cookies are golden brown.

4 Remove from the oven, then transfer to a wire rack and leave to cool before serving.

oatmeal & pecan nut cookies

ingredients

MAKES 15

115 g/4 oz unsalted butter, softened, plus extra for greasing
85 g/3 oz soft light brown sugar
1 egg, beaten
40 g/1^{1}/$_{2}$ oz pecan nuts, chopped
85 g/3 oz plain flour
^{1}/$_{2}$ tsp baking powder
55 g/2 oz rolled oats

method

1 Preheat the oven to 180°C/350°F/Gas Mark 4. Grease two baking sheets. Place the butter and sugar in a bowl and beat until light and fluffy. Gradually beat in the egg, then stir in the nuts.

2 Sift the flour and baking powder into the mixture and add the oats. Stir together until well combined. Drop dessertspoonfuls of the mixture onto the baking sheets, spaced well apart to allow for spreading.

3 Bake in the preheated oven for 15 minutes, or until pale golden. Remove from the oven and leave to cool on the baking sheets for 2 minutes, then cool completely on wire racks.

peanut butter cookies

ingredients

MAKES 26

115 g/4 oz butter, softened,
  plus extra for greasing
115 g/4 oz crunchy peanut
  butter
115 g/4 oz golden caster sugar
115 g/4 oz light muscovado
  sugar
1 egg, beaten
1/2 tsp vanilla extract
85 g/3 oz plain flour
1/2 tsp bicarbonate of soda
1/2 tsp baking powder
pinch of salt
115 g/4 oz rolled oats

method

1 Preheat the oven to 180°C/350°F/Gas Mark 4, then grease three baking trays.

2 Place the butter and peanut butter in a bowl and beat together. Beat in the caster sugar and muscovado sugar, then gradually beat in the egg and the vanilla extract.

3 Sift the flour, bicarbonate of soda, baking powder and salt into the mixture, add the oats and stir until just combined.

4 Place spoonfuls of the mixture onto the prepared baking trays, spaced well apart to allow for spreading. Flatten slightly with a fork.

5 Bake in the preheated oven for 12 minutes, or until lightly browned. Leave to cool on the baking trays for 2 minutes, then transfer to wire racks to cool completely.

pistachio & almond tuiles

ingredients

MAKES 12

1 egg white

55 g/2 oz golden caster sugar

25 g/1 oz plain flour

25 g/1 oz pistachio nuts,
   finely chopped

25 g/1 oz ground almonds

1/2 tsp almond extract

40 g/11/2 oz unsalted butter,
   melted and cooled

method

1 Preheat the oven to 160°C/325°F/Gas Mark 3. Line two baking trays with baking paper.

2 Whisk the egg white lightly with the sugar, then stir in the flour, pistachio nuts, ground almonds, almond extract and butter, mixing to a soft paste.

3 Place walnut-sized spoonfuls of the mixture on the prepared baking trays and use the back of the spoon to spread as thinly as possible. Bake in the preheated oven for 10–15 minutes, until pale golden.

4 Quickly lift each biscuit with a palette knife and place over the side of a rolling pin to shape into a curve. When set, transfer to a wire rack to cool.

fig & walnut cookies

ingredients

MAKES 20

225 g/8 oz unsalted butter or margarine, plus extra for greasing
55 g/2 oz dried figs
115 g/4 oz clear honey
4 tbsp demerara sugar
2 eggs, beaten
pinch of salt
1 tsp allspice
1 tsp bicarbonate of soda
1/2 tsp vanilla extract
2 tbsp dried dates, finely chopped
210 g/7 1/2 oz plain flour
175 g/6 oz rolled oats
55 g/2 oz walnuts, finely chopped
dried fig pieces, to decorate (optional)

method

1 Preheat the oven to 180°C/350°F/Gas Mark 4. Grease two large baking sheets.

2 Finely chop the figs. Mix the butter, honey, figs and sugar together in a large bowl. Beat the eggs into the mixture and mix thoroughly.

3 In a separate bowl, combine the salt, allspice, bicarbonate of soda, vanilla extract and dates. Gradually stir them into the creamed mixture. Sift the flour into the mixture and stir well. Finally, mix in the oats and walnuts.

4 Drop 20 rounded tablespoonfuls of the mixture onto the baking sheets, spaced well apart to allow for spreading. Decorate with fig pieces, if using. Bake in the preheated oven for 10–15 minutes, or until the cookies are golden brown.

5 Remove the cookies from the oven. Transfer to a wire rack and leave to cool before serving.

oat & hazelnut cookies

ingredients

MAKES 30

170 g/5³/4 oz unsalted butter
   or margarine, plus extra
   for greasing
250 g/9 oz demerara sugar
1 egg, beaten
4 tbsp milk
1 tsp vanilla extract
¹/2 tsp almond extract
85 g/3 oz hazelnuts
140 g/5 oz plain flour
1¹/2 tsp ground allspice
¹/4 tsp bicarbonate of soda
pinch of salt
170 g/5³/4 oz rolled oats
175 g/6 oz sultanas

method

1 Preheat the oven to 190°C/375°F/Gas Mark 5. Grease two large baking sheets.

2 Cream the butter and sugar together in a mixing bowl. Blend in the egg, milk, vanilla extract and almond extract until thoroughly combined. Finely chop the hazelnuts.

3 In a mixing bowl, sift the flour, allspice, bicarbonate of soda and salt together. Add to the creamed mixture slowly, stirring constantly. Mix in the oatmeal, sultanas and hazelnuts.

4 Put 30 rounded tablespoonfuls of the mixture onto the prepared baking sheets, spaced well apart to allow for spreading. Transfer to the preheated oven and bake for 12–15 minutes, or until the cookies are golden brown.

5 Remove the cookies from the oven and place on a wire rack to cool before serving.

almond biscotti

ingredients

MAKES 20–24

250 g/9 oz plain flour, plus
    extra for dusting
1 tsp baking powder
pinch of salt
150 g/5½ oz golden caster
    sugar
2 eggs, beaten
finely grated rind of 1 unwaxed
    orange
100 g/3½ oz whole blanched
    almonds, lightly toasted

method

1 Preheat the oven to 180°C/350°F/Gas Mark 4. Lightly dust a baking sheet with flour. Sift the flour, baking powder and salt into a bowl. Add the sugar, eggs and orange rind and mix to a dough, then knead in the almonds.

2 Using your hands, roll the dough into a ball, cut in half and roll each portion into a log about 4 cm/1½ inches in diameter. Place on the prepared baking sheet and bake in the preheated oven for 10 minutes. Remove from the oven and leave to cool for 5 minutes.

3 Using a serrated knife, cut the logs into 1-cm/½-inch diagonal slices. Arrange the slices on the baking sheet and return to the oven for 15 minutes or until slightly golden. Transfer to a wire rack to cool and crisp up.

nutty drizzles

ingredients

MAKES 24

200 g/7 oz unsalted butter,
    plus extra for greasing
250 g/9 oz demerara sugar
1 egg
125 g/4^{1}/$_{2}$ oz plain flour, sifted
1 tsp baking powder
1 tsp bicarbonate of soda
175 g/6 oz rolled oats
1 tbsp bran
1 tbsp wheatgerm
115 g/4 oz mixed nuts, toasted
    and coarsely chopped
200 g/7 oz plain chocolate
    chips
85 g/3 oz raisins and sultanas
175 g/6 oz plain chocolate,
    coarsely chopped

method

1 Preheat the oven to 180°C/350°F/Gas Mark 4. Grease two large baking sheets. In a large bowl, beat the butter, sugar and egg together. Add the flour, baking powder, bicarbonate of soda, oats, bran and wheatgerm and mix together until well combined. Stir in the nuts, chocolate chips and dried fruit.

2 Put 24 rounded tablespoonfuls of the mixture onto the prepared baking sheets. Transfer to the preheated oven and bake for 12 minutes, or until the cookies are golden.

3 Remove the cookies from the oven, then transfer to a wire rack and leave to cool. Meanwhile, heat the chocolate pieces in a heatproof bowl set over a saucepan of gently simmering water until melted. Stir the chocolate, then leave to cool slightly.

4 Use a spoon to drizzle the chocolate in waves over the cookies, or spoon it into a piping bag and pipe zigzag lines over the cookies. When the chocolate has set, store the cookies in an airtight container in the refrigerator until ready to serve.

almond crunchies

ingredients

MAKES ABOUT 50

225 g/8 oz butter, softened

140 g/5 oz caster sugar

1 egg yolk, lightly beaten

1/2 tsp almond extract

225 g/8 oz plain flour

225 g/8 oz blanched almonds, chopped

salt

method

1 Put the butter and sugar into a bowl and mix well with a wooden spoon, then beat in the egg yolk and almond extract. Sift the flour and a pinch of salt together into the mixture, add the almonds and stir until thoroughly combined. Halve the dough, shape it into balls, wrap in clingfilm and chill for 30–60 minutes.

2 Preheat the oven to 190°C/375°F/Gas Mark 5. Line two or three baking sheets with baking paper. Shape the dough into about 50 small balls and flatten them slightly between the palms of your hands. Place on the prepared baking sheets, spaced well apart.

3 Bake for 15–20 minutes, until golden brown. Leave to cool on the baking sheets for 5–10 minutes, then, using a palette knife, carefully transfer to wire racks to cool completely.

snickerdoodles

ingredients

MAKES ABOUT 40

225 g/8 oz butter, softened
140 g/5 oz caster sugar
2 large eggs, lightly beaten
1 tsp vanilla extract
400 g/14 oz plain flour
1 tsp bicarbonate of soda
$1/2$ tsp freshly grated nutmeg
pinch of salt
55 g/2 oz pecan nuts, finely
   chopped

cinnamon coating
1 tbsp caster sugar
2 tbsp ground cinnamon

method

1 Put the butter and sugar into a bowl and mix well with a wooden spoon, then beat in the eggs and vanilla extract. Sift the flour, bicarbonate of soda, nutmeg and salt together into the mixture, add the pecan nuts and stir until thoroughly combined. Shape the dough into a ball, wrap in clingfilm and leave to chill in the refrigerator for 30–60 minutes.

2 Preheat the oven to 190°C/375°F/Gas Mark 5. Line two baking trays with baking paper.

3 For the cinnamon coating, mix the caster sugar and cinnamon together in a shallow dish. Scoop up tablespoons of the dough and roll into balls. Roll each ball in the cinnamon mixture to coat and place on the prepared baking trays, spaced well apart.

4 Bake in the preheated oven for 10–12 minutes, until golden brown. Leave to cool on the baking trays for 5–10 minutes, then, using a palette knife, carefully transfer to wire racks to cool completely.

cashew nut & poppy seed cookies

ingredients

MAKES ABOUT 20

225 g/8 oz butter, softened

140 g/5 oz caster sugar

1 egg yolk, lightly beaten

280 g/10 oz plain flour

1 tsp ground cinnamon

115 g/4 oz cashew nuts, chopped

2–3 tbsp poppy seeds

salt

method

1 Put the butter and sugar into a bowl and mix well with a wooden spoon, then beat in the egg yolk. Sift the flour, cinnamon and a pinch of salt together into the mixture, add the nuts and stir until thoroughly combined. Shape the dough into a log. Spread out the poppy seeds in a shallow dish and roll the log in them until well coated. Wrap in clingfilm and chill in the refrigerator for 30–60 minutes.

2 Preheat the oven to 190°C/375°F/Gas Mark 5. Line two baking sheets with baking paper.

3 Unwrap the dough and cut into 1-cm/1/2-inch slices with a sharp serrated knife. Put them on the prepared baking sheets and bake in the preheated oven for 12 minutes, until golden brown. Leave to cool on the baking sheets for 5–10 minutes, then using a palette knife, carefully transfer to wire racks to cool completely.

walnut & coffee cookies

ingredients

MAKES ABOUT 30

2 sachets instant latte powder

1 tbsp hot water

225 g/8 oz butter, softened

140 g/5 oz caster sugar

1 egg yolk, lightly beaten

280 g/10 oz plain flour

100 g/3^1/$_2$ oz walnuts, finely
    chopped

salt

coffee sugar crystals,
    for sprinkling

method

1 Put the instant latte powder into a bowl and stir in the hot water to make a paste. Put the butter and sugar into a bowl and mix well with a wooden spoon, then beat in the egg yolk and coffee paste. Sift the flour and a pinch of salt together into the mixture, add the walnuts and stir until thoroughly combined. Halve the dough, shape into balls, wrap in clingfilm and chill in the refrigerator for 30–60 minutes.

2 Preheat the oven to 190°C/375°F/Gas Mark 5. Line two baking sheets with baking paper.

3 Unwrap the dough and roll out between two sheets of baking paper to about 3 mm/^{1}/$_8$ inch thick. Stamp out rounds with a 6-cm/2^1/$_2$-inch cutter and put them on the prepared baking sheets, spaced well apart.

4 Lightly brush the cookies with water, sprinkle with the coffee sugar crystals and bake for 10–12 minutes. Leave to cool on the baking sheets for 5–10 minutes, then, using a palette knife, carefully transfer the cookies to wire racks to cool completely.

pineapple & cherry florentines

ingredients

MAKES ABOUT 14

55 g/2 oz unsalted butter

40 g/1¹/₂ oz demerara sugar

1 tbsp golden syrup

50 g/1³/₄ oz plain flour, sifted

25 g/1 oz angelica, coarsely chopped

25 g/1 oz glacé cherries, coarsely chopped

55 g/2 oz flaked almonds, coarsely chopped

55 g/2 oz glacé pineapple, coarsely chopped

1 tsp lemon juice

115 g/4 oz plain chocolate, melted and cooled

method

1 Preheat the oven to 180°C/350°F/Gas Mark 4. Line two baking sheets with non-stick baking paper. Place the butter, sugar and syrup in a saucepan and heat gently until melted, then stir in the flour, angelica, cherries, almonds, pineapple and lemon juice.

2 Place walnut-sized mounds of the mixture, spaced well apart, on the prepared baking sheets and flatten gently with a fork. Bake in the preheated oven for 8–10 minutes, or until golden brown. Use a spatula to neaten the ragged edges. Leave to cool for 1 minute, then transfer to a wire rack to cool completely.

3 Spread the melted chocolate over the base of each Florentine, then place, chocolate-side up, on a wire rack. Use a fork to mark the chocolate with wavy lines. Leave to stand until set.

apricot & pecan nut cookies

ingredients

MAKES ABOUT 30

225 g/8 oz butter, softened

140 g/5 oz caster sugar

1 egg yolk, lightly beaten

2 tsp vanilla extract

280 g/10 oz plain flour

grated rind of 1 orange

55 g/2 oz ready-to-eat dried
    apricots, chopped

100 g/3$\frac{1}{2}$ oz pecan nuts,
    finely chopped

salt

method

1 Put the butter and sugar into a bowl and mix well with a wooden spoon, then beat in the egg yolk and vanilla extract. Sift the flour and a pinch of salt together into the mixture, add the orange rind and apricots and stir until thoroughly combined. Shape the dough into a log. Spread out the pecan nuts in a shallow dish. Roll the log in the nuts until well coated, then wrap in clingfilm and chill in the refrigerator for 30–60 minutes.

2 Preheat the oven to 190°C/375°F/Gas Mark 5. Line two baking sheets with baking paper.

Unwrap the dough and cut into 5-mm/$\frac{1}{4}$-inch slices with a sharp serrated knife. Put the slices on the prepared baking sheets, spaced well apart.

3 Bake in the preheated oven for 10–12 minutes. Leave to cool on the baking sheets for 5–10 minutes, then, using a palette knife, carefully transfer to wire racks to cool completely.

walnut & fig pinwheels

ingredients

MAKES ABOUT 30

225 g/8 oz butter, softened

200 g/7 oz caster sugar

1 egg yolk, lightly beaten

225 g/8 oz plain flour

55 g/2 oz ground walnuts

280 g/10 oz dried figs, finely
   chopped

5 tbsp freshly brewed mint tea

2 tsp finely chopped fresh
   mint

salt

method

1 Put the butter and 140 g/5 oz of the sugar into a bowl and mix well with a wooden spoon, then beat in the egg yolk. Sift the flour and a pinch of salt together into the mixture, add the ground walnuts and stir until thoroughly combined. Shape the dough into a ball, wrap in clingfilm and chill for 30–60 minutes.

2 Meanwhile, put the remaining sugar into a saucepan and stir in 125 ml/4 fl oz water, then add the figs, mint tea and chopped mint. Bring to the boil, stirring constantly, until the sugar has dissolved, then reduce the heat and simmer gently, stirring occasionally, for 5 minutes. Remove the pan from the heat and leave to cool.

3 Unwrap the dough and roll out between two sheets of baking paper into a 30-cm/ 12-inch square. Spread the fig filling evenly over the dough, then roll up like a Swiss roll. Wrap in clingfilm and chill in the refrigerator for 30 minutes.

4 Meanwhile, preheat the oven to 190°C/375°F/ Gas Mark 5. Line two baking sheets with baking paper. Unwrap the roll and cut into thin slices with a sharp serrated knife. Put the slices on the prepared baking sheets, spread well apart. Bake in the preheated oven for 10–15 minutes, until golden brown. Leave to cool on the baking sheets for 5–10 minutes, then using a palette knife, transfer to wire racks to cool completely.

mixed fruit cookies

ingredients

MAKES ABOUT 30

225 g/8 oz butter, softened
140 g/5 oz caster sugar
1 egg yolk, lightly beaten
280 g/10 oz plain flour
1/2 tsp mixed spice
25 g/1 oz ready-to-eat dried
apple, chopped
25 g/1 oz ready-to-eat dried
pear, chopped
25 g/1 oz ready-to-eat prunes,
chopped
grated rind of 1 orange
salt

method

1 Put the butter and sugar into a bowl and mix well with a wooden spoon, then beat in the egg yolk. Sift together the flour, mixed spice and a pinch of salt into the mixture, add the apple, pear, prunes and orange rind and stir until thoroughly combined. Shape the dough into a log, wrap in clingfilm and chill in the refrigerator for 30–60 minutes.

2 Preheat the oven to 190°C/375°F/Gas Mark 5. Line two baking sheets with baking paper.

3 Unwrap the log and cut it into 5-mm/1/4-inch thick slices with a sharp serrated knife. Put them on the prepared baking sheets spaced well apart.

4 Bake in the preheated oven for 10–15 minutes, until golden brown. Leave to cool on the baking sheets for 5–10 minutes, then, using a palette knife, carefully transfer the cookies to wire racks to cool completely.

tropical fruit & mascarpone cream cookie sandwiches

ingredients

MAKES ABOUT 15

225 g/8 oz butter, softened

140 g/5 oz caster sugar

1 egg yolk, lightly beaten

2 tsp passion fruit pulp

280 g/10 oz plain flour

40 g/1^{1}/$_{2}$ oz ready-to-eat dried
   mango, chopped

40 g/1^{1}/$_{2}$ oz ready-to-eat dried
   pawpaw, chopped

25 g/1 oz dried dates, stoned
   and chopped

3–4 tbsp shredded coconut,
   toasted

salt

mascarpone cream

85 g/3 oz mascarpone cheese

3 tbsp Greek-style yogurt

7 tbsp ready-made custard

^{1}/$_{2}$ tsp ground ginger

method

1 Put the butter and sugar into a bowl and mix well with a wooden spoon, then beat in the egg yolk and passion fruit pulp. Sift the flour and a pinch of salt together into the mixture, add the mango, pawpaw and dates and stir until thoroughly combined. Shape the dough into a log, wrap in clingfilm and chill in the refrigerator for 30–60 minutes.

2 Meanwhile, make the mascarpone cream. Put all the ingredients in a bowl and beat with a wooden spoon until thoroughly combined and smooth. Cover the bowl with clingfilm and chill in the refrigerator.

3 Preheat the oven to 190°C/375°F/Gas Mark 5. Line two baking sheets with baking paper.

4 Unwrap the dough and cut into slices with a sharp serrated knife. Put them on the prepared baking sheets spaced well apart.

5 Bake in the preheated oven for 10–15 minutes, until light golden brown. Leave to cool on the baking sheets for 5–10 minutes, then, using a palette knife, carefully transfer to wire racks to cool completely. When the cookies are cold spread the chilled mascarpone cream over half of them, sprinkle with the toasted coconut and top with the remaining cookies.

chocolate & apricot cookies

ingredients

MAKES ABOUT 30

225 g/8 oz butter, softened

140 g/5 oz caster sugar

1 egg yolk, lightly beaten

2 tsp amaretto liqueur

280 g/10 oz plain flour

55 g/2 oz plain chocolate
   chips

55 g/2 oz ready-to-eat dried
   apricots, chopped

100 g/3^{1}/$_{2}$ oz blanched
   almonds, chopped

salt

method

1 Put the butter and sugar into a bowl and mix well with a wooden spoon, then beat in the egg yolk and amaretto liqueur. Sift the flour and a pinch of salt together into the mixture, add the chocolate chips and apricots and stir until thoroughly combined.

2 Shape the mixture into a log. Spread out the almonds in a shallow dish and roll the log in them to coat. Wrap in clingfilm and chill in the refrigerator for 30–60 minutes.

3 Preheat the oven to 190°C/375°F/Gas Mark 5. Line two baking sheets with baking paper.

4 Unwrap the dough and cut into 5-mm/^{1}/$_{4}$-inch slices with a sharp serrated knife. Put them on the prepared baking sheets, spaced well apart.

5 Bake in the preheated oven for 12–15 minutes, until golden brown. Leave to cool on the baking sheets for 5–10 minutes, then, using a palette knife, carefully transfer to wire racks to cool completely.

orange & lemon cookies

ingredients

MAKES ABOUT 30

225 g/8 oz butter, softened
140 g/5 oz caster sugar
1 egg yolk, lightly beaten
280 g/10 oz plain flour
finely grated rind of 1 orange
finely grated rind of 1 lemon
salt

to decorate

1 tbsp lightly beaten egg white
1 tbsp lemon juice
115 g/4 oz icing sugar
few drops yellow food
     colouring
few drops orange food
     colouring
about 15 lemon jelly slices
about 15 orange jelly slices

method

1 Put the butter and sugar into a bowl and mix well with a wooden spoon, then beat in the egg yolk. Sift the flour and a pinch of salt together into the mixture and stir until thoroughly combined. Halve the dough and gently knead the orange rind into one half and the lemon rind into the other. Shape into balls, wrap in clingfilm and chill in the refrigerator for 30–60 minutes.

2 Preheat the oven to 190°C/375°F/Gas Mark 5. Line two baking sheets with baking paper.

3 Unwrap the orange-flavoured dough and roll out between two sheets of baking paper. Stamp out rounds with a 6-cm/2$\frac{1}{2}$-inch cutter and put them on a prepared baking sheet, spaced well apart. Repeat with the lemon-flavoured dough and stamp out crescents. Put them on the other prepared baking sheet spaced well apart.

4 Bake in the preheated oven for 10–15 minutes, until golden brown. Leave to cool for 5–10 minutes, then carefully transfer to wire racks to cool completely.

5 To decorate, mix together the egg white and lemon juice. Gradually beat in the icing sugar with a wooden spoon until smooth. Spoon half the icing into another bowl. Stir yellow food colouring into one bowl and orange food colouring into the other. Leave the cookies on the racks. Spread the icing over the cookies and decorate with the jelly slices. Leave to set.

grapefruit & apple mint cookies

ingredients

MAKES ABOUT 30

225 g/8 oz butter, softened

140 g/5 oz caster sugar, plus extra for sprinkling

1 egg yolk, lightly beaten

2 tsp grapefruit juice

280 g/10 oz plain flour

grated rind of 1 grapefruit

2 tsp finely chopped fresh apple mint

salt

method

1 Put the butter and sugar into a bowl and mix well with a wooden spoon, then beat in the egg yolk and grapefruit juice. Sift together the flour and a pinch of salt into the mixture, add the grapefruit rind and chopped mint and stir until thoroughly combined. Halve the dough, shape into balls, wrap in clingfilm and chill in the refrigerator for 30–60 minutes.

2 Preheat the oven to 190°C/375°F/Gas Mark 5. Line two baking sheets with baking paper.

3 Unwrap the dough and roll out between two sheets of baking paper to 3 mm/$1/8$ inch thick. Stamp out cookies with a 5-cm/2-inch flower cutter and place on the prepared baking sheets, spaced well apart. Sprinkle with caster sugar.

4 Bake in the preheated oven for 10–15 minutes, until golden brown. Leave to cool on the baking sheets for 5–10 minutes, then, using a palette knife, carefully transfer to wire racks to cool completely.

mango, coconut & ginger cookies

ingredients

MAKES ABOUT 30

225 g/8 oz butter, softened

140 g/5 oz caster sugar

1 egg yolk, lightly beaten

55 g/2 oz stem ginger, chopped, plus 2 tsp syrup from the jar

280 g/10 oz plain flour

55 g/2 oz ready-to-eat dried mango, chopped

100 g/3^1/$_2$ oz desiccated coconut

salt

method

1 Put the butter and sugar into a bowl and mix well with a wooden spoon, then beat in the egg yolk and ginger syrup. Sift the flour and a pinch of salt together into the mixture, add the stem ginger and mango and stir until thoroughly combined.

2 Spread out the coconut in a shallow dish. Shape the dough into a log and roll it in the coconut to coat. Wrap in clingfilm and chill in the refrigerator for 30–60 minutes.

3 Preheat the oven to 190°C/375°F/Gas Mark 5. Line two baking sheets with baking paper.

4 Unwrap the log and cut it into 5-mm/^{1}/$_4$-inch slices with a sharp serrated knife and place them on the prepared baking sheets, spaced well apart.

5 Bake in the preheated oven for 12–15 minutes. Leave to cool on the baking sheets for 5–10 minutes, then, using a palette knife, carefully transfer to wire racks to cool completely.

orange cream cheese biscuits

ingredients

MAKES ABOUT 30

225 g/8 oz butter, plus extra
for greasing
200 g/7 oz demerara sugar
85 g/3 oz cream cheese
1 egg, lightly beaten
350 g/12 oz plain flour
1 tsp bicarbonate of soda
1 tbsp fresh orange juice
demerara sugar, for sprinkling
1 tsp finely grated orange rind,
plus extra for decorating

method

1 Preheat the oven to 190°C/375°F/Gas Mark 5. Grease a large baking sheet.

2 Put the butter, sugar and cream cheese in a large bowl and beat until light and fluffy. Beat in the egg. Sift in the flour and bicarbonate of soda and add the orange juice and orange rind. Mix well.

3 Drop about 30 rounded tablespoonfuls of the mixture onto the prepared baking sheet, making sure that they are spaced well apart. Sprinkle with the demerara sugar.

4 Bake in the preheated oven for 10 minutes, or until light golden brown at the edges.

5 Leave to cool on a wire rack. Decorate with orange rind before serving.

jam rings

ingredients

MAKES ABOUT 15

225 g/8 oz butter, softened

140 g/5 oz caster sugar, plus
    extra for sprinkling

1 egg yolk, lightly beaten

2 tsp vanilla extract

280 g/10 oz plain flour

pinch of salt

1 egg white, lightly beaten

filling

55 g/2 oz butter, softened

100 g/3^1/$_2$ oz icing sugar

5 tbsp strawberry or raspberry
    jam, warmed

method

1 Put the butter and caster sugar into a bowl and mix well with a wooden spoon, then beat in the egg yolk and vanilla extract. Sift the flour and salt together into the mixture and stir until thoroughly combined. Halve the dough, shape into balls, wrap in clingfilm and chill in the refrigerator for 30–60 minutes.

2 Preheat the oven to 190°C/375°F/Gas Mark 5. Line two baking trays with baking paper.

3 Unwrap the dough and roll out between two sheets of baking paper. Stamp out biscuits with a 7-cm/2^3/$_4$-inch fluted round cutter and put half of them on one of the prepared baking trays, spaced well apart. Using a 4-cm/1^1/$_2$-inch plain round cutter, stamp out the centres of the remaining biscuits and remove. Put the rings on the other prepared baking tray, spaced well apart.

4 Bake in the preheated oven for 7 minutes, then brush the biscuit rings with beaten egg white and sprinkle with caster sugar. Bake for a further 5–8 minutes, until light golden brown. Leave to cool on the baking trays for 5–10 minutes, then carefully transfer to wire racks to cool completely.

5 To make the jam filling, beat the butter and icing sugar together in a bowl until smooth and combined. Spread the filling over the whole biscuits and top with a little jam. Place the rings on top and press gently together.

iced cherry rings

ingredients

MAKES ABOUT 18

115 g/4 oz unsalted butter,
    plus extra for greasing
85 g/3 oz golden caster sugar
1 egg yolk
finely grated rind of $\frac{1}{2}$ lemon
200 g/7 oz plain flour, plus
    extra for dusting
55 g/2 oz glacé cherries,
    finely chopped

i c i n g
85 g/3 oz icing sugar
1$\frac{1}{2}$ tbsp lemon juice

method

1 Preheat the oven to 200°C/400°F/Gas Mark 6. Lightly grease two baking trays.

2 Cream together the butter and caster sugar until pale and fluffy. Beat in the egg yolk and lemon rind. Sift in the flour, stir, then add the glacé cherries, mixing with your hands to a soft dough.

3 Roll out the dough on a lightly floured surface to about 5 mm/$\frac{1}{4}$ inch thick. Stamp out 8-cm/ 3$\frac{1}{4}$-inch rounds with a plain round cutter. Stamp out the centre of each with a 2.5-cm/ 1-inch cutter and place the rings on the prepared baking trays. Re-roll any trimmings and cut out more rings.

4 Bake in the preheated oven for 12–15 minutes, until firm and golden brown.

5 Allow to cool on the baking trays for 2 minutes, then transfer to a wire rack to finish cooling.

6 Mix the icing sugar to a smooth paste with the lemon juice. Drizzle over the biscuits and leave until set.

citrus crescents

ingredients

MAKES ABOUT 25

100 g/3$\frac{1}{2}$ oz butter, softened,
  plus extra for greasing
75 g/2$\frac{3}{4}$ oz caster sugar
1 egg, separated
200 g/7 oz plain flour, plus
  extra for dusting
grated rind of 1 orange
grated rind of 1 lemon
grated rind of 1 lime
2–3 tbsp orange juice

method

1 Preheat the oven to 200°C/400°F/Gas Mark 6. Lightly grease two baking trays. In a mixing bowl, cream together the butter and sugar until light and fluffy, then gradually beat in the egg yolk.

2 Sift the flour into the creamed mixture and mix until evenly combined. Add the orange rind, lemon rind and lime rind to the mixture with enough of the orange juice to make a soft dough.

3 Roll out the dough on a lightly floured surface. Stamp out rounds using a 7.5-cm/3-inch plain round cutter. Make crescent shapes by cutting away a quarter of each round. Re-roll the trimmings to make about 25 crescents in total.

4 Place the crescents on the prepared baking trays. Prick the surface of each crescent with a fork. Lightly whisk the egg white in a small bowl and brush it over the biscuits.

5 Bake in the preheated oven for 12–15 minutes. Leave to cool on a wire rack before serving.

chewy candied fruit cookies

ingredients

MAKES ABOUT 30

225 g/8 oz butter, softened
140 g/5 oz caster sugar
1 egg yolk, lightly beaten
2 tsp vanilla extract
280 g/10 oz plain flour
salt

candied topping

4 tbsp maple syrup
55 g/2 oz butter
55 g/2 oz caster sugar
115 g/4 oz ready-to-eat dried
     peaches, chopped
55 g/2 oz glacé cherries,
     chopped
55 g/2 oz chopped mixed peel
85 g/3 oz macadamia nuts,
     chopped
25 g/1 oz plain flour

method

1 Put the butter and sugar into a bowl and mix well with a wooden spoon, then beat in the egg yolk and vanilla extract. Sift the flour and a pinch of salt together into the mixture and stir until thoroughly combined. Halve the dough, shape into balls, wrap in clingfilm and chill for 30–60 minutes.

2 Preheat the oven to 190°C/375°F/Gas Mark 5. Line two baking sheets with baking paper.

3 Unwrap the dough and roll out between two sheets of baking paper. Stamp out rounds with a 6-cm/2$\frac{1}{2}$-inch plain round cutter and put them on the prepared baking sheets, spaced well apart.

4 For the candied topping, put the syrup, butter and sugar into a saucepan and melt over a low heat, stirring occasionally. Meanwhile, put the fruit, mixed peel, nuts and flour into a bowl and mix well. When the syrup mixture is thoroughly combined, stir it into the fruit mixture. Divide the candied topping between the cookies, gently spreading it out to the edges.

5 Bake for 10–15 minutes, until firm. Leave to cool on the baking sheets for 5–10 minutes, then, using a palette knife, carefully transfer the cookies to wire racks to cool completely.

classic saffron cookies

ingredients

MAKES ABOUT 30

100 g/3¹/₂ oz currants

125 ml/4 fl oz sweet white wine

225 g/8 oz butter, softened

140 g/5 oz caster sugar

1 egg yolk, lightly beaten

280 g/10 oz plain flour

¹/₂ tsp powdered saffron

salt

method

1 Put the currants in a bowl, pour in the wine and leave to soak for 1 hour. Drain the currants and reserve any remaining wine.

2 Preheat the oven to 190°C/375°F/Gas Mark 5. Line two baking sheets with baking paper.

3 Put the butter and sugar into a bowl and mix well with a wooden spoon, then beat in the egg yolk and 2 teaspoons of the reserved wine. Sift the flour, saffron and a pinch of salt together into the mixture and stir, until thoroughly combined.

4 Scoop up tablespoonfuls of the dough and put them on the prepared baking sheets, spaced well apart. Flatten gently and smooth the tops with the back of the spoon.

5 Bake in the preheated oven for 10–15 minutes, until light golden brown. Leave to cool on the baking sheets for 5–10 minutes, then, using a palette knife, carefully transfer to wire racks to cool completely.

camomile cookies

ingredients

MAKES ABOUT 30

225 g/8 oz butter, softened

140 g/5 oz golden caster
   sugar, plus extra for coating

1 tbsp (3–4 tea bags)
   camomile or camomile and
   lime flower infusion or tea

1 egg yolk, lightly beaten

1 tsp vanilla extract

280 g/10 oz plain flour

salt

method

1 Put the butter and sugar into a bowl and mix well with a wooden spoon. If necessary, remove the tea leaves from the tea bags. Stir the tea into the butter mixture, then beat in the egg yolk and vanilla extract. Sift the flour and a pinch of salt together into the mixture and stir until thoroughly combined.

2 Shape the dough into a log. Spread out 3–4 tablespoons of caster sugar in a shallow dish and roll the log in the sugar to coat. Wrap in clingfilm and chill for 30–60 minutes.

3 Preheat the oven to 190°C/375°F/Gas Mark 5. Line two baking sheets with baking paper.

4 Unwrap the log and cut into 5-mm/^{1}/$_{4}$-inch slices with a sharp serrated knife. Place them on the prepared baking sheets, spaced well apart to allow for spreading during cooking.

5 Bake for about 10 minutes, until golden. Leave to cool on the baking sheets for 5–10 minutes, then, using a palette knife, carefully transfer to wire racks to cool completely.

fennel & angelica cookies

ingredients

MAKES ABOUT 20

225 g/8 oz butter, softened

140 g/5 oz caster sugar

1 egg yolk, lightly beaten

1 tbsp finely chopped angelica

280 g/10 oz plain flour

1 tbsp fennel seeds

salt

method

1 Put the butter and sugar into a bowl and mix well with a wooden spoon, then beat in the egg yolk and angelica. Sift the flour and a pinch of salt together into the mixture, add the fennel seeds and stir until thoroughly combined. Shape the dough into a log, wrap in clingfilm and chill in the refrigerator for 30–60 minutes.

2 Preheat the oven to 190°C/375°F/Gas Mark 5. Line two baking sheets with baking paper.

3 Unwrap the dough and cut into 1-cm/$1/2$-inch slices with a sharp serrated knife. Put them on the prepared baking sheets, spaced well apart.

4 Bake in the preheated oven for 12–15 minutes, until golden brown. Leave to cool on the baking sheets for 5–10 minutes, then, using a palette knife, carefully transfer to wire racks to cool completely.

treacle & spice drizzles

ingredients

MAKES 25

200 g/7 oz butter, softened
2 tbsp treacle
140 g/5 oz caster sugar
1 egg yolk, lightly beaten
280 g/10 oz plain flour
1 tsp ground cinnamon
$1/2$ tsp grated nutmeg
$1/2$ tsp ground cloves
2 tbsp chopped walnuts
salt

icing
115 g/4 oz icing sugar
1 tbsp hot water
a few drops of yellow food
    colouring
a few drops of pink food
    colouring

method

1 Put the butter, treacle and sugar into a bowl and mix well with a wooden spoon, then beat in the egg yolk. Sift the flour, cinnamon, nutmeg, cloves and a pinch of salt together into the mixture, add the walnuts and stir until thoroughly combined. Halve the dough, shape into balls, wrap in clingfilm and chill in the refrigerator for 30–60 minutes.

2 Preheat the oven to 190°C/375°F/Gas Mark 5. Line two baking sheets with baking paper.

3 Unwrap the dough and roll out between two sheets of baking paper to about 5 mm/$1/4$ inch thick. Stamp out rounds with a 6-cm/$2^{1/2}$-inch fluted cutter and put them on the prepared baking sheets.

4 Bake in the preheated oven for 10–15 minutes, until firm. Cool on the baking sheets for 5–10 minutes, then, using a palette knife, carefully transfer to wire racks to cool completely.

5 For the icing, sift the icing sugar into a bowl, then gradually stir in the hot water until the icing has the consistency of thick cream. Spoon half the icing into another bowl and stir a few drops of yellow food colouring into one bowl and a few drops of pink food colouring into the other. Leave the cookies on the racks and, using teaspoons, drizzle the yellow icing over them in one direction and the pink icing over them at right angles. Leave to set.

cinnamon & caramel cookies

ingredients

MAKES ABOUT 25

225 g/8 oz butter, softened
140 g/5 oz caster sugar
1 egg yolk, lightly beaten
1 tsp vanilla extract
280 g/10 oz plain flour
1 tsp ground cinnamon
1/2 tsp allspice
25–30 caramel sweets
salt

method

1 Preheat the oven to 190°C/375°F/Gas Mark 5. Line two baking sheets with baking paper.

2 Put the butter and sugar into a bowl and mix well with a wooden spoon, then beat in the egg yolk and vanilla extract. Sift the flour, cinnamon, allspice and a pinch of salt together into the mixture and stir until thoroughly combined.

3 Scoop up tablespoons of the mixture, shape into balls and place on the prepared baking sheets, spaced well apart. Bake in the preheated oven for 8 minutes. Place a caramel sweet on top of each cookie, return to the oven and bake for a further 6–7 minutes.

4 Remove from the oven and leave to cool on the baking sheets for 5–10 minutes. Using a palette knife, carefully transfer the cookies to wire racks to cool completely.

brandy snaps

ingredients

MAKES ABOUT 20

85 g/3 oz unsalted butter

85 g/3 oz golden caster sugar

3 tbsp golden syrup

85 g/3 oz plain flour

1 tsp ground ginger

1 tbsp brandy

finely grated rind of 1/2 lemon

filling

150 ml/5 fl oz double cream
  or whipping cream

1 tbsp brandy (optional)

1 tbsp icing sugar

method

1 Preheat the oven to 160°C/325°F/Gas Mark 3. Line three large baking trays with baking paper.

2 Place the butter, sugar and golden syrup in a saucepan and heat gently over a low heat, stirring occasionally, until melted. Remove from the heat and leave to cool slightly. Sift the flour and ginger into the pan and beat until smooth, then stir in the brandy and lemon rind.

3 Drop small spoonfuls of the mixture onto the prepared baking trays, leaving plenty of room for spreading. Place one baking tray at a time in the preheated oven for 10–12 minutes, or until the snaps are golden brown.

4 Remove the first baking tray from the oven and leave to cool for about 30 seconds, then lift each round with a palette knife and wrap around the handle of a wooden spoon. If the brandy snaps start to become too firm to wrap, return them to the oven for about 30 seconds to soften again. When firm, remove from the spoon handles and finish cooling on a wire rack. Repeat with the remaining baking trays.

5 For the filling, whip the cream with the brandy, if using, and the icing sugar until thick. Just before serving, pipe the cream mixture into each end of the brandy snaps.

lavender cookies

ingredients

MAKES 12

55 g/2 oz golden caster sugar,
plus extra for dusting

1 tsp chopped lavender leaves

115 g/4 oz unsalted butter,
softened, plus extra
for greasing

finely grated rind of 1 lemon

140 g/5 oz plain flour

method

1 Preheat the oven to 150°C/300°F/Gas Mark 2, then grease a large baking sheet. Place the sugar and lavender leaves in a food processor. Process until the lavender is very finely chopped, then add the butter and lemon rind and continue to process until light and fluffy. Transfer to a large bowl. Sift in the flour and beat until the mixture forms a stiff dough.

2 Place the dough on a sheet of baking paper and place another sheet on top. Gently press down with a rolling pin and roll out to 3–5 mm/ $1/8$–$1/4$ inch thick. Remove the top sheet of paper and stamp out rounds from the dough using a 7-cm/$2^3/4$-inch plain round cutter. Re-knead and re-roll the trimmings and stamp out more rounds.

3 Using a spatula, transfer the cookies to the prepared baking sheet. Prick them with a fork and bake in the preheated oven for 12 minutes, or until pale brown. Remove from the oven and cool on the sheet for 2 minutes, then transfer to a wire rack to cool completely.

vanilla hearts

ingredients

MAKES 12

225 g/8 oz plain flour, plus extra for dusting

150 g/5½ oz butter, cut into small pieces, plus extra for greasing

125 g/4½ oz caster sugar, plus extra for dusting

1 tsp vanilla extract

method

1 Preheat the oven to 180°C/350°F/Gas Mark 4. Lightly grease a large baking sheet.

2 Sift the flour into a large bowl. Add the butter and rub it in with your fingertips until the mixture resembles fine breadcrumbs. Stir in the caster sugar and vanilla extract and mix together to form a firm dough.

3 Roll out the dough on a lightly floured work surface to a thickness of 2.5 cm/1 inch. Stamp out 12 hearts with a heart-shaped cutter measuring 5 cm/2 inches across and 2.5 cm/ 1 inch deep. Arrange the hearts on the prepared baking sheet.

4 Bake in the preheated oven for 15–20 minutes, or until the hearts are a light golden colour. Transfer the vanilla hearts to a wire rack to cool completely. Dust them with a little caster sugar just before serving.

gingerbread people

ingredients

MAKES ABOUT 20

450 g/1 lb plain flour, plus
   extra for dusting

2 tsp ground ginger

1 tsp allspice

2 tsp bicarbonate of soda

115 g/4 oz butter, plus extra
   for greasing

100 g/3½ oz golden syrup

115 g/4 oz brown sugar

1 egg, beaten

to decorate

currants

glacé cherries

85 g/3 oz icing sugar

3–4 tsp water

method

1 Preheat the oven to 160°C/325°F/Gas Mark 3. Grease three large baking sheets. Sift the flour, ginger, allspice and bicarbonate of soda into a large bowl. Place the butter, syrup and sugar in a saucepan over a low heat and stir until melted. Pour onto the dry ingredients and add the egg. Mix together to form a dough. The dough will be sticky to start with, but will become firmer as it cools.

2 On a lightly floured work surface, roll out the dough to about 3 mm/⅛ inch thick and stamp out gingerbread people shapes. Place on the prepared baking sheets. Re-knead and re-roll the trimmings and cut out more shapes until the dough is used up. Decorate with currants for eyes and pieces of cherry for mouths. Bake in the preheated oven for 15–20 minutes, or until firm and lightly browned.

3 Remove from the oven and cool on the baking sheets for a few minutes, then transfer to wire racks to cool completely. Mix the icing sugar with the water to a thick consistency. Place the icing in a small polythene bag and cut a tiny hole in one corner. Use to draw buttons or clothes shapes on the cooled biscuits.

gingernuts

ingredients

MAKES 30

350 g/12 oz self-raising flour

pinch of salt

200 g/7 oz caster sugar

1 tbsp ground ginger

1 tsp bicarbonate of soda

125 g/4^1/$_2$ oz butter, plus extra
    for greasing

75 g/2^3/$_4$ oz golden syrup

1 egg, beaten

1 tsp grated orange zest

method

1 Preheat the oven to 160°C/325°F/Gas Mark 3. Lightly grease several baking sheets. Sift the flour, salt, sugar, ginger and bicarbonate of soda into a mixing bowl.

2 Melt the butter and golden syrup together in a saucepan over a low heat. Remove the pan from the heat and cool the butter and syrup mixture slightly, then pour it onto the dry ingredients. Add the egg and orange zest and mix thoroughly to form a dough.

3 Using your hands, carefully shape the dough into 30 even-sized balls. Place the balls well apart on the baking sheets, then flatten them slightly with your fingers.

4 Bake in the preheated oven for 15–20 minutes, or until golden. Carefully transfer the biscuits to a wire rack to cool.

party biscuits

ingredients

MAKES 16

115 g/4 oz butter, softened,
  plus extra for greasing
115 g/4 oz brown sugar
1 tbsp golden syrup
1/2 tsp vanilla extract
175 g/6 oz self-raising flour
85 g/3 oz sugar-coated
  chocolate beans

method

1 Preheat the oven to 180°C/350°F/Gas Mark 4. Grease two baking sheets. Place the butter and sugar in a bowl and beat together with an electric whisk until light and fluffy, then beat in the syrup and vanilla extract.

2 Sift in half the flour and work it into the mixture. Stir in the chocolate beans and the remaining flour and work the dough together using a spatula.

3 Roll the dough into 16 balls and place them on the prepared baking sheets, spaced well apart to allow for spreading. Do not flatten them. Bake in the preheated oven for 10–12 minutes, or until pale golden at the edges. Remove from the oven and cool on the baking sheets for 2 minutes, then transfer to wire racks to cool completely.

traditional easter biscuits

ingredients

MAKES ABOUT 30

225 g/8 oz butter, softened
140 g/5 oz caster sugar, plus
    extra for sprinkling
1 egg yolk, lightly beaten
280 g/10 oz plain flour
1 tsp mixed spice
pinch of salt
1 tbsp chopped mixed peel
55 g/2 oz currants
1 egg white, lightly beaten

method

1 Put the butter and sugar into a bowl and mix well with a wooden spoon, then beat in the egg yolk. Sift together the flour, mixed spice and a pinch of salt into the mixture, add the mixed peel and currants and stir until thoroughly combined. Halve the dough, shape into balls, wrap in clingfilm and chill in the refrigerator for 30–60 minutes.

2 Preheat the oven to 190°C/375°F/Gas Mark 5. Line two baking trays with baking paper.

3 Unwrap the dough and roll out between two sheets of baking paper. Stamp out rounds with a 6-cm/2^1/$_2$-inch fluted round cutter and put them on the prepared baking trays, spaced well apart.

4 Bake in the preheated oven for 7 minutes, then brush with the egg white and sprinkle with caster sugar. Return to the oven and bake for a further 5–8 minutes, until light golden brown. Leave to cool on the baking trays for 5–10 minutes, then, using a palette knife, carefully transfer to wire racks to cool completely.

easter nest cookies

ingredients

MAKES ABOUT 20-25

225 g/8 oz butter, softened,
   plus extra for greasing
140 g/5 oz caster sugar
1 egg yolk, lightly beaten
2 tsp lemon juice
280 g/10 oz plain flour
1 tbsp chopped mixed peel
55 g/2 oz glacé cherries,
   finely chopped
salt

to decorate
200 g/7 oz icing sugar
few drops of edible yellow food
   colouring
mini sugar-coated Easter eggs
yellow sugar sprinkles

method

1 Put the butter and sugar into a bowl and mix well with a wooden spoon, then beat in the egg yolk and lemon juice. Sift together the flour and a pinch of salt into the mixture, add the mixed peel and glacé cherries and stir until thoroughly combined. Halve the dough, shape into balls, wrap in clingfilm and chill in the refrigerator for 30–60 minutes.

2 Preheat the oven to 190°C/375°F/Gas Mark 5. Generously grease several round-based bun tins with butter.

3 Unwrap the dough and roll out between two sheets of baking paper. Stamp out cookies with a 7–8-cm/2³/₄–3¹/₄-inch sun-shaped cutter and put them in the prepared tins.

4 Bake in the preheated oven for 10–15 minutes, until light golden brown. Leave to cool in the tins.

5 Sift the icing sugar into a bowl, add the food colouring and stir in just enough water to give the icing the consistency of thick cream. Put the cookies on wire racks and gently spread the icing on them. When it is just beginning to set, gently press 3–4 eggs into it and sprinkle the sugar sprinkles around them. Leave to set completely.

easter bunny cookies

ingredients

MAKES ABOUT 15

225 g/8 oz butter, softened

140 g/5 oz caster sugar,
	plus extra for sprinkling

1 egg yolk, lightly beaten

2 tsp vanilla extract

250 g/9 oz plain flour

25 g/1 oz cocoa powder

2 tbsp finely chopped stem
	ginger

1 egg white, lightly beaten

15 white mini marshmallows

140 g/5 oz icing sugar

few drops of edible pink food
	colouring

salt

method

1 Put the butter and sugar into a bowl and mix well with a wooden spoon, then beat in the egg yolk and vanilla extract. Sift the flour, cocoa powder and a pinch of salt together into the mixture, add the ginger and stir until thoroughly combined. Halve the dough, shape into balls, wrap in clingfilm and chill in the refrigerator for 30–60 minutes. Preheat the oven to 190°C/375°F/Gas Mark 5. Line two baking sheets with baking paper.

2 Unwrap the dough and roll out between two sheets of baking paper. Stamp out 15 rounds with a 5-cm/2-inch plain cutter (bodies), 15 rounds with a 3-cm/1$1/4$-inch plain cutter (heads), 30 rounds with a 2-cm/$3/4$-inch plain cutter (ears) and 15 rounds with a 1-cm/$1/2$-inch plain cutter (tails). Make up the bunnies on the baking sheets, spaced well apart.

3 Bake in the preheated oven for 7 minutes, then brush the bunnies with egg white and sprinkle with caster sugar. Return to the oven and bake for a further 5–8 minutes. Remove from the oven and put a mini marshmallow in the centre of each tail. Return to the oven for 1 minute. Leave to cool for 5–10 minutes, then transfer to wire racks to cool completely.

4 Sift the icing sugar into a bowl and stir in enough water to give the icing the consistency of thick cream. Add a few drops of food colouring. Pipe a collar where the heads and bodies join and add initials, if desired. Leave to set.

halloween spider's web cookies

ingredients

MAKES ABOUT 30

225 g/8 oz butter, softened
140 g/5 oz caster sugar
1 egg yolk, lightly beaten
1 tsp peppermint extract
250 g/9 oz plain flour
25 g/1 oz cocoa powder
salt

to decorate

175 g/6 oz icing sugar
few drops vanilla extract
1–1½ tbsp hot water
few drops edible black food
    colouring

method

1 Put the butter and sugar into a bowl and mix well, then beat in the egg yolk and peppermint extract. Sift the flour, cocoa powder and a pinch of salt together into the mixture and stir until thoroughly combined. Halve the dough, shape into balls, wrap in clingfilm and chill in the refrigerator for 30–60 minutes. Preheat the oven to 190°C/375°F/Gas Mark 5. Line two baking sheets with baking paper.

2 Unwrap the dough and roll out between two sheets of baking paper. Stamp out cookies with a 6-cm/2½-inch plain round cutter and put them on the baking sheets spaced well apart. Bake in the preheated oven for 10–15 minutes, until light golden brown. Leave to cool for 5–10 minutes, then transfer to wire racks to cool completely.

3 Sift the icing sugar into a bowl, add the vanilla extract and stir in the hot water until the icing is smooth and has the consistency of thick cream. Leave the cookies on the racks and spread the white icing over them. Add a few drops of black food colouring to the remaining icing and spoon it into a piping bag with a fine nozzle. Starting from the middle of the cookie, pipe a series of concentric circles. Then carefully draw a cocktail stick through the icing from the middle to the outside edge to divide the cookie first into quarters and then into eighths. Leave to set.

christmas angels

ingredients

MAKES ABOUT 25

225 g/8 oz butter, softened

140 g/5 oz caster sugar

1 egg yolk, lightly beaten

2 tsp passion fruit pulp

280 g/10 oz plain flour

55 g/2 oz desiccated coconut

salt

to decorate

175 g/6 oz icing sugar

1–1$\frac{1}{2}$ tbsp passion fruit pulp

edible silver glitter,
      for sprinkling

method

1 Put the butter and sugar into a bowl and mix well with a wooden spoon, then beat in the egg yolk and passion fruit pulp. Sift the flour and a pinch of salt together into the mixture, add the coconut and stir until thoroughly combined. Halve the dough, shape into balls, wrap in clingfilm and chill in the refrigerator for 30–60 minutes.

2 Preheat the oven to 190°C/375°F/Gas Mark 5. Line two baking sheets with baking paper.

3 Unwrap the dough and roll out between two sheets of baking paper. Stamp out shapes with a 7-cm/2$\frac{3}{4}$-inch angel-shaped cutter and put them on the prepared baking sheets spaced well apart.

4 Bake in the preheated oven for 10–15 minutes, until light golden brown. Leave to cool on the baking sheets for 5–10 minutes, then, using a palette knife, carefully transfer to wire racks to cool completely.

5 Sift the icing sugar into a bowl and stir in the passion fruit pulp until the icing has the consistency of thick cream. Leave the cookies on the racks and spread the icing over them. Sprinkle with the edible glitter and leave to set.

christmas bells

ingredients

MAKES ABOUT 30

25 g/8 oz butter, softened
140 g/5 oz caster sugar
finely grated rind of 1 lemon
1 egg yolk, lightly beaten
280 g/10 oz plain flour
1/2 tsp ground cinnamon
100 g/3 1/2 oz plain chocolate
    chips
salt

to decorate
2 tbsp lightly beaten egg white
2 tbsp lemon juice
225 g/8 oz icing sugar
30 silver balls
food colouring pens

method

1 Put the butter, sugar and lemon rind into a bowl and mix well with a wooden spoon, then beat in the egg yolk. Sift the flour, cinnamon and a pinch of salt together into the mixture, add the chocolate chips and stir, until thoroughly combined. Halve the dough, shape into balls, wrap in clingfilm and chill in the refrigerator for 30–60 minutes.

2 Preheat the oven to 190°C/375°F/Gas Mark 5. Line two baking sheets with baking paper.

3 Unwrap the dough and roll out between two sheets of baking paper. Stamp out cookies with a 5-cm/2-inch bell-shaped cutter and put them on the prepared baking sheets spaced well apart.

4 Bake in the preheated oven for 10–15 minutes, until light golden brown. Leave to cool on the baking sheets for 5–10 minutes, then, using a palette knife, carefully transfer to wire racks to cool completely.

5 Mix together the egg white and lemon juice in a bowl, then gradually beat in the icing sugar until smooth. Leave the cookies on the racks and spread the icing over them. Place a silver ball on the clapper shape at the bottom of the cookie and leave to set completely. When the icing is dry, use the food colouring pens to draw patterns on the cookies.

christmas tree decorations

ingredients

MAKES 20–25

225 g/8 oz butter, softened
140 g/5 oz caster sugar
1 egg yolk, lightly beaten
2 tsp vanilla extract
280 g/10 oz plain flour
1 egg white, lightly beaten
2 tbsp hundreds and
    thousands
400 g/14 oz fruit-flavoured
    boiled sweets in different
    colours
salt

method

1 Put the butter and sugar into a bowl and mix well with a wooden spoon, then beat in the egg yolk and vanilla extract. Sift the flour and a pinch of salt together into the mixture and stir until thoroughly combined. Halve the dough, shape into balls, wrap in clingfilm and chill in the refrigerator for 30–60 minutes.

2 Preheat the oven to 190°C/375°F/Gas Mark 5. Line two baking sheets with baking paper.

3 Unwrap the dough and roll out between two sheets of baking paper. Stamp out cookies with Christmas-themed cutters and place them on the prepared baking sheets, spaced well apart. Using the end of a large plain piping nozzle, stamp out rounds from each shape and remove them. Make a small hole in the top of each cookie with a skewer so that they can be threaded with ribbon. Brush with egg white and sprinkle with hundreds and thousands. Bake for 7 minutes.

4 Meanwhile, lightly crush the sweets by tapping them with a rolling pin. Unwrap and sort into separate bowls by colour.

5 Remove the cookies from the oven and fill the holes with the crushed sweets. Return to the oven and bake for a further 5–8 minutes, until the cookies are light golden brown and the sweets have melted and filled the holes. Leave to cool. Thread thin ribbon through the holes in the top and hang.

pastries & desserts

Today's hectic lifestyle, combined with concerns about healthy eating and the availability of convenience foods, mean that we have rather lost our grandmothers' habit of routinely baking tarts, pies, strudels and other desserts. However, this doesn't mean that we've lost our taste for them. While most of us are just too busy to make pastry and peel fruit or whisk egg whites and chop nuts in the middle of the week, there is something very rewarding about preparing a traditional baked dessert for family meals when there's a little more time at the weekend.

Of course, baked desserts include much more than classic apple pie, perennially popular though this is. Lots of cold desserts – from pavlovas to cheesecakes – must be baked first. The range of pastries is extensive, from a simple shortcrust dough to paper-thin layers of strudel, light-as-air puff pastry and mouthwatering choux puffs. Fillings include fresh fruit, nuts, honey, syrup, meringue, chocolate, caramel, cream, cheese and custard. Then, in addition to pastries there are lots of other sweet treats from meringue to fruit cobbler. Some are perfect for family meals, especially a traditional Sunday lunch, while others would make an impressive ending to a formal dinner party.

Some people are put off making pastry because they think it is difficult. This is not so but there are a few useful tips. Keep everything, including your

hands and the mixing bowl, cool. If the mixture begins to feel greasy when you are rubbing the fat into the flour, put the bowl into the refrigerator for 30 minutes before continuing. Handle the dough as little as possible. You'll soon see that it's as easy as pie.

chocolate fudge tart

ingredients

SERVES 6

350 g/12 oz ready-made
    shortcrust pastry
flour, for sprinkling
icing sugar, for dusting

filling

140 g/5 oz plain chocolate,
    finely chopped
175 g/6 oz butter, diced
275 g/9¾ oz granulated sugar
100 g/3½ oz plain flour
½ tsp vanilla extract
6 eggs, beaten
200 ml/7 fl oz whipping
    cream, whipped and mixed
    with ground cinnamon,
    to decorate

method

1 Preheat the oven to 200°C/400°F/Gas Mark 6. Roll out the pastry on a lightly floured work surface and use to line a 20-cm/8-inch deep loose-based tart tin. Prick the pastry lightly with a fork, then line with foil and fill with baking beans. Bake in the preheated oven for 12–15 minutes, or until the dough no longer looks raw. Remove the beans and foil and bake for a further 10 minutes, or until the dough is firm. Leave to cool. Reduce the oven temperature to 180°C/350°F/Gas Mark 4.

2 To make the filling, place the chocolate and butter in a heatproof bowl and set over a saucepan of gently simmering water until melted. Stir until smooth, then remove from the heat and leave to cool. Place the sugar, flour, vanilla extract and eggs in a separate bowl and whisk until well blended. Stir in the butter and chocolate mixture.

3 Pour the filling into the pastry case and bake in the oven for 50 minutes, or until the filling is just set. Transfer to a wire rack to cool completely. Dust with icing sugar before serving with the whipped cream.

fine chocolate tart

ingredients

SERVES 6

pastry

125 g/4¹/₂ oz plain flour, plus
    extra for dusting
2 tsp cocoa powder, plus extra
    for dusting
2 tsp icing sugar
pinch of salt
50 g/1³/₄ oz cold butter, cut
    into pieces, plus extra
    for greasing
1 egg yolk
ice-cold water
plain and white chocolate
    curls, to decorate

ganache filling

200 g/7 oz plain chocolate
    with 70% cocoa solids
25 g/1 oz unsalted butter,
    softened
225 ml/8 fl oz double cream
1 tsp dark rum (optional)

method

1 Lightly butter a 23-cm/9-inch loose-based fluted tart tin. Sift the flour, cocoa powder, icing sugar and salt into a food processor, add the butter and process until the mixture resembles fine breadcrumbs. Tip the mixture into a large bowl, add the egg yolk and a little ice-cold water, just enough to bring the dough together. Turn out onto a surface dusted with flour and cocoa powder and roll out the pastry 8 cm/3¹/₄ inches larger than the tin. Carefully lift the pastry into the tin and press to fit. Roll the rolling pin over the tin to neaten the edges and trim the excess pastry. Fit a piece of baking paper into the tart case, fill with baking beans and chill in the refrigerator for 30 minutes. Meanwhile, preheat the oven to 190°C/375°F/ Gas Mark 5.

2 Remove the pastry case from the refrigerator and bake the pastry for 15 minutes in the preheated oven, then remove the beans and paper and bake for a further 5 minutes.

3 To make the ganache filling, chop the chocolate and put in a bowl with the butter. Bring the cream to the boil then pour on to the chocolate, stirring well, add the rum, if using, and continue stirring to make sure the chocolate is melted completely. Pour into the pastry case and chill for 3 hours. Decorate with chocolate curls.

white chocolate & cardamom tart

ingredients

SERVES 6

pastry

125 g/4¹/₂ oz plain flour, plus
    extra for dusting
pinch of salt
75 g/2³/₄ oz cold butter,
    cut into pieces
cold water

filling

10 g/¹/₄ oz or 2 pieces fine leaf
    gelatine
cold water
seeds of 8 cardamom pods
350 g/12 oz white chocolate,
    chopped into small pieces
375 ml/13 fl oz whipping
    cream

method

1 Grease a 23-cm/9-inch loose-based fluted tart tin. Sift the flour and salt into a food processor, add the butter and process, until the mixture resembles fine breadcrumbs. Tip the mixture into a large bowl and add a little cold water, just enough to bring the dough together. Turn out onto a surface dusted with more flour and roll out the pastry 8 cm/3¹/₄ inches larger than the tin. Carefully lift the pastry into the tin and press to fit. Roll the rolling pin over the tin to neaten the edges and trim the excess pastry. Fit a piece of baking paper into the tart case, fill with baking beans and chill for 30 minutes. Meanwhile, preheat the oven to 190°C/375°F/Gas Mark 5.

2 Remove the pastry case from the refrigerator and bake blind for 15 minutes in the preheated oven then remove the beans and paper and bake for a further 10 minutes. Cool completely.

3 Soak the gelatine in a little cold water in a small heatproof bowl for 5 minutes. Heat a saucepan of water to simmering point. Crush the cardamom seeds and put in a large bowl with the chocolate. Place the bowl of gelatine over the simmering water and stir until dissolved. Meanwhile, in a separate saucepan, heat the cream until just boiling, then pour over the chocolate, using a whisk to stir the chocolate until it has melted. Add the gelatine and stir. Cool, pour into the tart case and chill.

baked chocolate alaska

ingredients

SERVES 4

butter, for greasing

2 eggs

150 g/5^1/$_2$ oz caster sugar,
    plus 4 tbsp

4 tbsp plain flour

2 tbsp cocoa powder

3 egg whites

450 g/1 lb good-quality
    chocolate ice cream

method

1 Preheat the oven to 220°C/425°F/Gas Mark 7. Grease and base-line an 18-cm/7-inch round cake tin.

2 Whisk the eggs and the 4 tablespoons of sugar in a mixing bowl until very thick and pale. Sift the flour and cocoa powder together and carefully fold in.

3 Pour into the prepared tin and bake in the preheated oven for 7 minutes, or until springy to the touch. Turn out and transfer to a wire rack to cool completely.

4 Whisk the egg whites in a clean, greasefree bowl until soft peaks form. Gradually add the remaining sugar, whisking until you have a thick, glossy meringue. Place the sponge on a baking sheet. Soften the ice cream in the refrigerator and pile it onto the centre to form a dome.

5 Pipe or spread the meringue over the ice cream, making sure it is completely enclosed. (At this point the dessert can be frozen, if wished.)

6 Return to the oven for 5 minutes, until the meringue is just golden. Serve at once.

mississippi mud pie

ingredients

SERVES 8

pastry

225 g/8 oz plain flour, plus
    extra for dusting
2 tbsp cocoa powder
140 g/5 oz butter
2 tbsp caster sugar
1–2 tbsp cold water

filling

175 g/6 oz butter
350 g/12 oz muscovado sugar
4 eggs, lightly beaten
4 tbsp cocoa powder, sifted
150 g/5$\frac{1}{2}$ oz plain chocolate
375 ml/13 fl oz single cream
1 tsp chocolate extract

to decorate

450 ml/16 fl oz double cream,
    whipped
chocolate flakes and curls

method

1 To make the pastry, sift the flour and cocoa powder into a mixing bowl. Rub in the butter with your fingertips until the mixture resembles fine breadcrumbs. Stir in the sugar and enough cold water to mix to a soft dough. Wrap and chill in the refrigerator for 15 minutes.

2 Preheat the oven to 190°C/375°F/Gas Mark 5. Roll out the dough on a lightly floured work surface and use to line a 23-cm/9-inch loose-based tart tin. Line with baking paper and fill with baking beans. Bake blind in the preheated oven for 15 minutes. Remove from the oven and take out the paper and beans. Bake the pastry case for a further 10 minutes.

3 To make the filling, beat the butter and sugar together in a bowl and gradually beat in the eggs with the cocoa powder. Melt the chocolate and beat it into the mixture with the cream and the chocolate extract.

4 Reduce the oven temperature to 160°C/325°F/Gas Mark 3. Pour the mixture into the pastry case and bake for 45 minutes, or until the filling has set gently.

5 Let the mud pie cool completely, then transfer it to a serving plate, if you like. Cover with the whipped cream.

6 Decorate the pie with chocolate flakes and curls, then leave to chill until ready to serve.

chocolate nut strudel

ingredients

SERVES 6

150 g/5½ oz mixed nuts,
    chopped
115 g/4 oz plain chocolate,
    chopped
115 g/4 oz milk chocolate,
    chopped
115 g/4 oz white chocolate,
    chopped
200 g/7 oz filo pastry, thawed
    if frozen
150 g/5½ oz butter, preferably
    unsalted, plus extra for
    greasing
3 tbsp golden syrup
100 g/3½ oz icing sugar
ice cream, to serve

method

1 Preheat the oven to 190°C/375°F/Gas Mark 5. Lightly grease a baking sheet with butter. Set aside 1 tablespoon of the nuts. Mix the three types of chocolate together.

2 Place 1 sheet of filo pastry on a clean tea towel. Melt the butter and brush the pastry with the butter, drizzle with a little syrup and sprinkle with some nuts and chocolate. Place another sheet on top and repeat until you have used all the nuts and chocolate.

3 Use the tea towel to help you carefully roll up the strudel and place on the baking sheet, then drizzle with a little more syrup and sprinkle with the reserved nuts. Bake in the preheated oven for 20–25 minutes. If the nuts start to brown too much, cover the strudel with a sheet of foil.

4 Sprinkle the strudel with icing sugar, cut into slices and serve warm with ice cream.

profiteroles & chocolate sauce

ingredients

SERVES 4

choux pastry
200 ml/7 fl oz water
70 g/2¹/₂ oz butter, plus extra
      for greasing
100 g/3¹/₂ oz plain flour, sifted
3 eggs, beaten

cream filling
300 ml/10 fl oz double cream
3 tbsp caster sugar
1 tsp vanilla extract

chocolate sauce
125 g/4¹/₂ oz plain chocolate,
      broken into small pieces
35 g/1¹/₄ oz butter
6 tbsp water
2 tbsp brandy

method

1 Preheat the oven to 200°C/400°F/Gas Mark 6. Grease a large baking tray.

2 To make the choux pastry, put the water and butter into a saucepan and bring to the boil. Immediately add all the flour, remove the pan from the heat and stir the mixture into a paste that leaves the sides of the pan clean. Leave to cool slightly. Beat in enough of the eggs to give the mixture a soft dropping consistency.

3 Transfer to a piping bag fitted with a 1-cm/¹/₂-inch plain tip. Pipe small balls onto the prepared baking tray. Bake in the preheated oven for 25 minutes. Remove from the oven. Pierce each ball with a skewer to allow the steam to escape.

4 To make the filling, whip together the cream, sugar and vanilla extract. Cut the pastry balls almost in half, then fill with cream.

5 To make the sauce, gently melt the chocolate and butter with the water in a heatproof bowl set over a saucepan of gently simmering water, stirring until smooth. Stir in the brandy. Pile the profiteroles into individual serving dishes or into a pyramid on a raised cake stand. Pour over the sauce and serve.

pains au chocolat

ingredients

MAKES 4

280 g/10 oz strong white flour, plus extra for dusting

1 tsp salt

2 tsp easy-blend dried yeast

175 ml/6 fl oz milk

2 tbsp golden caster sugar

1 tbsp oil, plus extra for brushing

100 g/3$\frac{1}{2}$ oz butter, plus extra for greasing

115 g/4 oz plain chocolate, coarsely chopped

glaze

1 egg yolk

2 tbsp milk

method

1 Grease a baking sheet. Sift the flour and salt into a bowl and stir in the yeast. Make a well in the centre. Heat the milk in a saucepan until tepid. Add the sugar and oil and stir until the sugar has dissolved. Stir into the flour and mix well. Turn out the dough onto a lightly floured work surface and knead until smooth, then place in an oiled bowl. Cover and leave to rise in a warm place for 2–3 hours, or until doubled in size.

2 Knead the dough on a floured work surface and roll into a rectangle three times as long as it is wide. Divide the butter into thirds. Dot one portion over the top two thirds of the dough, leaving a 1-cm/$\frac{1}{2}$-inch margin. Fold the lower third up and the top third down. Seal the edges. Give the dough a half-turn. Roll into a rectangle. Repeat the process twice, then fold in half. Put into an oiled polythene bag and chill for 1 hour.

3 Preheat the oven to 220°C/425°F/Gas Mark 7. Cut the dough in half and roll out into two rectangles of 30 x 15 cm/12 x 6 inches. Cut each half into two rectangles of 15 x 7.5 cm/ 6 x 3 inches. Sprinkle chocolate along one short end of each and roll up. Place on the baking sheet in a warm place for 2–3 hours, or until doubled in size. To glaze, mix the egg yolk and milk and brush over the rolls. Bake for 15–20 minutes, or until golden and well risen.

chocolate chiffon pie

ingredients

SERVES 8

nut base

225 g/8 oz whole Brazil nuts

4 tbsp granulated sugar

4 tsp melted butter

filling

225 ml/8 fl oz milk

2 tsp powdered gelatine

115 g/4 oz caster sugar

2 eggs, separated

225 g/8 oz plain chocolate,
    roughly chopped

1 tsp vanilla extract

150 ml/5 fl oz double cream

2 tbsp chopped Brazil nuts,
    to decorate

method

1 Preheat the oven to 220°C/425°F/Gas Mark 7. To make the base, process the whole Brazil nuts in a food processor until finely ground. Add the sugar and melted butter and process briefly to combine. Tip the mixture into a 23-cm/9-inch round tart tin and press it onto the base and side with a spoon. Bake in the preheated oven for 8–10 minutes or until light golden brown, then leave to cool.

2 Pour the milk into a bowl and sprinkle over the gelatine. Let it soften for 2 minutes, then set over a saucepan of gently simmering water. Stir in half of the caster sugar, both the egg yolks and all the chocolate. Stir constantly over a low heat for 4–5 minutes until the gelatine has dissolved and the chocolate has melted. Remove from the heat and beat until the mixture is smooth. Stir in the vanilla extract, wrap and chill in the refrigerator for 45–60 minutes until starting to set.

3 Whip the cream until it is stiff, then fold all but 3 tablespoons into the chocolate mixture. Whisk the egg whites in a separate, clean, greasefree bowl until soft peaks form. Add 2 teaspoons of the remaining sugar and whisk until stiff peaks form. Fold in the remaining sugar, then fold the egg whites into the chocolate mixture. Pour the filling into the nut case and chill in the refrigerator for 3 hours. Decorate with the remaining whipped cream and the chopped nuts before serving.

chocolate orange pie

ingredients

SERVES 4

pastry

200 g/7 oz plain flour, plus
    extra for dusting
100 g/3½ oz butter, cut into
    small pieces, plus extra for
    greasing
55 g/2 oz icing sugar, sifted
finely grated rind of 1 orange
1 egg yolk, beaten
3 tbsp milk

filling

200 g/7 oz plain chocolate,
    broken into small pieces
2 eggs, separated
125 ml/4 fl oz milk
100 g/3½ oz caster sugar
8 amaretti biscuits, crushed

orange cream

1 tbsp orange-flavoured
    liqueur, such as Cointreau
1 tbsp finely grated orange
    rind, plus extra to decorate
125 ml/4 fl oz double cream

method

1 To make the pastry, sift the flour into a bowl. Rub in the butter with your fingertips until the mixture resembles breadcrumbs. Mix in the icing sugar, orange rind, egg yolk and milk. Turn out onto a lightly floured work surface and knead briefly. Wrap the pastry and leave to chill in the refrigerator for 30 minutes.

2 Roll out two thirds of the pastry to a thickness of 5 mm/¼ inch and use it to line a greased 23-cm/9-inch tart tin.

3 Preheat the oven to 180°C/350°F/Gas Mark 4. To make the filling, melt the chocolate in a heatproof bowl set over a saucepan of barely simmering water. Beat in the egg yolks, then the milk. Remove from the heat. In a separate, greasefree bowl, whisk the egg whites until stiff, then stir in the caster sugar. Fold the egg whites into the chocolate mixture, then stir in the biscuits. Spoon into the pastry case.

4 Roll out the remaining pastry, cut into strips, and use to form a lattice over the pie. Bake in the preheated oven for 1 hour.

5 To make the orange cream, beat the liqueur, orange rind and cream together. Remove the pie from the oven, decorate with orange rind and serve with the orange cream.

toffee apple tart

ingredients

SERVES 6

pastry

75 g/2¹/₂ oz cold butter,
    cut into pieces, plus extra
    for greasing
100 g/3¹/₂ oz plain flour
pinch of salt
cold water

filling

1.3 kg/3 lb firm, sweet apples,
    peeled and cored
1 tsp lemon juice
35 g/1¹/₄ oz butter
100 g/3¹/₂ oz caster sugar
200 g/7 oz granulated sugar
90 ml/3 fl oz cold water
150 ml/5 fl oz double cream

method

1 Lightly grease a 23-cm/9-inch loose-based fluted tart tin. Sift the flour and salt into a food processor, add the butter, and process until the mixture resembles fine breadcrumbs. Put into a large bowl and add enough cold water to bring the pastry together. Turn out onto a floured work surface and roll out the pastry 8 cm/3¹/₄ inches larger than the tin. Fit the pastry into the tin, trimming the excess. Fit a piece of baking paper into the base, fill with baking beans and chill for 30 minutes. Meanwhile, preheat the oven to 190°C/375°F/Gas Mark 5.

2 Bake the pastry case blind for 10 minutes in the preheated oven, remove the beans and paper and return to the oven for 5 minutes.

3 Meanwhile, cut 4 apples into eighths and toss in the lemon juice. Melt the butter in a frying pan and sauté the apple pieces until caramelized and brown at the edges. Remove from the pan and reserve. Thinly slice the remaining apples, put them in a saucepan with the caster sugar, and cook for about 20–30 minutes. Spoon into the pastry case and arrange the reserved apple pieces on top in a circle. Bake for 30 minutes.

4 Put the granulated sugar and water in a saucepan and heat until the sugar dissolves. Boil to form a caramel. Remove from the heat and add the cream, stirring constantly to combine into toffee. Remove the tart from the oven, pour the toffee over the apples, and chill.

pear tarte tatin

ingredients

SERVES 6

75 g/2¾ oz butter

100 g/3½ oz caster sugar

6 pears, peeled, halved and
    cored

flour, for dusting

225 g/8 oz ready-made puff
    pastry

double cream, to serve
    (optional)

method

1 Preheat the oven to 200°C/400°F/Gas Mark 6. Melt the butter and sugar in an ovenproof frying pan over a medium heat. Stir carefully for 5 minutes, until it turns a light caramel colour. Take care, because it will get very hot.

2 Remove the pan from the heat, place on a heatproof surface and arrange the pears, cut side up, in the caramel. Place one half in the centre and surround it with the others.

3 On a lightly floured work surface, roll out the dough to a round, slightly larger than the pan, and place it on top of the pears. Tuck down the edges into the pan.

4 Bake near the top of the preheated oven for 20–25 minutes until the pastry is well risen and golden brown.

5 Remove from the oven and leave to cool for 2 minutes.

6 Invert the tart onto a serving dish that is larger than the pan and has enough depth to take any juices that may run out. Remember that this is very hot, so take care with this manoeuvre and use thick oven gloves.

7 Serve warm, with cream, if using.

sicilian marzipan tart with candied fruit

ingredients

SERVES 6

pastry

75 g/2¹/₂ oz cold butter,
    cut into pieces, plus extra
    for greasing
100 g/3¹/₂ oz plain flour, plus
    extra for dusting
pinch of salt
cold water

filling

300 g/10¹/₂ oz marzipan
250 g/9 oz ground almonds
150 g/5¹/₂ oz unsalted butter
100 g/3¹/₂ oz caster sugar
70 g/2¹/₂ oz plain flour
2 eggs
75 g/2³/₄ oz sultanas
25 g/1 oz mixed peel,
    chopped
25 g/1 oz natural glacé
    cherries, halved
55 g/2 oz flaked almonds

method

1 Lightly grease a 23-cm/9-inch loose-based fluted tart tin. Sift the flour and salt into a food processor, add the butter, and process until the mixture resembles fine breadcrumbs. Tip the mixture into a large bowl and add a little cold water, just enough to bring the dough together. Turn out onto a work surface dusted with flour and roll out the dough 8 cm/3¹/₄ inches larger than the tin. Press the pastry into the tin, trimming any excess. Fit a piece of baking paper into the pastry case, fill with baking beans, and chill for 30 minutes. Meanwhile, preheat the oven to 190°C/375°F/Gas Mark 5.

2 Remove the pastry case from the refrigerator and bake blind for 10 minutes in the preheated oven, then remove the beans and paper and bake for a further 5 minutes.

3 Reduce the oven temperature to 180°C/ 350°F/Gas Mark 4. Grate the marzipan straight onto the base, distributing evenly. Put the ground almonds, butter and sugar in a food processor and pulse until smooth. Add 1 tablespoon of flour and 1 egg and blend, then add another tablespoon of flour and the other egg and blend. Finally, add the remaining flour. Scoop the mixture into a bowl and stir in the sultanas, mixed peel and cherries. Spoon the mixture over the marzipan, sprinkle with the flaked almonds and bake for 40 minutes.

caramelized lemon tart

ingredients

SERVES 6

pastry

100 g/3½ oz cold butter,
    cut into pieces, plus extra
    for greasing
150 g/5½ oz plain flour
pinch of salt
2 tbsp caster sugar
1 egg yolk
cold water

filling

5 lemons
2 eggs
300 g/10½ oz caster sugar
225 g/8 oz ground almonds
90 ml/3 fl oz whipping cream
90 ml/3 fl oz water

method

1 Lightly grease a 23-cm/9-inch loose-based fluted tart tin. Sift the flour and salt into a food processor, add the butter, and process until the mixture resembles fine breadcrumbs. Tip the mixture into a large bowl, add the sugar, egg yolk and a little cold water, just enough to bring the dough together. Turn out onto a work surface dusted with flour and roll out the pastry 8 cm/3¼ inches larger than the tin. Press the pastry into the tin, trimming any excess. Fit a piece of baking paper into the pastry case, fill with baking beans and chill for 30 minutes. Meanwhile, preheat the oven to 190°C/375°F/ Gas Mark 5.

2 Bake the pastry case blind for 10 minutes in the preheated oven, then remove the beans and paper and bake for a further 5 minutes.

3 Put the juice and finely grated rind of 3 lemons in a large bowl and add the eggs, a third of the sugar, the ground almonds, and the cream, whisking to combine. Pour into the pastry case and bake for 25 minutes. Meanwhile, thinly slice the remaining lemons. Put the remaining sugar and water in a saucepan and heat until the sugar has melted. Simmer for 5 minutes, then add the lemon slices and boil for 10 minutes.

4 Remove the tart from the oven and arrange the lemon slices over the surface in a spiral pattern. Drizzle the remaining syrup over the slices. Serve warm or cold.

peach & stem ginger tarte tatin

ingredients

SERVES 6

250 g/9 oz ready-made puff pastry

flour, for dusting

filling

6–8 just ripe peaches

100 g/3^1/$_2$ oz golden caster sugar

50 g/1^3/$_4$ oz unsalted butter

3 pieces stem ginger in syrup, chopped

1 tbsp ginger syrup from the stem ginger jar

1 egg, beaten

thick cream or ice cream, to serve

method

1 Preheat the oven to 190°C/375°F/Gas Mark 5. Plunge the peaches into boiling water, then drain and peel. Cut each in half. Put the sugar in a 25-cm/10-inch heavy, ovenproof frying pan and heat gently until it caramelizes. Don't stir, just shake the pan if necessary. Once the sugar turns a dark caramel colour, remove from the heat immediately and drop 2 tablespoons of the butter into it.

2 Place the peaches cut-side up on top of the caramel, packing them as close together as possible and tucking the ginger pieces into any gaps. Dot with the remaining butter and drizzle with the ginger syrup.

3 Return to a gentle heat while you roll out the pastry in a circle larger than the frying pan you are using. Drape the pastry over the peaches and tuck it in well round the edges, brush with the beaten egg and bake in the preheated oven, for 20–25 minutes, or until the pastry is browned and puffed up. Remove from the oven and rest for 5 minutes, then invert on to a serving plate and serve with thick cream or ice cream.

plum & almond tart

ingredients

SERVES 8

butter, for greasing

plain flour, for dusting

400 g/14 oz ready-made sweet
   pastry

filling

1 egg

1 egg yolk

140 g/5 oz golden caster sugar

55 g/2 oz butter, melted

100 g/3½ oz ground almonds

1 tbsp brandy

900 g/2 lb plums, halved and
   stoned

whipped cream, to serve
   (optional)

method

1 Preheat the oven to 200°C/400°F/Gas Mark 6. Grease a 23-cm/9-inch tart tin. On a lightly floured work surface, roll out the pastry and use it to line the tart tin. Line with baking paper and fill with baking beans, then bake in the preheated oven for 15 minutes. Remove the paper and beans and return to the oven for a further 5 minutes. Place a baking sheet in the oven to heat.

2 To make the filling, place the egg, egg yolk, 100 g/3½ oz of the caster sugar, melted butter, ground almonds and brandy in a bowl and mix together to form a paste. Spread the paste in the pastry case.

3 Arrange the plum halves, cut-side up, on top of the almond paste, fitting them together tightly. Sprinkle with the remaining caster sugar. Place the tart tin on the preheated baking sheet and bake for 35–40 minutes or until the filling is set and the pastry case is brown. Serve warm with whipped cream, if using.

walnut custard tarts

ingredients

SERVES 4

40 g/1½ oz butter

8 sheets filo pastry (work with
one sheet at a time and
cover the remaining sheets
with a damp tea towel)

40 g/1½ oz walnut halves

150 g/5½ oz Greek-style
yogurt

4 tbsp honey

150 ml/5 fl oz double cream

2 tbsp caster sugar

2 eggs

1 tsp vanilla extract

icing sugar, for dusting

method

1 Preheat the oven to 180°C/350°F/Gas Mark 4.
Melt the butter. Brush four 10-cm/4-inch deep
tartlet tins with a little of the butter. Cut the
sheets of filo pastry in half to make 16 squares.

2 Take 1 square of pastry, brush it with a little of
the melted butter and use it to line one of the
tins. Repeat with three more pastry squares,
placing each of them at a different angle. Line
the remaining three tins and place all four tins
on a baking sheet.

3 To make the filling, finely chop 2 tablespoons
of the walnuts. Put the yogurt, honey, cream,
sugar, eggs and vanilla extract in a bowl and
beat together. Stir in the chopped walnuts until
well mixed.

4 Pour the yogurt filling into the pastry cases.
Roughly break the remaining walnuts and
scatter over the top. Bake in the preheated
oven for 25–30 minutes, until the filling is firm
to the touch.

5 Cool the tartlets, then carefully remove from
the tins and dust with icing sugar.

bakewell tart

ingredients

SERVES 4

pastry

150 g/5½ oz plain flour,
plus extra for dusting

50 g/1¾ oz butter, cut into
small pieces, plus extra
for greasing

25 g/1 oz icing sugar, sifted

finely grated rind of ½ lemon

½ egg yolk, beaten

1½ tbsp milk

4 tbsp strawberry jam

filling

100 g/3½ oz butter

100 g/3½ oz brown sugar

2 eggs, beaten

1 tsp almond extract

115 g/4 oz rice flour

3 tbsp ground almonds

3 tbsp flaked almonds, toasted

icing sugar, to decorate

method

1 Preheat the oven to 190°C/375°F/Gas Mark 5. To make the pastry, sift the flour into a bowl. Rub in the butter with your fingertips until the mixture resembles fine breadcrumbs. Mix in the icing sugar, lemon rind, egg yolk and milk. Knead briefly on a lightly floured work surface. Wrap the pastry and chill in the refrigerator for 30 minutes.

2 Grease a 20-cm/8-inch ovenproof tart tin. Roll out the pastry to a thickness of 5 mm/¼ inch and use it to line the base and side of the tin. Prick all over the base with a fork, then spread with the jam.

3 To make the filling, cream the butter and sugar together until fluffy. Gradually beat in the eggs, followed by the almond extract, rice flour and ground almonds. Spread the mixture evenly over the jam-covered pastry, then sprinkle over the flaked almonds. Bake in the preheated oven for 40 minutes, until golden. Remove from the oven, dust with icing sugar and serve warm.

honey and lemon tart

ingredients

SERVES 8–12

pastry

225 g/8 oz plain flour, plus
    extra for dusting

pinch of salt

1$\frac{1}{2}$ tsp caster sugar

150 g/5$\frac{1}{2}$ oz butter

3–4 tbsp cold water

filling

375 g/13 oz cottage cheese,
    cream cheese or ricotta
    cheese

6 tbsp Greek honey

3 eggs, beaten

$\frac{1}{2}$ tsp cinnamon

grated rind and juice of
    1 lemon

lemon slices, to decorate

method

1 To make the pastry, put the flour, salt, sugar and butter, cut into cubes, in a food processor. Mix in short bursts, until the mixture resembles fine breadcrumbs. Sprinkle over the water and mix until the mixture forms a smooth dough. Alternatively, make the pastry in a bowl and rub in with your hands. Wrap the pastry and chill in the refrigerator for 30 minutes.

2 Preheat the oven to 200°C/400°F/Gas Mark 6. Meanwhile, make the filling. (If using cottage cheese, push the cheese through a sieve into a bowl.) Add the honey to the cheese and beat until smooth. Add the eggs, cinnamon and the lemon rind and juice and mix well.

3 On a lightly floured work surface, roll out the pastry and use to line a 23-cm/9-inch tart tin. Place on a baking sheet and line with greaseproof paper. Fill with baking beans and bake in the preheated oven for 15 minutes. Remove the paper and beans and bake for a further 5 minutes or until the base is firm but not brown.

4 Reduce the oven temperature to 180°C/ 350°F/Gas Mark 4. Pour the filling into the pastry case and bake in the oven for about 30 minutes until set. Serve cold, decorated with lemon slices.

fig, ricotta & honey tart

ingredients

SERVES 6

pastry

150 g/5¹/₂ oz plain flour

pinch of salt

75 g/2³/₄ oz cold butter,
   cut into pieces, plus extra
   for greasing

25 g/1 oz ground almonds

cold water

filling

6 figs

100 g/3¹/₂ oz caster sugar

600 ml/1 pint water

4 egg yolks

¹/₂ tsp vanilla extract

500 g/1 lb 2 oz ricotta cheese,
   drained of any liquid

2 tbsp flower honey, plus
   1 tsp for drizzling

method

1 Lightly grease a 23-cm/9-inch loose-based fluted tart tin. Sift the flour and salt into a food processor, add the butter and process until the mixture resembles fine breadcrumbs. Tip the mixture into a bowl, stir in the almonds and add just enough cold water to bring the pastry together. Turn out onto a floured work surface and roll out the pastry 8 cm/3¹/₄ inches larger than the tin. Fit the pastry into the tin, trimming the excess. Fit a piece of baking paper into the pastry case, fill with baking beans and chill for 30 minutes.

2 Meanwhile, preheat the oven to 190°C/375°F/ Gas Mark 5. Bake the pastry case in the preheated oven for 15 minutes, then remove the beans and paper. Return to the oven for a further 5 minutes.

3 Put the figs, half the caster sugar and the water in a saucepan and bring to the boil. Poach gently for 10 minutes, then drain and cool. Stir the egg yolks and vanilla extract into the ricotta, add the remaining sugar and the honey and mix well. Spoon into the pastry case and bake for 30 minutes. Remove from the oven and, when you are ready to serve, cut the figs in half lengthways and arrange on the tart, cut-side up. Drizzle with the extra honey and serve at once.

brandied plum tart

ingredients

SERVES 6

pastry

75 g/2¾ oz cold butter
   cut into pieces, plus extra
   for greasing
125 g/4½ oz plain flour
pinch of salt
cold water

filling

150 ml/5 fl oz brandy or
   armagnac
100 g/3½ oz golden caster
   sugar
4–5 ripe but not soft plums,
   halved
1 whole egg, plus 2 egg yolks
300 ml/10 fl oz double cream

method

1 Grease a 23-cm/9-inch loose-based fluted tart tin. Sift the flour and salt into a food processor, add the butter and process until the mixture resembles fine breadcrumbs. Tip into a large bowl and add a little cold water. Turn out onto a surface dusted with flour and roll out the pastry 8 cm/3¼ inches larger than the tin. Fit the pastry into the tin, trimming the excess. Fit a piece of baking paper into the base, fill with baking beans and chill for 30 minutes. Meanwhile, preheat the oven to 190°C/375°F/Gas Mark 5.

2 Bake the pastry case blind for 10 minutes in the preheated oven, then remove the beans and paper and bake for a further 5 minutes.

3 Put the brandy and 2 tablespoons of the sugar into a saucepan and bring to a simmer. Add the plum halves, simmer for 5 minutes, then set aside to cool. Reduce the oven temperature to 160°C/325°F/Gas Mark 3.

4 Lift the plums out of the syrup with a slotted spoon, reserving the syrup. Slip the skins off the plums and slice each half plum into 3–4 slices, arranging the slices in the base of the pastry case. Beat the egg and the egg yolks with the remaining sugar and heat the cream until just boiling. Whisk into the eggs, stirring constantly. Spoon the custard over the plums, return the tart to the oven and cook for 30–40 minutes, until the custard is set. Leave in the tin until completely cold, then lift on to a serving plate. Serve with the reserved syrup on the side.

crème brûlée tarts

ingredients

SERVES 6

pastry

150 g/5½ oz plain flour, plus extra for dusting

1–2 tbsp caster sugar

125 g/4½ oz butter, cut into pieces

1 tbsp water

filling

4 egg yolks

50 g/1½ oz caster sugar

400 ml/14 fl oz double cream

1 tsp vanilla extract

demerara sugar, for sprinkling

method

1 To make the pastry, place the flour and sugar in a large bowl. Rub in the butter with your fingertips until the mixture resembles breadcrumbs. Add the water and mix to form a soft dough. Wrap and chill for 30 minutes.

2 Divide the pastry into six pieces. Roll out each piece on a lightly floured work surface to line six 10-cm/4-inch tart tins. Prick the base of the pastry with a fork and chill for 20 minutes. Meanwhile, preheat the oven to 190°C/375°F/ Gas Mark 5.

3 Line the pastry cases with foil and baking beans and bake in the preheated oven for 15 minutes. Remove the foil and beans and cook the pastry cases for a further 10 minutes or until crisp. Set aside to cool.

4 To make the filling, beat the egg yolks and sugar together in a bowl until pale. Heat the cream and vanilla extract in a saucepan until just below boiling point, then pour onto the egg mixture, whisking constantly. Return the mixture to a clean saucepan and bring to just below the boil, stirring, until thick. Do not allow the mixture to boil. Cool slightly, then pour it into the pastry cases. Cool, then chill overnight.

5 Preheat the grill. Sprinkle the tarts with the sugar. Cook under the grill for a few minutes. Cool, then chill for 2 hours before serving.

blackberry tart with cassis cream

ingredients

SERVES 6

pastry

300 g/10$\frac{1}{2}$ oz plain flour
pinch of salt
175 g/6 oz unsalted butter
55 g/2 oz caster sugar
cold water

filling

750 g/1 lb 10 oz blackberries
6 tbsp golden caster sugar
1 tbsp crème de cassis
5 tsp semolina
1 egg white

to serve

225 ml/8 fl oz double cream
1 tbsp crème de cassis
fresh mint leaves

method

1 To make the pastry, sift the flour and salt into a large bowl and rub in the butter. Stir in the sugar and add enough cold water to bring the dough together, then wrap in clingfilm and chill for 30 minutes.

2 Meanwhile, rinse and pick over the blackberries, then put them in a bowl with 4 tablespoons of the sugar and the crème de cassis, stirring to coat. Preheat the oven to 200°C/400°F/Gas Mark 6.

3 Roll out the dough to a large circle, handling carefully because it is quite a soft dough. Leave the edges ragged and place on a baking sheet. Sprinkle the dough with the semolina, leaving a good 6-cm/2$\frac{1}{2}$-inch margin. Pile the fruit into the centre and brush the edges of the pastry with the egg white. Fold in the edges of the pastry to overlap and enclose the fruit, making sure to press the pastry together in order to close any gaps. Brush with the remaining egg white, sprinkle with the remaining sugar and bake for 25 minutes.

4 Whip the cream until it starts to thicken and stir in the crème de cassis. Serve the tart hot, straight from the oven, with a good spoonful of the cassis cream, decorated with mint leaves.

banoffee pie

ingredients

SERVES 4

filling

1 litre/1³/4 pints canned
   condensed milk
4 ripe bananas
juice of ¹/2 lemon
1 tsp vanilla extract
450 ml/16 fl oz double cream,
   whipped
75 g/2³/4 oz plain chocolate,
   grated

crust

85 g/3 oz butter, melted, plus
   extra for greasing
150 g/5¹/2 oz digestive
   biscuits, crushed into
   crumbs
55 g/2 oz shelled almonds,
   toasted and ground
40 g/1¹/2 oz shelled hazelnuts,
   toasted and ground

method

1 Place the unopened cans of milk in a large saucepan and add enough water to cover them. Bring to the boil, then reduce the heat and simmer for 2 hours, topping up the water level to keep the cans covered. Carefully lift out the hot cans from the pan and leave to cool.

2 Preheat the oven to 180°C/350°F/Gas Mark 4. Grease a 23-cm/9-inch tart tin with butter. Place the remaining butter in a bowl and add the crushed biscuits and ground nuts. Mix together well, then press the mixture evenly into the base and side of the tart tin. Bake for 10–12 minutes, then remove from the oven and leave to cool.

3 Peel and slice the bananas and place in a bowl. Squeeze over the juice from the lemon, add the vanilla extract, and mix together. Spread the banana mixture over the crumb crust in the tin, then spoon the contents of the cooled cans of evaporated milk over the bananas. Sprinkle over two thirds of the chocolate, then top with a layer of whipped cream. Sprinkle over the remaining grated chocolate and serve the pie at room temperature.

forest fruit pie

ingredients

SERVES 4

250 g/9 oz blueberries

250 g/9 oz raspberries

250 g/9 oz blackberries

100 g/3 1/2 oz caster sugar

200 g/7 oz plain flour, plus
    extra for dusting

40 g/1 1/2 oz ground hazelnuts

115 g/4 oz butter, diced, plus
    extra for greasing

finely grated zest of 1 lemon

1 egg yolk, beaten

4 tbsp milk

2 tsp icing sugar,
    for dusting

whipped cream, to serve

method

1 Put the fruit into a saucepan with about 3 tablespoons of the caster sugar and simmer, stirring, for 5 minutes. Remove from the heat.

2 Sift the flour into a bowl, then add the ground hazelnuts. Rub in the butter, then sift in the remaining sugar. Add the lemon zest, egg yolk and 3 tablespoons of the milk, and mix. Turn out onto a lightly floured work surface and knead briefly. Leave to rest for 30 minutes.

3 Preheat the oven to 190°C/375°F/Gas Mark 5. Grease a 20-cm/8-inch ovenproof pie dish with butter. Roll out half the pastry to a thickness of 5 mm/1/4 inch and use it to line the dish. Spoon the fruit into the pie case. Brush the rim with water, then roll out the remaining pastry and use it to cover the pie. Trim and crimp the edges, make 2 small slits in the top, and decorate with 2 leaf shapes cut from the dough trimmings. Brush all over with the remaining milk. Bake for 40 minutes. Remove from the oven, sprinkle over the icing sugar and serve with whipped cream.

lemon meringue pie

ingredients

SERVES 8–10

plain flour, for dusting

250 g/9 oz ready-rolled pastry, thawed if frozen

3 tbsp cornflour

85 g/3 oz caster sugar

grated rind of 3 lemons

300 ml/10 fl oz cold water

150 ml/5 fl oz lemon juice

3 egg yolks

55 g/2 oz unsalted butter, cut into small cubes, plus extra for greasing

3 egg whites

175 g/6 oz caster sugar

1 tsp golden granulated sugar

method

1 Grease a 25-cm/10-inch fluted flan tin. On a lightly floured work surface, roll out the pastry into a circle 5 cm/2 inches larger than the flan tin. Press the pastry into the tin, trimming the excess. Prick the base and chill, uncovered, in the refrigerator for 20–30 minutes.

2 Preheat the oven to 200°C/400°F/Gas Mark 6. Line the pastry case with baking paper and fill with baking beans. Bake on a heated baking tray for 15 minutes. Remove the beans and paper and return to the oven for 10 minutes. Remove from the oven and reduce the temperature to 150°C/300°F/Gas Mark 2.

3 Put the cornflour, sugar and lemon rind into a saucepan. Pour in a little water and blend to a smooth paste. Gradually add the remaining water and the lemon juice. Place the saucepan over a medium heat and bring to the boil, stirring constantly. Simmer gently for 1 minute, until smooth and glossy. Remove from the heat and beat in the egg yolks, one at a time, then beat in the butter. Place the saucepan in a bowl of cold water to cool the filling. When cool, spoon the mixture into the pastry case.

4 Whisk the egg whites until soft peaks form. Add the caster sugar gradually, whisking well with each addition. Spoon the meringue over the filling to cover it completely, making a seal with the pastry case and swirling the meringue into peaks. Sprinkle with the granulated sugar and bake for 20–30 minutes. Serve warm.

traditional apple pie

ingredients

SERVES 6

pastry

350 g/12 oz plain flour

pinch of salt

85 g/3 oz butter or margarine,
cut into small pieces

85 g/3 oz lard or vegetable
shortening, cut into
small pieces

about 6 tbsp cold water

beaten egg or milk, for glazing

filling

750 g–1 kg /1 lb 10 oz–2 lb
4 oz cooking apples,
peeled, cored and sliced

115 g/4 oz caster sugar, plus
extra for sprinkling

1/2–1 tsp ground cinnamon,
allspice or ginger

1–2 tbsp water (optional)

double cream, to serve

method

1 To make the pastry, sift the flour and salt into a large bowl. Add the butter and fat and rub in with your fingertips until the mixture resembles fine breadcrumbs. Add the water and gather the mixture together into a dough. Wrap the pastry and chill in the refrigerator for 30 minutes.

2 Preheat the oven to 220°C/425°F/Gas Mark 7. Roll out almost two thirds of the pastry thinly and use to line a 23-cm/9-inch deep pie plate or pie tin.

3 Mix the apples with the sugar and spice and pack into the pastry case; the filling can come up above the rim. Add the water, if needed, particularly if the apples are a dry variety.

4 Roll out the remaining pastry to form a lid. Dampen the edges of the pie rim with water and position the lid, pressing the edges firmly together. Trim and crimp the edges.

5 Use the trimmings to cut out leaves or other shapes to decorate the top of the pie, dampen and attach. Glaze the top of the pie with beaten egg or milk, make 1–2 slits in the top and place the pie on a baking sheet.

6 Bake in the preheated oven for 20 minutes, reduce the temperature to 180°C/350°F/Gas Mark 5 and bake for a further 30 minutes, or until the pastry is a light golden brown. Sprinkle with sugar and serve hot or cold, with cream.

apple lattice pie

ingredients

SERVES 4

pastry

280 g/10 oz plain flour,
    plus extra for dusting
pinch of salt
55 g/2 oz caster sugar
250 g/9 oz butter, cut into
    small pieces
1 egg
1 egg yolk
1 tbsp water

filling

3 tbsp blackcurrant or
    plum jam
55 g/2 oz chopped toasted
    mixed nuts
950 g/2 lb 2 oz cooking apples
1 tbsp lemon juice
1 tsp mixed spice
55 g/2 oz sultanas
50 g/1^3/$_4$ oz grapes, halved
    and deseeded
75 g/2^3/$_4$ oz soft light brown
    sugar

icing sugar, for dusting
custard, to serve

method

1 To make the pastry, sift the flour and salt into a bowl. Make a well in the centre and add the sugar, butter, egg, egg yolk and water. Mix together to form a smooth dough, adding more water if necessary. Wrap the pastry and chill in the refrigerator for 1 hour.

2 Preheat the oven to 220°C/425°F/Gas Mark 7. Shape about three quarters of the pastry into a ball and roll out on a lightly floured work surface into a circle large enough to line a shallow 25-cm/10-inch tart tin. Fit it into the tin and trim the edges. Roll out the remaining pastry and cut into long strips about 1 cm/ 1/2 inch wide.

3 To make the filling, spread the jam evenly over the base of the pastry case, then sprinkle over the toasted nuts. Peel and core the apples, then cut them into thin slices. Place them in a bowl with the lemon juice, mixed spice, sultanas, grapes and brown sugar. Mix together gently. Spoon the mixture into the pastry case, spreading it out evenly.

4 Arrange the pastry strips in a lattice over the top of the pie. Moisten with a little water, seal and trim the edges. Bake in the preheated oven for 50 minutes, or until golden. Dust with icing sugar. Serve at once with custard.

one roll fruit pie

ingredients

SERVES 8

175 g/6 oz plain flour, plus
    extra for dusting
100 g/3^1/$_2$ oz butter, diced,
    plus extra for greasing
1 tbsp water
1 egg, separated
crushed sugar cubes,
    for sprinkling

filling

600 g/1 lb 5 oz prepared
    fruit, such as rhubarb,
    gooseberries or plums
85 g/3 oz soft light brown
    sugar
1 tbsp ground ginger

method

1 Place the flour in a large bowl, add the butter and rub in with your fingertips until the mixture resembles breadcrumbs. Add the water and mix together to form a soft dough. Cover and leave to chill in the refrigerator for 30 minutes.

2 Preheat the oven to 200°C/400°F/Gas Mark 6. Grease a large baking tray. Roll out the dough on a lightly floured work surface, to a round 35 cm/14 inches in diameter. Transfer the round to the centre of the prepared baking tray and brush with the egg yolk.

3 To make the filling, mix the fruit with the sugar and ground ginger and pile it into the centre of the pastry. Turn in the edges of the pastry all the way around. Brush the surface of the pastry with the egg white and sprinkle with the crushed sugar cubes.

4 Bake in the preheated oven for 35 minutes, or until golden brown. Transfer to a serving plate and serve warm.

pumpkin pie

ingredients

SERVES 6

1.8 kg/4 lb sweet pumpkin, halved and the stem, seeds and stringy insides removed and discarded

150 g/5 oz plain flour, plus extra for dusting

1/4 tsp baking powder

1 tsp salt

1 1/2 tsp ground cinnamon

3/4 tsp ground nutmeg

3/4 tsp ground cloves

55 g/2 oz caster sugar

4 tbsp unsalted butter, diced, plus extra for greasing

3 eggs

400 ml/14 fl oz canned condensed milk

1/2 tsp vanilla extract

1 tbsp demerara sugar

streusel topping

2 tbsp plain flour

4 tbsp demerara sugar

1 tsp ground cinnamon

2 tbsp cold unsalted butter, in small pieces

55 g/2 oz shelled pecan nuts, chopped

55 g/2 oz shelled walnuts, chopped

method

1 Preheat the oven to 190°C/375°F/Gas Mark 5. Place the pumpkin halves, face down, in a baking tin and cover with foil. Bake in the preheated oven, for 1 1/2 hours, then remove and leave to cool. Purée the flesh in a food processor, drain away any excess liquid, then cover with clingfilm and leave to chill.

2 Grease a 23-cm/9-inch round pie dish. Sift the flour and baking powder into a bowl with 1/2 teaspoon each of salt and cinnamon and 1/4 teaspoon each of nutmeg and cloves. Add the caster sugar and rub in the butter until the mixture resembles fine breadcrumbs. Add 1 egg, lightly beaten, and mix to a soft dough. Roll out on a lightly floured counter, use to line the prepared pie dish, then trim the edge. Cover with clingfilm and leave to chill for 30 minutes. Preheat the oven to 220°C/425°F/Gas Mark 7.

3 To make the filling, place the pumpkin purée in a bowl, then stir in the condensed milk and the remaining eggs. Add the remaining spices and salt, then stir in the vanilla extract and demerara sugar. Pour into the pastry case and bake in the preheated oven for 15 minutes.

4 Meanwhile, make the topping. Combine the flour, sugar and cinnamon in a bowl, rub in the butter until crumbly, then stir in the nuts. Remove the pie from the oven and reduce the oven temperature to 180°C/350°F/Gas Mark 4. Sprinkle over the topping, bake for 35 minutes and serve hot or cold.

sweet potato pie

ingredients

SERVES 8

pastry

175 g/6 oz plain flour, plus
   extra for dusting

1/2 tsp salt

1/4 tsp caster sugar

50 g/1 3/4 oz butter, diced

40 g/1 1/2 oz white vegetable
   fat, diced

1–2 1/2 tbsp cold water

filling

500 g/1 lb 2 oz orange-fleshed
   sweet potatoes, peeled

3 eggs, beaten

100 g/3 1/2 oz soft light brown
   sugar

350 ml/12 fl oz canned
   condensed milk

40 g/1 1/2 oz butter, melted

2 tsp vanilla extract

1 tsp ground cinnamon

1 tsp ground nutmeg

1/2 tsp salt

method

1 To make the pastry, sift the flour, salt and caster sugar into a bowl. Add the butter and white vegetable fat to the bowl and rub in with your fingertips until the mixture resembles fine breadcrumbs. Sprinkle over 2 tablespoons of the water and mix with a fork to make a soft dough. Wrap in clingfilm and chill in the refrigerator for at least 1 hour.

2 Meanwhile, bring a large saucepan of water to the boil over a high heat. Add the sweet potatoes and cook for 15 minutes. Drain, then cool under cold running water. Cut each potato into eight wedges, place in a bowl and beat in the eggs and sugar until very smooth. Beat in the remaining ingredients, then set aside.

3 Preheat the oven to 220°C/425°F/Gas Mark 7. Roll out the pastry on a lightly floured work surface into a thin 28-cm/11-inch round and use to line a 23-cm/9-inch round tart tin, about 4 cm/1 1/2 inches deep. Trim off the excess pastry and press a floured fork around the edge. Prick the base of the pastry case with the fork. Line with baking paper and fill with baking beans. Bake in the preheated oven for 12 minutes, until lightly golden. Remove from the oven and take out the paper and beans.

4 Pour the filling into the pastry case and return to the oven for 10 minutes. Reduce the oven temperature to 160°C/325°F/Gas Mark 3 and bake for a further 35 minutes. Cool on a wire rack. Serve warm or at room temperature.

peach cobbler

ingredients

SERVES 4–6

filling

6 peaches, peeled and sliced

4 tbsp caster sugar

1/2 tbsp lemon juice

1 1/2 tsp cornflour

1/2 tsp almond extract or
  vanilla extract

pie topping

175 g/6 oz plain flour

100 g/3 1/2 oz caster sugar

1 1/2 tsp baking powder

1/2 tsp salt

85 g/3 oz butter, diced

1 egg

5–6 tbsp milk

vanilla ice cream or pecan nut
  ice cream, to serve

method

1 Preheat the oven to 220°C/425°F/Gas Mark 7. Place the peaches in a 23-cm/9-inch square ovenproof dish that is also suitable for serving. Add the sugar, lemon juice, cornflour and almond extract and toss together. Bake the peaches in the oven for 20 minutes.

2 Meanwhile, to make the topping, sift the flour, all but 2 tablespoons of the sugar, the baking powder and salt into a bowl. Rub in the butter with your fingertips until the mixture resembles breadcrumbs. Mix the egg and 5 tablespoons of the milk in a jug, then mix into the dry ingredients with a fork until a soft, sticky dough forms. If the dough seems too dry, stir in the extra tablespoon of milk.

3 Reduce the oven temperature to 200°C/400°F/ Gas Mark 6. Remove the peaches from the oven and drop spoonfuls of the topping over the surface, without smoothing. Sprinkle with the remaining sugar, return to the oven, and bake for a further 15 minutes, or until the topping is golden brown and firm – the topping will spread as it cooks. Serve hot or at room temperature with ice cream.

cherry clafoutis

ingredients

SERVES 6

450 g/1 lb ripe fresh cherries, stoned

100 g/3½ oz caster sugar

2 large eggs

1 egg yolk

100 g/3½ oz plain flour

pinch of salt

400 ml/14 fl oz milk

4 tbsp double cream

1 tsp vanilla extract or almond extract

method

1 Preheat the oven to 200°C/400°F/Gas Mark 6. Lightly grease a 1.2-litre/2-pint ovenproof serving dish or a 25-cm/10-inch quiche dish. Scatter the cherries over the base of the dish, then place the dish on a baking sheet.

2 Using an electric mixer, whisk the sugar, eggs and egg yolk together until blended and a pale yellow colour, scraping down the sides of the bowl as necessary.

3 Beat in the flour and salt, then slowly beat in the milk, cream and vanilla extract until a light, smooth batter forms. Pour the batter into the dish.

4 Transfer the filled dish on the baking sheet to the preheated oven and bake for 45 minutes, or until the top is golden brown and the batter is set.

5 Leave the pudding to stand for at least 5 minutes, then serve hot, lukewarm or at room temperature.

pear & pecan nut strudel

ingredients

SERVES 4

2 ripe pears

50 g/1³/₄ oz butter

85 g/3 oz fresh white
    breadcrumbs

40 g/1¹/₂ oz shelled pecan
    nuts, chopped

25 g/1 oz muscovado sugar

finely grated rind of 1 orange

100 g/3¹/₂ oz filo pastry,
    thawed if frozen

6 tbsp orange blossom honey

2 tbsp orange juice

sifted icing sugar,
    for dusting

Greek-style yogurt, to serve
    (optional)

method

1 Preheat the oven to 200°C/400°F/Gas Mark 6. Peel, core and chop the pears. Melt 1 tablespoon of the butter in a frying pan and gently sauté the breadcrumbs until golden. Transfer the breadcrumbs to a bowl and add the pears, nuts, sugar and orange rind. Place the remaining butter in a small saucepan and heat until melted.

2 Set aside 1 sheet of filo pastry, keeping it well wrapped, and brush the remaining sheets with a little melted butter. Spoon some of the nut filling onto the first sheet, leaving a 2.5-cm/ 1-inch margin. Build up the strudel by placing buttered filo sheets on top of the first, spreading each one with nut filling as you build up the layers. Drizzle the honey and orange juice over the top.

3 Fold the short ends over the filling, then roll up, starting at a long side. Carefully lift onto a baking sheet, with the join facing upwards. Brush with any remaining melted butter and crumple the reserved sheet of filo pastry around the strudel. Bake in the preheated oven for 25 minutes, or until golden and crisp. Dust with sifted icing sugar and serve warm with yogurt, if using.

pear pie

ingredients

SERVES 6

pastry

280 g/10 oz plain flour

pinch of salt

125 g/4½ oz caster sugar

115 g/4 oz butter, cut into
    small pieces

1 egg

1 egg yolk

few drops vanilla extract

2–3 tsp water

filling

4 tbsp apricot jam

55 g/2 oz amaretti biscuits or
    ratafia biscuits, crumbled

850 g–1 kg/1 lb 14 oz–2 lb 4 oz
    pears, peeled and cored

1 tsp ground cinnamon

85 g/3 oz raisins

85 g/3 oz soft light brown
    sugar or demerara sugar

sifted icing sugar, for sprinkling

method

1 To make the pastry, sift the flour and salt onto a work surface, make a well in the centre and add the sugar, butter, egg, egg yolk, vanilla extract and most of the water. Using your fingers, gradually work the flour into the other ingredients to form a smooth dough, adding more water if necessary. Wrap the pastry and chill in the refrigerator for at least 1 hour.

2 Preheat the oven to 200°C/400°F/Gas Mark 6. Roll out three quarters of the pastry and use to line a shallow 25-cm/10-inch square cake tin or deep tart tin. To make the filling, spread the jam over the base and sprinkle with the crushed biscuits.

3 Slice the pears very thinly. Arrange over the biscuits in the pastry case. Sprinkle with cinnamon, then with raisins and, finally, with brown sugar.

4 Roll out a thin sausage shape using a third of the remaining pastry and place around the edge of the pie. Roll the remainder into thin sausages and arrange in a lattice over the pie, 4 or 5 strips in each direction, attaching them to the strip around the edge.

5 Cook in the preheated oven for 50 minutes, until golden brown and cooked through. Cool, then serve warm or chilled, sprinkled with sifted icing sugar.

paper-thin fruit pies

ingredients

MAKES 4

1 eating apple

1 ripe pear

2 tbsp lemon juice

4 tbsp melted butter

4 sheets filo pastry, thawed
if frozen

2 tbsp apricot jam

1 tbsp unsweetened orange
juice

1 tbsp finely chopped
pistachio nuts

2 tsp icing sugar, for dusting

custard, to serve

method

1 Core and thinly slice the apple and pear and immediately toss them in the lemon juice to prevent them turning brown. Melt the butter in a saucepan over a low heat.

2 Cut each sheet of pastry into four and cover with a clean, damp tea towel. Brush a four-cup muffin tin with a little of the butter.

3 Preheat the oven to 200°C/400°F/Gas Mark 6. Brush four small sheets of pastry with melted butter. Press a sheet of pastry into the base of one cup. Arrange the other sheets of pastry on top at slightly different angles. Repeat with the other sheets of pastry to make another three pies. Arrange alternate slices of apple and pear in the centre of each pastry case and lightly crimp the edges of the pastry.

4 Stir the jam and orange juice together until smooth and brush over the fruit. Bake in the preheated oven for 12–15 minutes. Sprinkle with the pistachio nuts, dust lightly with icing sugar and serve hot with custard.

mixed fruit pavlova

ingredients

SERVES 4

6 egg whites

pinch of cream of tartar

pinch of salt

300 g/10$^1/_2$ oz caster sugar

600 ml/1 pint double cream

1 tsp vanilla extract

2 kiwi fruit, peeled and sliced

250 g/9 oz strawberries, hulled
    and sliced

3 ripe peaches, sliced

1 ripe mango, peeled and
    sliced

2 tbsp orange liqueur, such as
    Cointreau

fresh mint leaves, to decorate

method

1 Preheat the oven to 110°C/225°F/Gas Mark
$^1/_4$. Line three baking sheets with baking paper,
then draw a 22-cm/8$^1/_2$-inch circle in the
centre of each one. Beat the egg whites into
stiff peaks. Mix in the cream of tartar and salt.
Gradually add 200 g/7 oz of sugar. Beat for
2 minutes until glossy. Fill a piping bag with
the mixture and use it to fill each circle, making
them slightly domed in the centre. Place in the
preheated oven and bake for 3 hours. Remove
from the oven and leave to cool.

2 Whip together the cream and vanilla extract
with all but 2 tablespoons of the remaining
sugar. Put the fruit into a separate bowl and stir
in the liqueur. Put one meringue circle onto a
serving plate, then spread over one third of the
sugared cream. Spread over one third of the
fruit, then top with a meringue. Spread over
another third of cream, then another third of
fruit. Top with the last meringue. Spread over
the remaining cream, followed by the remaining
fruit. Decorate with mint leaves and serve.

chestnut, maple syrup & pecan nut tart

ingredients

SERVES 6

pastry

115 g/4 oz plain flour, plus
	extra for dusting
pinch of salt
75 g/2¹/₂ oz cold butter,
	cut into pieces, plus extra
	for greasing
cold water

filling

1 kg/2 lb 4 oz canned
	sweetened chestnut purée
300 ml/10 fl oz double cream
25 g/1 oz butter
2 tbsp maple syrup
175 g/6 oz pecan nuts

method

1 Preheat the oven to 190°C/375°F/Gas Mark 5. Lightly grease a 23-cm/9-inch loose-based fluted tart tin. Sift the flour and salt into a food processor, add the butter and process until the mixture resembles fine breadcrumbs. Tip the mixture into a large bowl and add a little cold water, just enough to bring the pastry together. Turn out onto a work surface dusted with flour and roll out the pastry 8 cm/3¹/₂ inches larger than the tin. Carefully lift the dough into the tin and press to fit. Roll the rolling pin over the tin to neaten the edges and trim the excess pastry. Fit a piece of baking paper into the pastry case, fill with baking beans and chill in the refrigerator for 30 minutes.

2 Remove from the refrigerator and bake in the oven for 15 minutes, then remove the beans and paper and bake for a further 10 minutes.

3 Empty the chestnut purée into a large bowl. Whip the cream until stiff and fold into the chestnut purée. Spoon into the cold pastry case and chill for 2 hours. Melt the butter with the maple syrup and, when bubbling, add the pecan nuts and stir for 1–2 minutes. Spoon onto baking paper and let cool. When ready to serve, arrange the pecan nuts on the chestnut cream.

florentine praline tartlets

ingredients

MAKES 6

praline
100 g/3¹/₂ oz sugar
3 tbsp water
40 g/1¹/₂ oz flaked almonds
butter

pastry
100 g/3¹/₂ oz plain flour, plus
    extra for dusting
pinch of salt
75 g/2¹/₂ oz cold butter,
    cut into pieces, plus extra
    for greasing
1 tsp icing sugar
cold water

frangipane
70 g/2¹/₂ oz butter
2 eggs
70 g/2¹/₂ oz caster sugar
2 tbsp plain flour
150 g/5¹/₂ oz ground almonds

topping
8 natural glacé cherries,
    chopped
2 tbsp mixed candied peel,
    chopped
100 g/3¹/₂ oz plain chocolate,
    chopped

method

1 First make the praline. Put the sugar and the water in a saucepan and dissolve the sugar over a low heat. Do not stir, just boil for 10 minutes, until the sugar turns to caramel, then stir in the nuts and turn out onto buttered foil. Leave to cool and harden. When cold break up the praline and chop into smallish pieces.

2 Grease six 9-cm/3¹/₂-inch loose-based fluted tart tins. Sift the flour and salt into a food processor, add the butter and process until the mixture resembles fine breadcrumbs. Tip the mixture into a large bowl, add the sugar, and a little cold water, just enough to bring the dough together. Turn out onto a floured work surface and divide into six equal-sized pieces. Roll each piece to fit the tart tins. Carefully fit the pastry into the tins. Roll the rolling pin over the tins to neaten the edges and trim the excess dough. Put in the freezer for 30 minutes. Meanwhile, preheat the oven to 200°C/400°F/ Gas Mark 6.

3 While the tarts are in the freezer, make the frangipane. Melt the butter and beat the eggs and sugar together. Stir the melted butter into the egg and sugar mixture, then add the flour and almonds. Bake the pastry cases blind, straight from the freezer, for 10 minutes in the preheated oven. Divide the frangipane between the tart shells and return to the oven for 8–10 minutes. Leave to cool completely.

almond tart

ingredients

MAKES 1

pastry

280 g/10 oz plain flour

175 g/6 oz caster sugar

1 tsp finely grated lemon rind

pinch of salt

150 g/5½ oz unsalted butter, chilled and cut into small dice, plus extra for greasing

1 egg, beaten lightly

1 tbsp chilled water

filling

175 g/6 oz unsalted butter, at room temperature

175 g/6 oz caster sugar

3 large eggs

225 g/8 oz finely ground almonds

2 tsp plain flour

1 tbsp finely grated orange rind

½ tsp almond extract

icing sugar, to decorate

soured cream, to serve (optional)

method

1 Preheat the oven to 220°C/425°F/Gas Mark 7. Grease a 25-cm/10-inch loose-based tart tin with butter. To make the pastry, put the flour, sugar, lemon rind and salt into a bowl. Rub or cut in the butter until the mixture resembles fine breadcrumbs. Combine the egg and water, then slowly pour into the flour, stirring with a fork until a coarse mass forms. Shape into a ball and leave to chill for at least 1 hour.

2 Roll out the pastry on a lightly floured work surface until 3 mm/⅛ inch thick. Use to line the prepared tart tin. Return the tart tin to the fridge for at least 15 minutes.

3 Cover the pastry case with foil and fill with baking beans. Place in the preheated oven and bake for 12 minutes. Remove the beans and foil and return the pastry case to the oven for 4 minutes to dry the base. Remove from the oven and reduce the oven temperature to 200°C/400°F/Gas Mark 6.

4 Meanwhile, make the filling. Beat the butter and sugar until creamy. Beat in the eggs, 1 at a time. Add the almonds, flour, orange rind and almond extract and beat until blended. Spoon the filling into the pastry case and smooth the surface. Bake for 30–35 minutes until the top is golden and the tip of a knife inserted in the centre comes out clean. Leave to cool completely on a wire rack, then dust with sifted icing sugar. Serve with soured cream, if using.

truffled honey tart

ingredients

SERVES 6

pastry

115 g/4 oz plain flour

pinch of salt

75 g/2^1/$_2$ oz cold butter,
    cut into pieces, plus extra
    for greasing

1 tsp icing sugar

cold water

filling

250 g/9 oz curd cheese

115 g/4 oz cream cheese

125 ml/4 fl oz double cream

2 egg yolks, plus 1 whole egg

2 tbsp caster sugar

4 tbsp flower honey, plus extra
    for drizzling

sugared rose petals or
    crystallized violets,
    to decorate

method

1 Lightly grease a 23-cm/9-inch loose-based fluted tart tin. Sift the flour and salt into a food processor, add the butter and process until the mixture resembles fine breadcrumbs. Tip the mixture into a large bowl, add the sugar, and a little cold water, just enough to bring the dough together. Turn out onto a work surface dusted with more flour and roll out the pastry 8 cm/3^1/$_4$ inches larger than the tin. Carefully lift the pastry into the tin and press to fit. Roll a rolling pin over the tin to neaten the edges and trim the excess pastry. Fit a piece of baking paper into the pastry case, fill with baking beans and leave to chill in the refrigerator for 30 minutes. Meanwhile, preheat the oven to 190°C/375°F/Gas Mark 5.

2 Remove the pastry case from the refrigerator and bake blind for 10 minutes in the preheated oven, then remove the beans and paper and bake for a further 5 minutes.

3 Mix the curd cheese, cream cheese and cream together until smooth, then stir in the egg yolks, whole egg, sugar and honey until completely smooth. Pour into the pastry case and bake for 30 minutes. Remove from the oven and leave to cool in the tin for 10 minutes. Drizzle with more honey and decorate with sugared rose petals.

custard pie

ingredients

SERVES 8

pastry

200 g/7 oz plain flour

2 tbsp caster sugar

115 g/4 oz butter, cut into
    small pieces

1 tbsp water

filling

3 eggs

85 g/3 oz caster sugar

150 ml/5 fl oz single cream

150 ml/5 fl oz milk

freshly grated nutmeg

whipped cream, to serve
    (optional)

method

1 To make the pastry, place the flour and sugar in a mixing bowl. Rub in the butter with your fingertips until the mixture resembles fine breadcrumbs. Add the water and mix together until a soft dough has formed. Wrap the pastry and chill in the refrigerator for 30 minutes, then roll out to a circle slightly larger than a 24-cm/9^1/$_2$-inch loose-based tart tin.

2 Meanwhile, preheat the oven to 190°C/375°F/ Gas Mark 5. Line the tin with the pastry, trimming off the edge. Prick all over the base with a fork and chill in the refrigerator for about 30 minutes.

3 Line the pastry case with baking paper and fill with baking beans. Bake in the preheated oven for 15 minutes. Remove the paper and beans and bake for a further 15 minutes.

4 To make the filling, whisk the eggs, sugar, cream, milk and nutmeg together. Pour the filling into the prepared pastry case.

5 Return the pie to the oven and cook for a further 25–30 minutes or until the filling is just set. Serve with whipped cream, if you like.

treacle tart

ingredients

SERVES 8

250 g/9 oz ready-made pastry,
   thawed if frozen
350 g/12 oz golden syrup
100 g/3¹/₂ oz fresh white
   breadcrumbs
125 ml/4 fl oz double cream
finely grated rind of ¹/₂ lemon
   or orange
2 tbsp lemon juice or orange
   juice
custard or single cream,
   to serve

method

1 Roll out the pastry to line a 20-cm/8-inch loose-based flan tin, reserving the trimmings. Prick the base of the pastry with a fork and leave to chill in the refrigerator for 30 minutes. Preheat the oven to 190°C/375°F/Gas Mark 5.

2 Cut out small shapes from the reserved pastry trimmings, such as hearts, leaves or stars, to decorate the top of the tart.

3 In a bowl, combine the golden syrup, breadcrumbs, double cream, grated lemon rind and lemon juice.

4 Pour the mixture into the pastry case and decorate the edges of the tart with the reserved pastry shapes.

5 Bake in the preheated oven for 35–40 minutes, or until the filling is just set.

6 Leave the tart to cool slightly in the tin. Turn out and serve hot or cold, with custard.

coconut tart

ingredients

SERVES 8

butter, for greasing
plain flour, for dusting
400 g/14 oz ready-made sweet
    pastry

filling

2 eggs
grated rind and juice of
    2 lemons
200 g/7 oz golden caster sugar
375 ml/13 fl oz double cream
250 g/9 oz desiccated coconut

method

1 Preheat the oven to 200°C/400°F/Gas Mark 6. Grease a 23-cm/ 9-inch tart tin. On a lightly floured work surface, roll out the pastry and use it to line the prepared tin. Line with baking paper and fill with baking beans, then bake in the preheated oven for 15 minutes. Remove the paper and beans and return to the oven for a further 5 minutes. Reduce the oven temperature to 160°C/325°F/Gas Mark 3 and place a baking sheet in the oven to heat.

2 To make the filling, place the eggs, lemon rind and sugar in a bowl and beat together for 1 minute. Gently stir in the cream, then the lemon juice and, finally, the coconut.

3 Spoon the filling into the pastry case and place the tart tin on the preheated baking sheet. Bake for 40 minutes or until set and golden. Cool for 1 hour to firm up. Serve at room temperature.

pecan pie

ingredients

SERVES 8

pastry

225 g/8 oz plain flour

pinch of salt

115 g/4 oz butter, cut into
   small pieces

1 tbsp lard or vegetable
   shortening, cut into small
   pieces

55 g/2 oz golden caster sugar

6 tbsp cold milk

filling

3 eggs

200 g/7 oz muscovado sugar

1 tsp vanilla extract

pinch of salt

85 g/3 oz butter, melted

3 tbsp golden syrup

3 tbsp treacle

140 g/5 oz shelled pecan nuts,
   roughly chopped

halved pecan nuts, to decorate

whipped cream or vanilla ice
   cream, to serve

method

1 To make the pastry, sift the flour and salt into a mixing bowl and rub in the butter and lard with your fingertips until the mixture resembles fine breadcrumbs. Work in the caster sugar and add the milk. Work the mixture into a soft dough. Wrap the dough and leave to chill in the refrigerator for 30 minutes.

2 Preheat the oven to 200°C/400°F/Gas Mark 6. Roll out the pastry and use it to line a 23–25-cm/9–10-inch tart tin. Trim off the excess by running the rolling pin over the top of the tart tin. Line with baking paper, and fill with baking beans. Bake in the oven for 20 minutes. Remove from the oven and remove the paper and beans. Reduce the oven temperature to 180°C/350°F/Gas Mark 4. Place a baking sheet in the oven.

3 To make the filling, place the eggs in a bowl and beat lightly. Beat in the sugar, vanilla extract and salt. Stir in the butter, golden syrup, treacle and chopped nuts. Pour into the pastry case and decorate with the halved pecan nuts.

4 Place on the heated baking sheet and bake in the oven for 35–40 minutes until the filling is set. Serve warm or at room temperature with whipped cream.

croissants

ingredients

MAKES 12

500 g/1 lb 2 oz strong white
   flour, plus extra for dusting
55 g/2 oz caster sugar
1 tsp salt
2 tsp easy-blend dried yeast
300 ml/10 fl oz milk, heated
   until just warm to the touch
280 g/10 oz butter, softened,
   plus extra for greasing
1 egg, lightly beaten with
1 tbsp milk, to glaze
jam, to serve (optional)

method

1 Stir the dry ingredients into a large bowl, make a well in the centre, and add the milk. Mix to a soft dough. Knead on a lightly floured work surface until smooth and elastic. Leave to rise in a greased bowl, covered, in a warm place, until doubled in size. Meanwhile, flatten the butter with a rolling pin between 2 sheets of greaseproof paper to form a rectangle 5-mm/1/4-inch thick, then leave to chill. Knead the dough for 1 minute. Remove the butter from the refrigerator.

2 Roll out the dough on a well-floured work surface to 46 x 15 cm/18 x 6 inches. Place the butter in the centre, fold up the sides and squeeze the edges together gently. With the short end of the dough towards you, fold the top third down towards the centre of the dough, then fold the bottom third up. Rotate 45° clockwise so that the fold is to your left and the top flap is towards your right. Roll out to a rectangle and fold again. Repeat twice. Cut the dough in half. Roll out half into a triangle 5 mm/1/4 inch thick (keep the other half refrigerated). Use a triangular template, base 18 cm/7 inches and sides 20 cm/ 8 inches, to cut out the croissants.

3 Preheat the oven to 200°C/400°F/Gas Mark 6. Brush the triangles lightly with the glaze. Roll into croissant shapes, starting at the base and tucking the point underneath. Brush with the glaze. Place on an ungreased baking sheet. When doubled in size bake for 15–20 minutes until golden brown. Serve with jam, if using.

new york cheesecake

ingredients

SERVES 9–10

sunflower or corn oil,
    for oiling
75 g/2¾ oz butter
200 g/7 oz digestive biscuits,
    crushed
400 g/14 oz cream cheese
2 large eggs
150 g/5½ oz caster sugar
1½ tsp vanilla extract
450 ml/16 fl oz soured cream

blueberry topping

55 g/2 oz caster sugar
4 tbsp water
250 g/9 oz fresh blueberries
1 tsp arrowroot

method

1 Preheat the oven to 190°C/375°F/Gas Mark 5. Brush a 20-cm/8-inch springform cake tin with oil. Melt the butter in a saucepan over a low heat. Stir in the biscuit crumbs, then spread in the tin. Place the cream cheese, eggs, two thirds of the sugar and ½ teaspoon of the vanilla extract in a food processor. Process until smooth. Pour over the crumb layer and smooth the top. Place on a baking sheet and bake for 20 minutes, or until set. Remove from the oven and leave to stand for 20 minutes. Leave the oven switched on.

2 Mix the cream with the remaining sugar and vanilla extract in a bowl. Spoon over the cheesecake. Return to the oven for 10 minutes, leave to cool, then chill in the refrigerator for 8 hours, or overnight.

3 To make the topping, put the sugar in a saucepan with half of the water, place over a low heat and stir until the sugar has dissolved. Increase the heat, add the blueberries, cover and cook until they start to soften.

4 Remove from the heat. Mix the arrowroot and remaining water in a bowl, add to the fruit, and stir until smooth. Return to a low heat. Cook until the juice thickens and turns translucent. Leave to cool. Remove the cheesecake from the tin 1 hour before serving. Spoon the fruit on top and chill until ready to serve.

hot chocolate cheesecake

ingredients

SERVES 8–10

pastry

150 g/5¹/₂ oz plain flour, plus
    extra for dusting

2 tbsp cocoa powder

50 g/1³/₄ oz butter, plus extra
    for greasing

2 tbsp golden caster sugar

25 g/1 oz ground almonds

1 egg yolk

filling

2 eggs, separated

75 g/2³/₄ oz golden caster
    sugar

350 g/12 oz cream cheese

4 tbsp ground almonds

150 ml/5 fl oz double cream

25 g/1 oz cocoa powder, sifted

1 tsp vanilla extract

icing sugar, for dusting

method

1 Grease a 20-cm/8-inch loose-based cake tin. To make the pastry, sift the flour and cocoa powder into a bowl and rub in the butter until the mixture resembles fine breadcrumbs. Stir in the sugar and ground almonds. Add the egg yolk and sufficient water to make a soft dough.

2 Roll out the pastry on a lightly floured work surface and use to line the prepared tin. Leave to chill for 30 minutes. Preheat the oven to 160°C/325°F/Gas Mark 3. To make the filling, put the egg yolks and sugar into a large bowl and whisk until thick and pale. Whisk in the cream cheese, ground almonds, cream, cocoa powder and vanilla extract until well combined.

3 Put the egg whites in a large bowl and whisk until stiff but not dry. Stir a little of the egg white into the cheese mixture, then fold in the remainder. Pour into the pastry case. Bake in the oven for 1 hour 30 minutes, until well risen and just firm to the touch. Carefully remove from the tin and dust with icing sugar. Serve the cheesecake warm.

chocolate amaretto cheesecake

ingredients

SERVES 10–12

base
vegetable oil, for oiling
175 g/6 oz digestive biscuits
55 g/2 oz amaretti biscuits
85 g/3 oz butter

filling
225 g/8 oz plain chocolate,
    broken into pieces
400 g/14 oz cream cheese,
    at room temperature
115 g/4 oz golden caster sugar
4 eggs
300 ml/10 fl oz double cream
50 ml/2 fl oz amaretto

topping
1 tbsp amaretto
300 ml/10 fl oz soured cream

crushed amaretti biscuits,
    to decorate

method

1 Line the base of a 23-cm/9-inch springform cake tin with foil and brush the sides of the tin with oil. Place the biscuits in a polythene bag and crush with a rolling pin. Put the butter in a saucepan and heat gently until just melted, then stir in the biscuits. Press into the base of the tin and chill for 1 hour.

2 Melt the chocolate in a heatproof bowl set over a saucepan of gently simmering water, then set aside to cool slightly. Preheat the oven to 160°C/325°F/Gas Mark 3. To make the filling, put the cream cheese in a bowl and beat until fluffy, then add the sugar and beat until smooth. Gradually add the eggs, beating until well blended. Blend in the melted chocolate, cream and amaretto. Pour the mixture over the biscuit case and bake in the oven for 50–60 minutes, until set.

3 Leave the cheesecake in the oven with the door slightly ajar, until cold. Run a knife round the inside of the tin to loosen the cheesecake. Chill for 2 hours, then remove from the tin and place the cheesecake on a serving plate. To make the topping, stir the amaretto into the soured cream and spread over the cheesecake. Sprinkle the crushed biscuits round the edge to decorate.

irish cream cheesecake

ingredients

SERVES 12

oil, for oiling

175 g/6 oz chocolate chip
    cookies

55 g/2 oz butter

filling

225 g/8 oz plain chocolate

225 g/8 oz g milk chocolate

55 g/2 oz golden caster sugar

250 g/9 oz cream cheese

425 ml/15 fl oz double cream,
    whipped

3 tbsp Irish cream liqueur

crème fraîche or soured cream
    and fresh fruit, to serve

method

1 Line the base of a 20-cm/8-inch springform tin with foil and brush the sides with oil. Place the biscuits in a polythene bag and crush with a rolling pin. Put the butter in a saucepan and heat gently until just melted, then stir in the crushed biscuits. Press the mixture into the base of the tin and chill in the refrigerator for 1 hour.

2 To make the filling, melt the plain and milk chocolate together, stir to combine and leave to cool. Place the sugar and cream cheese in a large bowl and beat together until smooth, then fold in the whipped cream. Fold the mixture gently into the melted chocolate, then stir in the Irish cream liqueur.

3 Spoon the filling over the chilled biscuit base and smooth the surface. Cover and chill in the refrigerator for 2 hours, or until quite firm. Transfer to a serving plate and cut into small slices. Serve with a spoonful of crème fraîche and fresh fruit.

chocolate cheesecake

ingredients

SERVES 12

175 g/6 oz margarine, plus
    extra for greasing
100 g/3¹/₂ oz plain flour
85 g/3 oz ground almonds
85 g/3 oz molasses sugar
675 g/1 lb 8 oz firm tofu
175 ml/6 fl oz vegetable oil
125 ml/4 fl oz orange juice
175 ml/6 fl oz brandy
6 tbsp cocoa powder, plus
    extra to decorate
2 tsp almond extract
icing sugar, for dusting
cape gooseberries, to decorate

method

1 Preheat the oven to 160°C/325°F/Gas Mark 3. Lightly grease and line the base of a 23-cm/9-inch springform cake tin. Put the flour, ground almonds and 1 tablespoon of the sugar in a bowl and mix well. Rub the margarine into the mixture to form a dough.

2 Press the pastry into the base of the tin to cover, pushing the pastry right up to the edge of the tin.

3 Coarsely chop the tofu and put into a food processor with the vegetable oil, orange juice, brandy, cocoa, almond extract and remaining sugar and process until smooth and creamy. Pour into the pastry case and cook in the preheated oven for about 1–1¹/₄ hours, or until set.

4 Leave to cool in the tin for 5 minutes, then remove from the tin and chill in the refrigerator. Dust with icing sugar and cocoa. Decorate with cape gooseberries and serve.

ginger cheesecake

ingredients

SERVES 6–8

175 g/6 oz gingernut biscuits

sunflower oil, for oiling

55 g/2 oz butter, preferably
    unsalted

400 g/14 oz plain chocolate

55 g/2 oz icing sugar

2 tbsp maple syrup or
    golden syrup

3 bay leaves

seeds from 1 vanilla pod,
    soaked in 4 tsp milk or
    dark rum

200 g/7 oz cream cheese

125 ml/4 fl oz double cream,
    whipped

70 g/2½ oz crystallized ginger
    pieces, sliced thinly, plus
    extra to decorate

to serve

whipped cream

cocoa powder

method

1 To make the base, crush the gingernut biscuits in a food processor, or place them in a polythene bag, loosely seal the end and pound with a rolling pin to reduce them to crumbs. Oil a 20-cm/8-inch loose-based cake tin, line the base with greaseproof paper and oil again.

2 Melt the butter, stir in the crushed biscuits, then press the mixture over the base of the tin. Refrigerate to set while you make the filling.

3 Break the chocolate into pieces and place in a large heatproof bowl set over a saucepan of gently simmering water. Add the icing sugar, syrup, bay leaves, vanilla seeds and their soaking liquid and stir, until the chocolate has melted and the mixture is smooth and glossy. Remove from the heat and leave to cool, stirring occasionally. Remove and discard the bay leaves.

4 Beat in the cream cheese, then fold in the lightly whipped cream and the crystallized ginger. Pour into the saucepan, cover with clingfilm and return to the refrigerator for about 3 hours. When it is firm, carefully remove the cheesecake from the tin.

5 Decorate the cheesecake with slices of crystallized ginger and serve with cream, dusted with cocoa.

marble cheesecake

ingredients

SERVES 10

base

225 g/8 oz toasted oat cereal

75 g/2³/₄ oz toasted hazelnuts, chopped

50 g/1³/₄ oz butter

25 g/1 oz plain chocolate

filling

350 g/12 oz cream cheese

100 g/3¹/₂ oz caster sugar

200 ml/7 fl oz natural yogurt

300 ml/10 fl oz double cream

10 g/¹/₄ oz powdered gelatine

3 tbsp water

175 g/6 oz plain chocolate, melted

175 g/6 oz white chocolate, melted

method

1 Place the toasted oat cereal in a polythene bag and crush with a rolling pin. Pour the crushed cereal into a mixing bowl and stir in the hazelnuts.

2 Melt the butter and chocolate together over a low heat and stir into the cereal mixture, stirring until well coated.

3 Using the base of a glass, press the cereal mixture into the base and up the sides of a 20-cm/8-inch springform tin.

4 Beat the cheese and sugar together with a wooden spoon until smooth. Beat in the yogurt. Whip the cream until just holding its shape and fold into the mixture. Sprinkle the gelatine over the water in a heatproof bowl and leave until spongy. Place over a saucepan of hot water and stir until dissolved. Stir into the cheese mixture.

5 Divide the mixture in half and beat the plain chocolate into one half and the white chocolate into the other half.

6 Place alternate spoonfuls of filling on the cereal base. Swirl the filling together with the tip of a knife to give a marbled effect. Decorate the top using a serrated scraper. Leave to chill for at least 2 hours, until set, before serving.

strawberry cheesecake

ingredients

SERVES 8

base

55 g/2 oz butter, preferably
    unsalted

200 g/7 oz crushed digestive
    biscuits

85 g/3 oz chopped walnuts

filling

450 g/1 lb mascarpone
    cheese

2 eggs, beaten

3 tbsp caster sugar

250 g/9 oz white chocolate,
    broken into pieces

300 g/10½ oz strawberries,
    hulled and quartered

topping

175 g/6 oz mascarpone
    cheese

chocolate caraque

16 whole strawberries

method

1 Melt the butter over a low heat and stir in the crushed biscuits and the nuts. Spoon the mixture into a 23-cm/9-inch springform cake tin and press evenly over the base with the back of a spoon. Set aside.

2 Preheat the oven to 150°C/300°F/Gas Mark 2. To make the filling, beat the cheese until smooth, then beat in the eggs and sugar. Put the chocolate in a heatproof bowl set over a saucepan of gently simmering water. Stir over a low heat until melted and smooth. Remove from the heat and cool slightly, then stir into the cheese mixture. Finally, stir in the strawberries.

3 Spoon the mixture into the cake tin, spread out evenly and smooth the surface. Bake in the preheated oven for 1 hour, until the filling is just firm. Turn off the oven and leave the cheesecake to cool inside with the door slightly ajar until completely cold.

4 Transfer the cheesecake to a serving plate and spread the mascarpone cheese on top. Decorate with the chocolate caraque and some whole strawberries.

berry cheesecake

ingredients

SERVES 8

base

85 g/3 oz margarine

175 g/6 oz oatmeal biscuits

70 g/2¹/₂ oz desiccated
    coconut

topping

1¹/₂ tsp powdered gelatine

150 ml/5 fl oz cold water

125 ml/4 fl oz evaporated milk

1 egg

6 tbsp soft light brown sugar

450 g/1 lb soft cream cheese

350 g/12 oz mixed berries

2 tbsp honey

method

1 Melt the margarine in a saucepan. Put the biscuits into a food processor and process until crushed, or crush finely with a rolling pin. Stir the crumbs into the margarine with the coconut.

2 Press the mixture evenly into a base-lined 20-cm/8-inch springform cake tin and set aside to chill in the refrigerator.

3 To make the topping, sprinkle the gelatine over the water in a heatproof bowl and leave until spongy. Place over a saucepan of hot water and stir until dissolved. Set aside to cool slightly.

4 Beat the milk with the egg, sugar and cream cheese until smooth. Stir in 55 g/2 oz of the berries. Add the gelatine in a thin stream, stirring constantly.

5 Spoon the mixture on to the biscuit base and return to the refrigerator to chill for 2 hours, or until set.

6 Remove the cheesecake from the tin and transfer to a serving plate. Arrange the remaining berries on top of the cheesecake and drizzle the honey over the top. Serve.

mascarpone cheesecake

ingredients

SERVES 8

55 g/2 oz butter, preferably
  unsalted, plus extra
  for greasing
350 g/12 oz gingernut biscuit
  crumbs
1 tbsp chopped stem ginger
500 g/1 lb 2 oz mascarpone
  cheese
finely grated rind and juice of
  2 lemons
100 g/3½ oz caster sugar
2 large eggs, separated
fruit coulis, to serve

method

1 Preheat the oven to 180°C/350°F/Gas Mark 4. Grease and base-line a 25-cm/10-inch springform cake tin or loose-based cake tin.

2 Melt the butter in a saucepan and stir in the biscuit crumbs and chopped ginger. Use to line the tin, pressing the mixture about 5 mm/¼ inch up the sides.

3 Beat together the cheese, lemon rind and juice, sugar and egg yolks until quite smooth.

4 Whisk the egg whites until stiff and fold into the cheese and lemon mixture.

5 Pour the mixture into the tin and bake in the preheated oven for 35–45 minutes, until just set. Don't worry if it cracks or sinks – this is quite normal.

6 Leave the cheesecake in the tin to cool. Serve with fruit coulis.

ricotta lemon cheesecake

ingredients

SERVES 6–8

70 g/2½ oz sultanas

3 tbsp Marsala or grappa

butter, for greasing

2 tbsp semolina, plus extra for
  dusting

350 g/12 oz ricotta cheese,
  drained

3 large egg yolks, beaten

100 g/3½ oz caster sugar

3 tbsp lemon juice

2 tbsp candied orange peel,
  finely chopped

finely grated rind of 2 large
  lemons

to decorate

icing sugar

fresh mint sprigs

redcurrants or berries
  (optional)

method

1 Soak the sultanas in the Marsala or grappa in a small bowl for about 30 minutes, or until the liquid has been absorbed and the fruit is swollen.

2 Preheat the oven to 180°C/350°F/Gas Mark 4. Cut out a circle of baking paper to fit the base of a loose-based 20-cm/8-inch round cake tin about 5 cm/2 inches deep. Grease the sides and base of the tin and line the base. Lightly dust with semolina and tip out the excess.

3 Using a wooden spoon, press the ricotta cheese though a nylon sieve into a bowl. Beat in the egg yolks, sugar, semolina and lemon juice and continue beating until blended.

4 Fold in the sultanas, orange peel and lemon rind. Pour into the prepared tin and smooth the surface.

5 Bake the cheesecake in the centre of the preheated oven for 30–40 minutes, until firm to the touch and coming away slightly from the side of the tin.

6 Turn off the oven and open the door. Leave the cheesecake inside to cool for 2–3 hours. Remove from the tin and transfer to a plate. Sift over a layer of icing sugar from at least 30 cm/12 inches above the cheesecake to dust the top and sides lightly. Decorate with mint leaves and redcurrants, if using.

breads & savoury

You might ask why make bread yourself when supermarket shelves are packed with a huge variety of different loaves. There are several reasons, the first being that it's utterly delicious and as fresh as it's possible to be. Secondly, it's a very pleasurable and rewarding activity – and much easier than many people think. Then, given that bread is a staple, making your own is cost-saving and, finally, it's very likely to be healthier. Commercially made bread is one of the main sources of unhealthily high levels of salt in the diet and some loaves also contain large quantities of sugar, although only small amounts of both are required to ensure that yeast doughs rise successfully.

There are lots of recipes for all kinds of leavened bread – from a classic white loaf to Italian focaccia, including loaves made with raising agents other than yeast, such as soda bread. Some are plain, while others are flavoured with cheese, nuts, seeds, olives, tomatoes and herbs. In addition, there are flat breads, bagels, breadsticks and other tasty treats. It's a truly international compilation of this most basic, yet infinitely varied of foods.

Finally, there is a superb collection of recipes for mouthwatering savoury baking, from snacks to serve with pre-dinner drinks, party

foods and crackers to more substantial tarts, pies, quiches and gratins. The choice is vast with a wide range of ingredients to suit all tastes: cheese, fish, bacon, chicken, herbs, spices, nuts and all kinds of different vegetables, from artichokes to watercress.

crusty white bread

ingredients

MAKES 1 MEDIUM LOAF

1 egg

1 egg yolk

lukewarm water, as required

500 g/1 lb 2 oz strong white
    flour, plus extra for dusting

1¹/₂ tsp salt

2 tsp sugar

1 tsp easy-blend dried yeast

25 g/1 oz butter, diced

corn oil, for oiling

method

1 Place the egg and egg yolk in a jug and beat lightly to mix. Add enough lukewarm water to make up to 300 ml/10 fl oz. Stir well.

2 Place the flour, salt, sugar and yeast in a large bowl. Add the butter and rub it in with your fingertips until the mixture resembles breadcrumbs. Make a well in the centre, add the egg mixture and work to a smooth dough.

3 Turn out the dough onto a lightly floured work surface and knead for 10 minutes, or until the dough is smooth and elastic. Place the dough in an oiled bowl, cover with clingfilm and leave to rise in a warm place for 1 hour, or until it has doubled in size.

4 Preheat the oven to 220°C/425°F/Gas Mark 7. Oil a loaf tin. Turn out the dough onto a lightly floured work surface and knead for 1 minute until smooth. Shape the dough the length of the tin and three times the width. Fold the dough in three lengthways and place it in the tin with the join underneath. Cover and leave in a warm place for 30 minutes, until the dough has risen above the tin.

5 Bake in the preheated oven for 30 minutes, or until firm and golden brown. Test that the loaf is cooked by tapping it on the base – it should sound hollow. Transfer to a wire rack to cool completely before serving.

wholemeal harvest bread

ingredients

MAKES 1 LOAF

225 g/8 oz strong wholemeal
   flour, plus extra for dusting

1 tbsp skimmed milk powder

1 tsp salt

2 tbsp soft light brown sugar

1 tsp easy-blend dried yeast

1^{1}/$_{2}$ tbsp sunflower oil,
   plus extra for greasing

175 ml/6 fl oz lukewarm water

method

1 Place the flour, milk powder, salt, sugar and yeast in a large bowl. Pour in the oil and add the water, then mix well to make a smooth dough.

2 Turn out onto a lightly floured surface and knead well for about 10 minutes, until smooth. Brush a bowl with oil. Shape the dough into a ball, place it in the bowl and cover with a damp tea towel. Leave to rise in a warm place for 1 hour, until the dough has doubled in volume.

3 Preheat the oven to 220°C/425°F/Gas Mark 7. Oil a 900-g/2-lb loaf tin. Turn out the dough onto a lightly floured surface and knead for 1 minute, until smooth. Shape the dough the length of the tin and three times the width. Fold the dough in three lengthways and place in the tin with the join underneath. Cover and leave in a warm place for 30 minutes, until it has risen above the tin.

4 Bake in the preheated oven for 30 minutes, or until firm and golden brown. Test that the loaf is cooked by tapping on the base with your knuckles – it should sound hollow. Transfer to a wire rack to cool.

pitta breads

ingredients

MAKES 6–8

350 g/12 oz strong white
    bread flour, plus extra
    for dusting

1^1/$_2$ tsp salt

1 tsp caster sugar

1 tsp easy-blend dried yeast

1 tbsp olive oil, plus extra
    for oiling

200 ml/7 fl oz lukewarm water

method

1 Sift the flour and salt together into a bowl and stir in the sugar and yeast. Make a well in the centre and pour in the oil and lukewarm water. Stir with a wooden spoon until the dough begins to come together, then knead until it leaves the side of the bowl. Turn out onto a lightly floured surface and knead well for 10 minutes, until smooth and elastic.

2 Brush a bowl with oil. Shape the dough into a ball, put it in the bowl and put the bowl into a plastic bag or cover with a damp tea towel. Leave to rise in a warm place for 1 hour, until the dough has doubled in volume. Turn out on to a lightly floured surface and knock back with your fist. Divide the dough into 6 to 8 equal pieces, shape each piece into a ball and place on a tray. Put the tray into a polythene bag and leave to rest for 10 minutes.

3 With floured hands, slightly flatten a dough ball and roll out on a lightly floured surface to an oval 15 cm/6 in long and 5 mm/1/4 inch thick. Place on a lightly floured tea towel, sprinkle lightly with flour and cover with a tea towel. Repeat with the remaining balls and leave to rise for 30 minutes.

4 Meanwhile, put three baking sheets in the oven and preheat to 230°C/450°F/Gas Mark 8. Transfer the pitta breads to the baking sheets, spacing them well apart, and bake for 5 minutes, until puffed and golden brown. Transfer to wire racks to cool slightly, then cover with a tea towel to keep them soft.

plaited poppy seed bread

ingredients

MAKES 1 LOAF

225 g/8 oz strong white flour,
    plus extra for dusting

1 tsp salt

2 tbsp skimmed milk powder

1¹/₂ tbsp caster sugar

1 tsp easy-blend dried yeast

175 ml/6 fl oz lukewarm water

2 tbsp vegetable oil, plus extra
    for brushing

5 tbsp poppy seeds

topping

1 egg yolk

1 tbsp milk

1 tbsp caster sugar

2 tbsp poppy seeds

method

1 Sift the flour and salt together into a bowl and stir in the milk powder, sugar and yeast. Make a well in the centre and pour in the lukewarm water and oil. Stir well with a wooden spoon until the dough begins to come together. Add the poppy seeds and knead with your hands until the dough leaves the side of the bowl. Turn out onto a lightly floured surface and knead well for about 10 minutes, until smooth and elastic.

2 Brush a bowl with oil. Shape the dough into a ball, put it in the bowl and cover with a damp tea towel. Leave to rise in a warm place for 1 hour, until the dough has doubled in volume.

3 Brush a baking tray with oil. Turn out the dough onto a lightly floured surface, knock back with your fist and knead for 1–2 minutes. Divide the dough into three equal pieces and shape each into a rope 25–30 cm/10–12 inches long. Place the ropes side by side and press them together at one end. Plait the dough, pinch the other end together and tuck it underneath. Put the loaf on the baking tray, cover with a damp tea towel and leave to rise in a warm place for 30 minutes.

4 Preheat the oven to 200°C/400°F/Gas Mark 6. To make the topping, beat the egg yolk with the milk and sugar. Brush over the top of the loaf and sprinkle with the poppy seeds. Bake in the preheated oven for 30–35 minutes, until golden brown and the loaf sounds hollow when tapped on the base with your knuckles. Transfer to a wire rack to cool.

rye bread

ingredients

MAKES 1 LARGE LOAF

450 g/1 lb rye flour

225 g/8 oz strong white flour,
plus extra for dusting

2 tsp salt

2 tsp soft light brown sugar

1½ tsp easy-blend dried yeast

425 ml/15 fl oz lukewarm
water

2 tsp vegetable oil, plus extra
for brushing

1 egg white

method

1 Sift the flours and salt together into a bowl. Add the sugar and yeast and stir to mix. Make a well in the centre and pour in the lukewarm water and oil. Stir with a wooden spoon until the dough begins to come together, then knead with your hands until it leaves the side of the bowl. Turn out onto a lightly floured surface and knead for 10 minutes, until elastic and smooth.

2 Brush a bowl with oil. Shape the dough into a ball, put it in the bowl and cover with a damp tea towel. Leave to rise in a warm place for 2 hours, until the dough has doubled in volume.

3 Brush a baking tray with oil. Turn out the dough onto a lightly floured surface and knock back with your fist, then knead for a further 10 minutes. Shape the dough into a ball, put it on the baking tray and cover with a damp tea towel. Leave to rise in a warm place for 40 minutes, until the dough has doubled in volume.

4 Meanwhile, preheat the oven to 190°C/ 375°F/Gas Mark 5. Beat the egg white with 1 tablespoon of water in a bowl. Bake the loaf in the preheated oven for 20 minutes, then remove from the oven and brush the top with the egg white glaze. Return to the oven and bake for a further 20 minutes. Brush the top of the loaf with the glaze again and return to the oven for a further 20–30 minutes, until the crust is a rich brown colour and the loaf sounds hollow when tapped on the base with your knuckles. Transfer to a wire rack to cool.

walnut & seed bread

ingredients

MAKES 2 LARGE LOAVES

450 g/1 lb wholemeal flour

450 g/1 lb granary flour

115 g/4 oz strong white flour, plus extra for dusting

2 tbsp sesame seeds

2 tbsp sunflower seeds

2 tbsp poppy seeds

115 g/4 oz walnuts, chopped

2 tsp salt

15 g/^{1}/$_2$ oz easy-blend dried yeast

2 tbsp olive oil or walnut oil

700 ml/1^1/$_4$ pints lukewarm water

1 tbsp melted butter or oil, for greasing

method

1 In a mixing bowl, mix together the flours, seeds, walnuts, salt and yeast. Add the oil and lukewarm water and stir well to form a soft dough. Turn out the dough onto a lightly floured surface and knead well for 5–7 minutes. The dough should look smooth and feel elastic.

2 Return the dough to the bowl, cover with a damp tea towel and leave to rise in a warm place for 1–1^1/$_2$ hours. When the dough has doubled in size, turn it out onto a lightly floured surface and knead again for 1 minute.

3 Grease two 900-g/2-lb loaf tins well with melted butter or oil. Divide the dough in two. Shape one piece the length of the tin and three times the width. Fold the dough in three lengthways and place in one of the tins with the join underneath. Repeat with the other piece of dough.

4 Cover and leave to rise again in a warm place for about 30 minutes, until the bread is well risen above the tins. Meanwhile, preheat the oven to 230°C/450°F/Gas Mark 8.

5 Bake in the centre of the preheated oven for 25–30 minutes. If the loaves are getting too brown, reduce the temperature to 220°C/425°F/Gas Mark 7. Test that the bread is cooked by tapping on the base with your knuckles – it should sound hollow. Transfer to a wire rack to cool.

irish soda bread

ingredients

MAKES 1 LOAF

butter, for greasing
450 g/1 lb plain flour,
    plus extra for dusting
1 tsp salt
1 tsp bicarbonate of soda
400 ml/14 fl oz buttermilk

method

1 Preheat the oven to 220°C/425°F/Gas Mark 7. Lightly grease a baking tray.

2 Sift the flour, salt and bicarbonate of soda into a mixing bowl. Make a well in the centre of the dry ingredients and pour in most of the buttermilk. Mix well together using your hands. The dough should be very soft but not too wet. If necessary, add the remaining buttermilk.

3 Turn out the dough onto a lightly floured surface and knead it lightly. Shape into a 20-cm/8-inch round.

4 Place the bread on the prepared baking tray, cut a cross in the top and bake in the preheated oven for 25–30 minutes. Test that the loaf is cooked by tapping on the base with your knuckles – it should sound hollow.

corn bread

ingredients

MAKES 1 LOAF

vegetable oil, for oiling
175 g/6 oz plain flour
1 tsp salt
4 tsp baking powder
1 tsp caster sugar
280 g/10 oz polenta
115 g/4 oz butter, softened
4 eggs
250 ml/8 fl oz milk
3 tbsp double cream

method

1 Preheat the oven to 200°C/400°F/Gas Mark 6. Brush a 20-cm/8-inch square cake tin with oil.

2 Sift the flour, salt and baking powder together into a bowl. Add the sugar and polenta and stir to mix. Add the butter, cut it into the dry ingredients, then rub in with your fingertips until the mixture resembles breadcrumbs.

3 Lightly beat the eggs in a bowl with the milk and cream, then stir into the polenta mixture until thoroughly combined.

4 Spoon the mixture into the prepared tin and smooth the surface. Bake in the preheated oven for 30–35 minutes, until a skewer inserted into the centre of the loaf comes out clean. Remove the tin from the oven and leave to cool for 5–10 minutes, then cut into squares and serve warm.

coriander & garlic naan

ingredients

MAKES 3

280 g/10 oz strong white flour, plus extra for dusting

1 tsp salt

1 tbsp ground coriander

1 garlic clove, very finely chopped

1 tsp easy-blend dried yeast

2 tsp clear honey

100 ml/3½ fl oz lukewarm water

4 tbsp natural yogurt

1 tbsp vegetable oil, plus extra for brushing

1 tsp black onion seeds

1 tbsp chopped fresh coriander

method

1 Sift the flour, salt and ground coriander together into a bowl and stir in the garlic and yeast. Make a well in the centre and pour in the honey, water, yogurt and oil. Stir well with a wooden spoon until the dough begins to come together, then knead with your hands until it leaves the side of the bowl. Turn out onto a lightly floured surface and knead well for about 10 minutes, until smooth and elastic.

2 Brush a bowl with oil. Shape the dough into a ball, put it in the bowl and cover with a damp tea towel. Leave to rise in a warm place for 1–2 hours, until the dough has doubled in volume.

3 Put three baking trays in the oven and preheat to 240°C/475°F/Gas Mark 9. Preheat the grill. Turn out the dough onto a lightly floured surface and knock back with your fist. Divide into three pieces, shape each piece into a ball and cover two of them with oiled clingfilm.

4 Roll out the uncovered piece of dough into a teardrop shape about 8 mm/3/8 inch thick and cover with oiled clingfilm. Roll out the other pieces of dough in the same way. Place the naan on the preheated baking trays and sprinkle with the onion seeds and chopped coriander. Bake in the preheated oven for 5 minutes, until puffed up. Transfer the naan bread to the grill pan, brush with oil and grill for 2–3 minutes. Serve warm.

turkish flatbread

ingredients

MAKES 8

750 g/1 lb 10 oz plain flour, plus extra for dusting

1½ tsp salt

1 tsp ground cumin

½ tsp ground coriander

1 tsp caster sugar

10 g/¼ oz easy-blend dried yeast

2 tbsp olive oil, plus extra for oiling

400 ml/14 fl oz lukewarm water

method

1 Sift the flour, salt, cumin and coriander together into a bowl and stir in the sugar and yeast. Make a well in the centre and pour in the oil and lukewarm water. Stir well with a wooden spoon until the dough begins to come together, then knead with your hands until it leaves the side of the bowl. Turn out onto a lightly floured surface and knead well for about 10 minutes, until smooth and elastic.

2 Brush a bowl with oil. Shape the dough into a ball, put it in the bowl and cover with a damp tea towel. Leave to rise in a warm place for 1 hour, until the dough has doubled in volume.

3 Lightly oil a baking tray. Turn out the dough onto a lightly floured surface, knock back with your fist and knead for 1–2 minutes. Divide the dough into eight equal pieces, shape each piece into a ball, then roll out to a 20-cm/8-inch round. Cover the rounds with a damp tea towel and leave to rest for 20 minutes.

4 Heat a heavy-based frying pan and brush the base with oil. Add one dough round, cover and cook for 2–3 minutes, until lightly browned on the underside. Turn over with a fish slice, re-cover the pan and cook for a further 2 minutes, until lightly browned on the second side. Remove from the pan and cook the remaining dough rounds in the same way.

vegetable & hazelnut loaf

ingredients

SERVES 4

2 tbsp sunflower oil, plus extra for oiling

1 onion, chopped

1 garlic clove, finely chopped

2 celery sticks, chopped

1 tbsp plain flour

200 ml/7 fl oz strained canned tomatoes

115 g/4 oz fresh wholemeal breadcrumbs

2 carrots, grated

115 g/4 oz toasted hazelnuts, ground

1 tbsp dark soy sauce

2 tbsp chopped fresh coriander

1 egg, lightly beaten

salt and pepper

mixed red and green lettuce leaves, to serve

method

1 Preheat the oven to 180°C/350°F/Gas Mark 4. Oil and line a 450-g/1-lb loaf tin. Heat the oil in a heavy-based frying pan over a medium heat. Add the onion and cook, stirring frequently, for 5 minutes, or until soft. Add the garlic and celery and cook, stirring frequently, for 5 minutes. Add the flour and cook, stirring constantly, for 1 minute. Gradually stir in the tomatoes and cook, stirring constantly, until thick. Remove the pan from the heat.

2 Put the breadcrumbs, carrots, ground hazelnuts, soy sauce and coriander in a bowl. Add the tomato mixture and stir well. Cool slightly, then beat in the egg and season with salt and pepper.

3 Spoon the mixture into the prepared tin and smooth the surface. Cover with foil and bake in the preheated oven for 1 hour. If serving hot, turn out the loaf onto a warmed serving dish and serve immediately with mixed red and green salad leaves. Alternatively, cool the loaf in the tin before turning out.

focaccia with roasted cherry tomatoes, basil & crispy pancetta

ingredients

SERVES 4–6

500 g/1 lb 2 oz strong white flour, plus extra for kneading and rolling
1 tbsp dried basil
1/2 tsp sugar
2 tsp easy-blend dried yeast
2 tsp salt
300 ml/10 fl oz lukewarm water
2 tbsp olive oil, plus extra for oiling
fresh basil, to garnish

topping
400 g/14 oz cherry tomatoes
1 tbsp olive oil, plus extra for oiling and drizzling
200 g/7 oz thick pancetta, diced
4 tbsp chopped fresh basil
salt and pepper

method

1 Place the flour, dried basil, sugar, yeast and salt in a bowl. Combine the water and oil and mix with the dry ingredients to form a soft dough, adding more water if the dough appears too dry. Turn out onto a lightly floured work surface and knead for 10 minutes, or until the dough bounces back when pressed lightly with your finger. Place the dough in a lightly oiled bowl and cover with clingfilm. Leave in a warm place for 1 hour, or until doubled in size.

2 Preheat the oven to 140°C/275°F/Gas Mark 1. Place the tomatoes on a baking sheet covered with baking paper, sprinkle with oil and season with salt and pepper. Bake for 30 minutes.

3 Increase the oven temperature to 220°C/425°F/Gas Mark 7. Remove the dough from the bowl and knead again briefly. Shape into a rectangle and place on a lightly oiled baking sheet, turning over the dough to oil both sides. Make rough indentations in the dough using your fingers. Top with the tomatoes and pancetta. Sprinkle with salt and pepper. Leave in a warm place for 10 minutes for the dough to rise again. Bake for 15–20 minutes, or until golden brown and cooked through. Drizzle with oil and top with fresh basil. Serve warm.

olive & sun-dried tomato bread

ingredients

MAKES 2 LOAVES

400 g/14 oz plain flour, plus
   extra for dusting

1 tsp salt

1 sachet easy-blend dried
   yeast

1 tsp soft light brown sugar

1 tbsp chopped fresh thyme

225 ml/8 fl oz water, heated to
   50°C/122°F

4 tbsp olive oil, plus extra
   for oiling

100 g/3½ oz black olives,
   stoned and sliced

100 g/3½ oz green olives,
   stoned and sliced

200 g/7 oz sun-dried tomatoes
   in oil, drained and sliced

1 egg yolk, beaten

method

1 Place the flour, salt and yeast in a bowl and mix together, then stir in the sugar and thyme. Make a well in the centre. Slowly stir in enough water and oil to make a dough. Mix in the olives and sun-dried tomatoes. Knead the dough for 5 minutes, then form it into a ball. Brush a bowl with oil, add the dough and cover with clingfilm. Leave to rise in a warm place for about 1½ hours, or until it has doubled in size.

2 Dust a baking sheet with flour. Knead the dough lightly, then cut in half and shape both halves into ovals or circles. Place on the baking sheet, cover with clingfilm and leave to rise again in a warm place for 45 minutes, or until they have doubled in size.

3 Preheat the oven to 200°C/400°F/Gas Mark 6. Make three shallow diagonal cuts on the top of each piece of dough. Brush with the egg. Bake for 40 minutes, or until cooked through – they should be golden on top and sound hollow when tapped on the base. Transfer to wire racks to cool. Store in an airtight container for up to 3 days.

black olive focaccia

ingredients

SERVES 12

550 g/1 lb 4 oz strong white
   flour, plus extra for dusting
1 tsp salt
2 tsp easy-blend dried yeast
350 ml/12 fl oz lukewarm
   water
6 tbsp extra virgin olive oil,
   plus extra for oiling
200 g/7 oz stoned black olives,
coarsely chopped
1 tsp rock salt

method

1 Sift the flour and salt into a warmed bowl and stir in the yeast. Pour in the water and 2 tablespoons of the olive oil and mix to a soft dough. Knead the dough on a lightly floured work surface for 5–10 minutes, or until it becomes smooth and elastic. Transfer it to a clean, warmed, oiled bowl and cover with clingfilm. Leave to stand in a warm place for 1 hour, or until the dough has doubled in size.

2 Brush two baking sheets with oil. Knock back the dough, then knead on a lightly floured work surface for 1 minute. Add the olives and knead until combined. Divide the dough in half and shape into two ovals 28 x 23-cm/ 11 x 9 inches long, and place on the baking sheets. Cover with oiled clingfilm and leave to stand in a warm place for 1 hour, or until the dough is puffy.

3 Preheat the oven to 200°C/400°F/Gas Mark 6. Press your fingers into the dough to make dimples, drizzle over 2 tablespoons of oil and sprinkle with the rock salt. Bake in the preheated oven for 30–35 minutes, or until golden. Drizzle with the remaining olive oil and cover with a cloth to give a soft crust. Slice each loaf into six pieces and serve warm.

mixed seed bread

ingredients

MAKES 1 MEDIUM LOAF

450 g/1 lb strong white flour

150 g/5 1/2 oz rye flour

1 1/2 tbsp skimmed milk powder

1 1/2 tsp salt

1 tbsp soft light brown sugar

1 tsp easy-blend dried yeast

1 1/2 tbsp sunflower oil

2 tsp lemon juice

300 ml/10 fl oz lukewarm water

1 tsp caraway seeds

1/2 tsp poppy seeds

1/2 tsp sesame seeds

topping

1 egg white

1 tbsp water

1 tbsp sunflower or pumpkin seeds

method

1 Place the flours, milk, salt, sugar and yeast in a large bowl. Pour in the oil and add the lemon juice and water. Stir in the seeds and mix well to make a smooth dough.

2 Turn out the dough onto a lightly floured work surface and knead for 10 minutes, or until the dough is smooth and elastic. Place the dough in an oiled bowl, cover with clingfilm and leave to rise in a warm place for 1 hour, or until it has doubled in size.

3 Oil a 900-g/2-lb loaf tin. Turn out the dough onto a lightly floured work surface and knead for 1 minute until smooth. Shape the dough the length of the tin and three times the width. Fold the dough into three lengthways and place it in the tin with the join underneath. Cover and leave in a warm place for 30 minutes until it has risen above the tin.

4 Preheat the oven to 220°C/425°F/Gas Mark 7. For the topping, lightly beat the egg white with the water to make a glaze. Just before baking, brush the glaze over the loaf, then gently press the sunflower seeds all over the top.

5 Bake in the preheated oven for 30 minutes, or until firm and golden brown. Test that the loaf is cooked by tapping it on the base – it should sound hollow. Transfer to a wire rack to cool completely before serving.

cheese & chive plait

ingredients

SERVES 10

500 g/1 lb 4 oz strong white
    flour, plus extra for dusting

1 tsp salt

1 tsp caster sugar

1½ tsp easy-blend dried yeast

25 g/1 oz butter

115 g/4 oz Cheddar cheese,
    coarsely grated

3 tbsp snipped fresh chives

4 spring onions, chopped

150 ml/5 fl oz lukewarm milk

175 ml/6 fl oz lukewarm water

vegetable oil, for oiling

beaten egg, for glazing

method

1 Sift the flour and salt into a warmed bowl and stir in the sugar and yeast. Rub in the butter, then stir in the cheese, chives and spring onions. Make a well in the centre. Mix together the milk and water and pour into the well. Mix to make a soft dough. Turn out the dough onto a lightly floured work surface and knead for 10 minutes, or until it is smooth and elastic.

2 Transfer the dough to a clean, oiled bowl and cover with clingfilm. Leave to stand in a warm place for 1 hour, or until doubled in size. Preheat the oven to 220°C/425°F/Gas Mark 7, then brush a large baking sheet with oil. Turn out the dough onto a floured work surface and knead for 1 minute. Divide the dough into three pieces. Roll out each piece into a rope shape and plait the three pieces together, pinching the ends to seal.

3 Place on the prepared baking sheet and cover with oiled clingfilm. Leave to stand in a warm place for 45 minutes, or until doubled in size. Brush with beaten egg and bake in the preheated oven for 20 minutes.

4 Reduce the oven temperature to 180°C/350°F/Gas Mark 4 and bake for a further 15 minutes, or until golden brown and the loaf sounds hollow when tapped on the base. Serve warm or cold.

english muffins

ingredients

MAKES 10–12

10 g/¼ oz easy-blend
    dried yeast
250 ml/9 fl oz lukewarm water
125 ml/4 fl oz natural yogurt
450 g/1 lb strong white flour
½ tsp salt
50 g/1¾ oz fine semolina
oil, for greasing

to serve
butter and jam (optional)

method

1 Mix the yeast with half the water in a bowl until it has dissolved.

2 Add the remaining water and the yogurt and mix well.

3 Sift the flour into a large bowl and add the salt. Pour in the yeast liquid and mix well to a soft dough.

4 Turn out onto a floured surface and knead well until very smooth. Put the dough back into the bowl, cover with clingfilm and leave to rise for 30–40 minutes in a warm place until it has doubled in size.

5 Turn out again onto the surface and knead lightly. Roll out the dough to a thickness of 2 cm/¾ inch.

6 Using a 7.5-cm/3-inch cutter, cut into rounds and scatter the semolina over each muffin. Re-roll the trimmings of the dough and make further muffins until it is all used up. Place them on a lightly floured baking sheet, cover and allow to rise again for 30–40 minutes.

7 Heat a griddle pan or a large frying pan and lightly grease with a little oil. Cook half the muffins for 7–8 minutes on each side, taking care not to burn them. Repeat with the remaining muffins. Serve freshly cooked with lots of butter and jam, if using.

bagels

ingredients

MAKES 10

350 g/12 oz strong white flour, plus extra for dusting

2 tsp salt

10 g/¼ oz easy-blend dried yeast

1 tbsp lightly beaten egg

200 ml/7 fl oz lukewarm water

vegetable oil, for oiling

1 egg white

2 tsp water

2 tbsp caraway seeds

method

1 Sift the flour and salt together into a bowl and stir in the yeast. Make a well in the centre, pour in the egg and the lukewarm water and mix to a dough. Turn out onto a lightly floured surface and knead well for about 10 minutes. Brush a bowl with oil. Shape the dough into a ball, place it in the bowl, cover with a damp tea towel and leave to rise in a warm place for 1 hour.

2 Brush two baking trays with oil and dust a tray with flour. Turn out the dough onto a lightly floured surface and knock back with your fist. Knead for 2 minutes, then divide into ten pieces. Shape each piece into a ball and leave to rest for 5 minutes. Gently flatten each ball with a lightly floured hand and make a hole in the centre with the handle of a wooden spoon. Put the bagels on the floured tray, cover with a damp tea towel and leave to rise in a warm place for 20 minutes.

3 Preheat the oven to 220°C/425°F/Gas Mark 7 and bring a large saucepan of water to the boil. Reduce the heat until the water is barely simmering, add two bagels, poach for 1 minute, then turn over and poach for a further 30 seconds. Remove with a slotted spoon and drain on a tea towel. Repeat with the remaining bagels. Transfer the bagels to the prepared baking trays. Beat the egg white with the water in a bowl and brush it over the bagels. Sprinkle with caraway seeds and bake in the preheated oven for 25–30 minutes, until golden brown. Transfer to a wire rack to cool.

breadsticks

ingredients

MAKES 30

350 g/12 oz strong white flour,
   plus extra for dusting
1½ tsp salt
1½ tsp easy-blend dried yeast
200 ml/7 fl oz lukewarm water
3 tbsp olive oil, plus extra
   for oiling
sesame seeds, for coating

method

1 Sift the flour and salt together into a warmed bowl. Stir in the yeast. Make a well in the centre. Add the water and oil to the well and mix to form a soft dough.

2 Turn out the dough onto a lightly floured work surface and knead for 5–10 minutes, or until smooth and elastic. Put the dough in an oiled bowl, cover with a damp tea towel and leave to rise in a warm place for 1 hour, or until doubled in size.

3 Preheat the oven to 200°C/400°F/Gas Mark 6. Lightly oil two baking trays.

4 Turn out the dough again and knead lightly. Roll out into a rectangle measuring 23 x 20 cm/ 9 x 8 inches. Cut the dough into three strips, each 20 cm/8 inches long, then cut each strip across into ten equal pieces.

5 Gently roll and stretch each piece of dough into a stick about 30 cm/12 inches long, then brush with oil. Spread out the sesame seeds on a large shallow plate or tray. Roll each breadstick in the sesame seeds to coat, then place on the prepared baking trays, spaced well apart. Brush with oil, cover with a damp tea towel and leave to prove in a warm place for 15 minutes.

6 Bake the breadsticks in the preheated oven for 10 minutes. Turn over and bake for a further 5–10 minutes, until golden. Transfer to a wire rack and leave to cool.

cheese straws

ingredients

MAKES 24

115 g/4 oz plain flour, plus extra for dusting

pinch of salt

1 tsp curry powder

55 g/2 oz butter, plus extra for greasing

55 g/2 oz Cheddar cheese, grated

1 egg, beaten

poppy seeds and cumin seeds, for sprinkling

method

1 Sift the flour, salt and curry powder into a bowl. Add the butter and rub in until the mixture resembles breadcrumbs. Add the cheese and half the egg and mix to form a dough. Wrap in clingfilm and chill in the refrigerator for 30 minutes.

2 Preheat the oven to 200°C/400°F/Gas Mark 6, then grease several baking sheets. On a floured work surface, roll out the dough to 5 mm/1/4 inch thick. Cut into three 7.5 x 1-cm/ 3 x 1/2-inch strips. Pinch the strips lightly along the sides and place on the baking sheets.

3 Brush the straws with the remaining egg and sprinkle half with poppy seeds and half with cumin seeds. Bake in the preheated oven for 10–15 minutes, or until golden. Transfer to wire racks to cool.

savoury oatcakes

ingredients

MAKES 12–14

100 g/3$^{1}/_{2}$ oz unsalted butter,
 plus extra for greasing
90 g/3$^{1}/_{4}$ oz rolled oats
25 g/1 oz wholemeal flour
$^{1}/_{2}$ tsp coarse sea salt
1 tsp dried thyme
40 g/1$^{1}/_{2}$ oz walnuts, finely
 chopped
1 egg, beaten
40 g/1$^{1}/_{2}$ oz sesame seeds

method

1 Preheat the oven to 180°C/350°F/Gas Mark 4. Lightly grease two baking trays.

2 Rub the butter into the oats and flour, using your fingertips. Stir in the salt, thyme and walnuts, then add the egg and mix to a soft dough. Spread out the sesame seeds on a large shallow plate or tray. Break off walnut-sized pieces of dough and roll into balls, then roll in the sesame seeds to coat lightly and evenly.

3 Place the balls of dough on the prepared baking trays, spaced well apart, and roll the rolling pin over them to flatten them as much as possible. Bake in the preheated oven for 12–15 minutes, or until firm and pale golden.

4 Cool on the baking trays for 3–4 minutes, then transfer to a wire rack to finish cooling.

cheese & mustard scones

ingredients

MAKES 8

225 g/8 oz self-raising flour, plus extra for dusting

1 tsp baking powder

pinch of salt

50 g/1³/₄ oz butter, diced, plus extra for greasing

125 g/4¹/₂ oz mature Cheddar cheese, grated

1 tsp mustard powder

150 ml/5 fl oz milk, plus extra for brushing

pepper

method

1 Preheat the oven to 220°C/425°F/Gas Mark 7. Lightly grease a baking tray.

2 Sift the flour, baking powder and salt into a mixing bowl. Rub in the butter with your fingertips until the mixture resembles breadcrumbs.

3 Stir in the cheese, mustard and enough milk to form a soft dough.

4 On a lightly floured surface, knead the dough very lightly, then flatten it out with the palm of your hand to a depth of about 2.5 cm/1 inch.

5 Cut the dough into eight wedges with a knife. Brush each one with a little milk and sprinkle with pepper to taste.

6 Bake in the preheated oven for 10–15 minutes, until golden brown. Transfer the scones to a wire rack and leave to cool slightly before serving.

blinis

ingredients

MAKES 8

100 g/3^{1}/$_{2}$ oz buckwheat flour

100 g/3^{1}/$_{2}$ oz strong white flour

5 g/^{1}/$_{8}$ oz easy-blend
    dried yeast

1 tsp salt

400 ml/14 fl oz lukewarm milk

2 eggs, 1 whole and
    1 separated

vegetable oil, for oiling

soured cream and smoked
    salmon, to serve

method

1 Sift the flours into a large, warmed bowl. Stir in the yeast and salt. Beat in the milk, whole egg and egg yolk until smooth. Cover the bowl and leave to stand in a warm place for 1 hour.

2 Place the egg white in a spotlessly clean bowl and whisk until soft peaks form. Fold into the batter. Brush a heavy-based frying pan with oil and place over a medium–high heat. When the pan is hot, pour enough batter onto the surface to make a blini about the size of a saucer.

3 When bubbles rise, turn the blini over with a spatula and cook the other side until light brown. Wrap in a clean tea towel to keep warm while cooking the remainder. Serve the warm blinis with soured cream and smoked salmon.

spiced cocktail bites

ingredients

MAKES ABOUT 20

140 g/5 oz plain flour, plus extra for dusting

2 tsp curry powder

115 g/4 oz butter, plus extra for greasing

90 g/3¼ oz Cheddar cheese, grated

2 tsp poppy seeds

1 tsp black onion seeds

1 egg yolk

cumin seeds, for sprinkling

method

1 Preheat the oven to 190°C/375°F/Gas Mark 5, then grease 2 baking sheets. Sift the flour and curry powder into a bowl. Cut the butter into pieces and add to the flour. Rub in with your fingertips until the mixture resembles breadcrumbs, then stir in the cheese, poppy seeds and black onion seeds. Stir in the egg yolk and mix to a firm dough.

2 Wrap the dough in clingfilm and chill in the refrigerator for 30 minutes. Roll out the dough on a floured work surface, to 3 mm/⅛ inch thick. Stamp out shapes with a cutter. Re-roll the trimmings and stamp out more shapes until the dough is used up.

3 Place on the prepared baking sheets and sprinkle with the cumin seeds. Leave to chill for 15 minutes. Bake in the preheated oven for 20 minutes, or until crisp and golden. Serve warm or transfer to wire racks to cool.

curried cheese bites

ingredients

MAKES 40

100 g/3½ oz plain flour, plus
    extra for dusting
1 tsp salt
2 tsp curry powder
115 g/4 oz mild Cheddar
    cheese, grated
115 g/4 oz Parmesan cheese,
    freshly grated
115 g/4 oz butter, softened,
    plus extra for greasing

method

1 Preheat the oven to 180°C/350°F/Gas Mark 4. Lightly grease about four baking sheets.

2 Sift the flour and salt into a mixing bowl. Stir in the curry powder and both the grated cheeses. Rub in the softened butter with your fingertips, then bring the mixture together to form a soft dough.

3 Roll out the dough thinly on a lightly floured work surface to form a rectangle.

4 Cut out 40 rounds using a 5-cm/2-inch fluted round cutter and arrange on the baking sheets.

5 Bake in the preheated oven for 10–15 minutes, until golden brown.

6 Leave to cool slightly on the baking sheets. Transfer to a wire rack to cool completely and crispen, then serve.

pesto palmiers

ingredients

MAKES 20

plain flour, for dusting

250 g/9 oz ready-made puff
   pastry

3 tbsp green or red pesto

butter, for greasing

1 egg yolk, beaten with
   1 tbsp water

30 g/1 oz Parmesan cheese,
   freshly grated

method

1 On a floured work surface, roll out the pastry to a 35 x 15-cm/14 x 6-inch rectangle and trim the edges with a sharp knife. Spread the pesto evenly over the pastry. Roll up the ends tightly to meet in the centre of the pastry.

2 Wrap in clingfilm and chill in the refrigerator for 20 minutes, until firm, then remove from the refrigerator and unwrap. Meanwhile, preheat the oven to 200°C/400°F/Gas Mark 6, then grease a baking sheet. Brush with the beaten egg yolk on all sides. Cut into 1 cm/$1/2$ inch thick slices. Place the slices on the prepared baking sheet.

3 Bake in the preheated oven for 10 minutes, or until crisp and golden. Remove from the oven and immediately sprinkle over the Parmesan cheese. Serve the palmiers warm or transfer to a wire rack and leave to cool to room temperature.

cheese & rosemary bites

ingredients

MAKES 40

225 g/8 oz cold butter, diced, plus extra for greasing

250 g/9 oz plain flour

280 g/10 oz Gruyère cheese, grated

1/2 tsp cayenne pepper

2 tsp finely chopped fresh rosemary leaves

1 egg yolk, beaten with 1 tbsp water

method

1 Preheat the oven to 180°C/350°F/Gas Mark 4, then grease two baking sheets. Place the flour, butter, cheese, cayenne pepper and rosemary in a food processor. Pulse until the mixture forms a dough, adding a little cold water, if necessary, to bring the mixture together.

2 On a floured work surface, roll out the dough to 5 mm/1/4 inch thick. Stamp out shapes, such as stars and hearts, with 6-cm/21/2-inch cutters.

3 Place the shapes on the prepared baking sheets, then cover with clingfilm and leave to chill in the refrigerator for 30 minutes, or until firm. Brush with the beaten egg yolk and bake in the oven for 10 minutes, or until golden brown. Leave to cool on the baking sheets for 2 minutes, then serve warm or transfer to wire racks to cool.

spicy chicken muffins

ingredients

MAKES 12

125 ml/4 fl oz sunflower oil or groundnut oil, plus extra for oiling

2 onions, chopped

3 spring onions, chopped

1 small fresh red chilli, deseeded and finely chopped

3 skinless, boneless chicken thighs, chopped into small pieces

1 tsp paprika

325 g/11$\frac{1}{2}$ oz self-raising flour

1 tsp baking powder

2 large eggs

1 tbsp lemon juice

1 tbsp grated lemon rind

125 ml/4 fl oz soured cream

125 ml/4 fl oz natural yogurt

salt and pepper

method

1 Preheat the oven to 190°C/375°F/Gas Mark 5. Oil a 12-cup muffin tin or line with paper muffin cases. Heat a little oil in a frying pan, add the onions, spring onions and chilli and cook over a low heat, stirring constantly, for 3 minutes. Remove from the heat, lift out the onions and chilli, and set aside. Heat a little more oil in the pan, add the chicken and paprika, and cook, stirring, over a medium heat for 5 minutes. Remove from the heat and set aside.

2 Sift the flour and baking powder into a large mixing bowl. In a separate bowl, lightly beat the eggs, then stir in the remaining oil and the lemon juice and lemon rind. Pour in the soured cream and the yogurt and mix together. Add the egg mixture to the flour mixture, then gently stir in the onions, spring onions, chilli and chicken. Season to taste with salt and pepper. Do not overstir the batter – it is fine for it to be a little lumpy.

3 Divide the muffin batter evenly between the 12 cups in the muffin tin, then transfer to the preheated oven. Bake for 20 minutes, or until risen and golden. Remove the muffins from the oven and serve warm, or place them on a wire rack and leave to cool.

leek & ham muffins

ingredients

MAKES 12

2 tbsp sunflower oil or
  groundnut oil, plus extra
  for oiling
1 leek, washed, trimmed
  and finely chopped
280 g/10 oz plain flour
2 tsp baking powder
$1/2$ tsp bicarbonate of soda
1 large egg, lightly beaten
300 ml/10 fl oz Greek-style
  yogurt
55 g/2 oz butter, melted
25 g/1 oz Cheddar cheese,
  grated
25 g/1 oz fresh chives,
  finely snipped
150 g/$5^1/2$ oz cooked ham,
  chopped

method

1 Preheat the oven to 200°C/ 400°F/Gas Mark 6. Oil a 12-cup muffin tin or line with paper muffin cases. Heat the oil in a frying pan, add the chopped leek and cook, stirring, over a low heat for 2 minutes. Remove from the heat and leave to cool.

2 Sift the flour, baking powder and bicarbonate of soda into a large mixing bowl. In a separate bowl, lightly mix the egg, yogurt and melted butter together. Add the cheese, chives, cooked leek and half of the chopped ham, then mix together well. Add the cheese mixture to the flour mixture and then gently stir together until just combined. Do not overstir the batter – it is fine for it to be a little lumpy.

3 Divide the muffin batter evenly between the 12 cups in the muffin tin. Sprinkle over the remaining chopped ham, then transfer to the oven. Bake for 20 minutes, or until risen and golden. Remove the muffins from the oven and serve warm, or place them on a wire rack and leave to cool.

potato & pancetta muffins

ingredients

MAKES 12

1 tbsp sunflower oil or
  groundnut oil, plus extra
  for oiling
3 shallots, finely chopped
350 g/12 oz self-raising flour
1 tsp salt
450 g/1 lb potatoes, cooked
  and mashed
2 large eggs
350 ml/12 fl oz milk
125 ml/4 fl oz soured cream
1 tbsp finely snipped fresh
  chives
150 g/5^1/$_2$ oz pancetta, grilled
  and crumbled into pieces
4 tbsp grated Cheddar cheese

method

1 Preheat the oven to 200°C/400°F/Gas Mark 6. Oil a 12-cup muffin tin or line with paper muffin cases. Heat the oil in a frying pan, add the chopped shallots and cook, stirring, over a low heat for 2 minutes. Remove from the heat and leave to cool.

2 Sift the flour and salt into a large mixing bowl. In a separate bowl, mix the mashed potatoes, eggs, milk, soured cream, chives and half of the pancetta together. Add the potato mixture to the flour mixture and then gently stir together until just combined. Do not overstir the batter – it is fine for it to be a little lumpy.

3 Divide the muffin batter evenly between the 12 cups in the muffin tin. Sprinkle over the remaining pancetta, then sprinkle over the grated cheese. Transfer to the preheated oven and bake for 20 minutes, or until risen and golden. Remove the muffins from the oven and serve warm, or place them on a wire rack and leave to cool.

crab & cream cheese muffins

ingredients

MAKES 12

sunflower oil or groundnut oil, for oiling

280 g/10 oz plain flour

1½ tsp baking powder

½ tsp bicarbonate of soda

½ tsp salt

1 large egg

150 ml/5 fl oz natural yogurt

150 ml/5 fl oz soured cream

25 g/1 oz Cheddar cheese, grated

3 tsp chopped fresh parsley

3 tsp chopped fresh dill

filling

200 g/7 oz canned crabmeat, drained

200 g/7 oz cream cheese

2 tbsp mayonnaise

salt and pepper

method

1 Preheat the oven to 200°C/400°F/Gas Mark 6. Oil a 12-cup muffin tin. Sift the flour, baking powder, bicarbonate of soda and salt into a large mixing bowl.

2 In a separate bowl, lightly beat the egg, then pour in the yogurt and soured cream and mix together. Stir in the grated cheese and chopped herbs. Add the soured cream and cheese mixture to the flour mixture, then gently stir together. Do not overstir the batter – it is fine for it to be a little lumpy. Divide the muffin batter evenly between the 12 cups in the muffin tin, then transfer to the preheated oven. Bake for 20 minutes, or until risen and golden.

3 Meanwhile, make the filling. Place the crabmeat in a mixing bowl and flake with a fork. Add the cream cheese and mayonnaise and mix together well. Season to taste with salt and pepper. Cover the bowl with clingfilm and leave to chill in the refrigerator until ready for use.

4 When the muffins are cooked, remove them from the oven, place them on a wire rack, and leave to cool to room temperature. When cool, cut them in half horizontally. Remove the crabmeat filling from the refrigerator and spread it over the bottom halves of the muffins. Replace the top halves, so that the filling is sandwiched in the middle, and serve.

herb muffins with smoked cheese

ingredients

MAKES 12

sunflower oil or groundnut oil,
    for oiling
280 g/10 oz plain flour
2 tsp baking powder
1/2 tsp bicarbonate of soda
25 g/1 oz smoked hard
    cheese, grated
50 g/1¾ oz fresh parsley,
    finely chopped
1 large egg, lightly beaten
300 ml/10 fl oz Greek-style
    yogurt
55 g/2 oz butter, melted

method

1 Preheat the oven to 200°C/400°F/Gas Mark 6. Oil a 12-cup muffin tin or line with paper muffin cases. Sift the flour, baking powder and bicarbonate of soda into a large mixing bowl. Add the smoked cheese and the parsley and mix together well.

2 In a separate bowl, lightly mix the egg, yogurt and melted butter together. Add the yogurt mixture to the flour mixture and then gently stir together until just combined. Do not overstir the batter – it is fine for it to be a little lumpy.

3 Divide the muffin batter evenly between the 12 cups in the muffin tin, then transfer to the oven. Bake for 20 minutes, or until risen and golden. Remove the muffins from the oven and serve warm, or place them on a wire rack and leave to cool.

soured cream muffins with chives

ingredients

MAKES 12

1 tbsp sunflower oil or
    groundnut oil, for oiling
280 g/10 oz plain flour
2 tsp baking powder
1/2 tsp bicarbonate of soda
25 g/1 oz Cheddar cheese,
    grated
35 g/1 1/4 oz fresh chives,
    finely snipped, plus extra
    to garnish
1 large egg, lightly beaten
225 ml/8 fl oz soured cream
90 ml/3 fl oz natural yogurt
55 g/2 oz butter, melted

method

1 Preheat the oven to 200°C/400°F/Gas Mark 6. Oil a 12-cup muffin tin. Sift the flour, baking powder and bicarbonate of soda into a large mixing bowl. Add the cheese and chives and mix together well.

2 In a separate bowl, lightly mix the egg, soured cream, yogurt and melted butter together. Add the soured cream mixture to the flour mixture and then gently stir together until just combined. Do not overstir the batter – it is fine for it to be a little lumpy.

3 Divide the muffin batter evenly between the 12 cups in the muffin tin. Sprinkle over the remaining snipped chives to garnish and transfer to the preheated oven. Bake for 20 minutes, or until risen and golden. Remove the muffins from the oven and serve warm, or place them on a wire rack and leave to cool.

parmesan & pine kernel muffins

ingredients

MAKES 12

oil or melted butter,
    for greasing
280 g/10 oz plain flour
1 tbsp baking powder
1/8 tsp salt
85 g/3 oz freshly grated
    Parmesan cheese
60 g/2¼ oz pine kernels
2 eggs
250 ml/9 fl oz buttermilk
6 tbsp sunflower oil or
    85 g/3 oz butter, melted
    and cooled
pepper

topping
10 g/¼ oz freshly grated
    Parmesan cheese
35 g/1¼ oz pine kernels

method

1 Preheat the oven to 200°C/400°F/Gas Mark 6. Grease a 12-cup muffin tin or line with 12 paper muffin cases.

2 To make the topping, mix together the cheese and pine kernels and set aside.

3 To make the muffins, sift together the flour, baking powder, and salt and pepper to taste into a large bowl. Stir in the Parmesan cheese and pine kernels.

4 Lightly beat the eggs in a large jug or bowl then beat in the buttermilk and oil. Make a well in the centre of the dry ingredients and pour in the beaten liquid ingredients. Stir gently until just combined; do not over-mix.

5 Spoon the mixture into the prepared muffin tin. Scatter the topping over the muffins. Bake in the preheated oven for about 20 minutes, until well risen, golden brown and firm to the touch.

6 Leave the muffins in the tin for 5 minutes, then serve warm.

caramelized onion muffins

ingredients

MAKES 12

oil or melted butter,
    for greasing
7 tbsp sunflower oil
3 onions, finely chopped
1 tbsp red wine vinegar
2 tsp sugar
280 g/10 oz plain flour
1 tbsp baking powder
1/8 tsp salt
2 eggs
250 ml/9 fl oz buttermilk
pepper

method

1 Preheat the oven to 200°C/400°F/Gas Mark 6. Grease a 12-cup muffin tin or line with 12 paper muffin cases.

2 Heat 2 tablespoons of the oil in a frying pan. Add the onions and cook for about 3 minutes, until beginning to soften. Add the vinegar and sugar and cook, stirring occasionally, for a further 10 minutes, until golden brown. Remove from the heat and leave to cool.

3 Meanwhile, sift together the flour, baking powder, and salt and pepper to taste into a large bowl.

4 Lightly beat the eggs in a large jug or bowl then beat in the buttermilk and the remaining oil. Make a well in the centre of the dry ingredients, pour in the beaten liquid ingredients and add the onion mixture, reserving 4 tablespoons for the topping. Stir gently until just combined; do not over-mix.

5 Spoon the mixture into the prepared muffin tin. Sprinkle the reserved onion mixture on top of the muffins. Bake in the preheated oven for about 20 minutes, until well risen, golden brown and firm to the touch.

6 Leave the muffins in the tin for 5 minutes, then serve warm.

quiche lorraine

ingredients

SERVES 4

flour, for dusting

300 g/10½ oz ready-made
    shortcrust pastry

15 g/½ oz butter

1 small onion, finely chopped

4 streaky bacon rashers, diced

55 g/2 oz Gruyère cheese or
    Cheddar cheese, grated

2 eggs, beaten

300 ml/10 fl oz single cream

pepper

method

1 Roll out the pastry on a lightly floured work surface to a round slightly larger than a 23-cm/9-inch loose-based round tart tin, 3 cm/1¼ inches deep. Lift the pastry onto the tin and press it down into the fluted edge, using the back of your finger. Trim off the excess pastry and prick the base all over with a fork. Chill in the refrigerator for at least 10 minutes to allow the pastry to rest and prevent shrinkage.

2 Preheat the oven to 200°C/400°F/Gas Mark 6 and preheat a baking tray. Place a sheet of baking paper in the pastry-lined tin and fill with baking beans. Place on the baking tray and bake blind for 10 minutes. Remove the paper and beans and bake for a further 10 minutes.

3 Melt the butter in a frying pan and cook the onion and bacon over a medium heat for about 5 minutes, stirring occasionally, until the onion is soft and lightly browned. Spread the mixture evenly in the hot pastry case and sprinkle with half the cheese. Beat together the eggs and cream in a small bowl and season to taste with pepper. Pour into the pastry case and sprinkle with the remaining cheese.

4 Reduce the oven temperature to 190°C/375°F/Gas Mark 5. Place the quiche in the oven and bake for 25–30 minutes, or until golden brown and just set. Cool for 10 minutes before turning out.

triple tomato tart

ingredients

SERVES 6

flour, for dusting

250 g/9 oz ready-made puff
    pastry

3 tbsp sundried tomato purée

250 g/9 oz vine-ripened
    tomatoes, sliced

150 g/5½ oz cherry tomatoes,
    halved

2 sprigs fresh rosemary

2 tbsp extra virgin olive oil

1 tbsp balsamic vinegar

1 egg yolk

125 g/4½ oz Italian sliced
    salami, chopped

salt and pepper

handful thyme sprigs, to
    garnish

method

1 Preheat the oven to 190°C/375°F/Gas Mark 5. Roll out the pastry to form a rectangle 35 cm/14 inches long and 25 cm/10 inches wide and lift onto a heavy-duty baking sheet. Spread the tomato purée over the dough, leaving a 3-cm/1¼-inch margin.

2 Arrange the tomato slices over the tomato purée, sprinkle over the cherry tomato halves, top with the rosemary and drizzle with 1 tablespoon of the oil and the balsamic vinegar. Brush the edges of the dough with the egg yolk, place in the preheated oven and bake for 10 minutes. Sprinkle over the salami and bake for a further 10–15 minutes.

3 Remove the tart from the oven and season with salt and pepper. Drizzle with the remaining oil and sprinkle with thyme.

crab & watercress tart

ingredients

SERVES 6

pastry

75 g/2³/4 oz cold butter, cut into pieces, plus extra for greasing

100 g/3¹/2 oz plain flour, plus extra for dusting

pinch of salt

cold water

filling

300 g/10¹/2 oz prepared white and brown crabmeat

1 bunch watercress, washed and leaves picked from stems

60 ml/2 fl oz milk

2 large eggs, plus 3 egg yolks

225 ml/8 fl oz double cream

¹/2 tsp ground nutmeg

¹/2 bunch fresh chives, snipped

2 tbsp finely grated Parmesan cheese

salt and pepper

method

1 Lightly grease a 23-cm/9-inch loose-based fluted tart tin. Sift the flour and salt into a food processor, add the butter, and process until the mixture resembles fine breadcrumbs. Tip the mixture into a large bowl and add a little cold water, just enough to bring the dough together. Turn out onto a floured work surface and roll out the dough 8 cm/3¹/4 inches larger than the tin. Carefully lift the dough into the tin and press to fit. Roll the rolling pin over the tin to neaten the edges and trim the excess dough. Fit a piece of baking paper into the tart case, fill with baking beans and chill in the refrigerator for 30 minutes. Meanwhile, preheat the oven to 190°C/375°F/Gas Mark 5.

2 Remove the pastry case from the refrigerator and bake blind for 10 minutes in the preheated oven, then remove the beans and paper. Return to the oven for 5 minutes. Remove the tin from the oven and reduce the oven temperature to 160°C/325°F/Gas Mark 3.

3 Arrange the crabmeat and watercress in the tart tin. Whisk the milk, eggs and egg yolks together in a bowl. Bring the cream to simmering point in a saucepan and pour over the egg mixture, whisking all the time. Season with salt and pepper and nutmeg and stir in the chives. Carefully pour this mixture over the crab and watercress and sprinkle over the cheese. Bake for 35–40 minutes, until golden and set. Leave to stand for 10 minutes before serving.

goat's cheese & thyme tart

ingredients

SERVES 6

flour, for dusting

250 g/9 oz ready-made puff
    pastry

500 g/1 lb 2 oz goat's cheese,
    such as chèvre, sliced

3–4 sprigs fresh thyme, leaves
    picked from stalks

50 g/1¾ oz black olives,
    stoned

50 g/1¾ oz canned anchovies
    in olive oil

1 tbsp olive oil

1 egg yolk

salt and pepper

method

1 Preheat the oven to 190°C/375°F/Gas Mark 5. Roll out the pastry into a large circle or rectangle and place on a baking sheet.

2 Arrange the cheese slices on the pastry, leaving a 2.5-cm/1-inch margin. Sprinkle over the thyme and olives, and arrange the anchovies over the cheese. Drizzle over the olive oil. Season well and brush the edges of the pastry with the egg yolk.

3 Bake in the preheated oven for 20–25 minutes, until the cheese is bubbling and the pastry is browned.

spring vegetable tart

ingredients

SERVES 6

butter, for greasing

flour, for dusting

250 g/9 oz ready-made
    shortcrust pastry

300 g/10½ oz selection of
    baby spring vegetables,
    such as carrots, asparagus,
    peas, broad beans, spring
    onions, corn, leeks

300 ml/10 fl oz double cream

125 g/4½ oz mature Cheddar
    cheese, grated

2 eggs plus 3 egg yolks

handful fresh tarragon and
    flatleaf parsley, chopped

salt and pepper

method

1 Meanwhile, preheat the oven to 200°C/400°F/ Gas Mark 6. Grease a 25-cm/10-inch loose-based tart tin. Roll out the pastry on a floured work surface to 8 cm/3¼ inches larger than the tin. Carefully lift the pastry into the tin and press to fit. Roll the rolling pin over the tin to neaten the edges and trim the excess pastry. Fit a piece of baking paper into the tart case, fill with baking beans and leave to chill in the refrigerator for 30 minutes.

2 Bake the pastry case blind for 15 minutes in the preheated oven, then remove the beans and paper and bake for a further 5 minutes. Remove from the oven and leave to cool. Reduce the oven temperature to 180°C/350°F/Gas Mark 4. Bring a saucepan of water to the boil.

3 Prepare the vegetables by trimming and peeling where necessary, then cut them into bite-sized pieces and blanch them in the boiling water. Drain and leave to cool. Put the cream in a saucepan and bring to simmering point. Place the cheese, eggs and egg yolks in a heatproof bowl and pour the warm cream over the mixture. Stir to combine, season well with salt and pepper and stir in the tarragon and parsley. Arrange the vegetables in the pastry case, pour over the cheese filling and bake for 30–40 minutes, until set. Leave to cool in the tin for 10 minutes before serving.

yellow courgette tart

ingredients

SERVES 6

50 g/1³/₄ oz unsalted butter,
   plus extra for greasing
250 g/9 oz ready-made
   shortcrust pastry
2 large yellow courgettes
1 bunch spring onions,
   trimmed and finely sliced
150 ml/5 fl oz double cream
3 large eggs
1 small bunch fresh chives,
   chopped
salt and white pepper

method

1 Grease a 25-cm/10-inch loose-based tart tin. Roll out the pastry 8 cm/3¹/₄ inches larger than the tin. Carefully lift the pastry into the tin and press to fit. Roll the rolling pin over the tin to neaten the edges and trim the excess pastry. Fit a piece of baking paper into the tart case, fill with baking beans and leave to chill in the refrigerator for 30 minutes. Meanwhile, preheat the oven to 200°C/400°F/Gas Mark 6.

2 Bake the pastry case blind in the preheated oven for 15 minutes, then remove the beans and paper and bake for a further 5 minutes. Remove from the oven and leave to cool. Reduce the oven temperature to 180°C/350°F/Gas Mark 4.

3 Meanwhile, grate the courgettes and put in a sieve with 1 tablespoon of salt. Leave to drain for 20 minutes, then rinse and put in a clean tea towel, squeezing all the moisture from the courgettes. Keep dry.

4 Melt the butter in a wide frying pan, add the spring onions and sauté until soft, then add the courgettes and cook over a medium heat for 5 minutes, until any liquid has evaporated. Leave to cool slightly. Whisk the cream and eggs together with some salt and pepper and chives. Spoon the courgettes into the tart case and pour in the cream mixture, making sure it settles properly, and bake for 30 minutes. Serve hot or cold.

squash, sage & gorgonzola tart

ingredients

SERVES 6

1/2 small butternut squash or
   1 slice pumpkin, weighing
   250 g/9 oz
1 tsp olive oil
butter, for greasing
flour, for dusting
250 g/9 oz ready-made
   shortcrust pastry
225 ml/8 fl oz double cream
175 g/6 oz Gorgonzola cheese
2 eggs, plus 1 egg yolk
6–8 fresh sage leaves
salt and pepper

method

1 Preheat the oven to 190°/375°F/Gas Mark 5. Cut the squash in half and brush the cut side with the oil. Place cut-side up on a baking sheet and bake in the preheated oven for 30–40 minutes, until browned and very soft. Leave to cool. Remove the seeds and scoop out the flesh into a large bowl, discarding the skin.

2 Lightly grease a 23-cm/9-inch loose-based fluted tart tin. Roll out the pastry on a floured work surface to 8 cm/3 1/4 inches larger than the tin. Carefully lift the pastry into the tin and press to fit, trimming the excess pastry. Fit a piece of baking paper into the pastry case, fill with baking beans, and chill in the refrigerator for 30 minutes.

3 Remove the pastry case from the refrigerator and bake blind for 10 minutes, then remove the beans and paper. Return to the oven for 5 minutes.

4 Mash the squash and mix with half the cream, season with salt and pepper and spread in the pastry case. Slice the cheese and lay it on top. Whisk the remaining cream with the eggs and egg yolk and pour the mixture into the case, making sure it settles evenly. Arrange the sage leaves in a circle on the surface. Bake for 30–35 minutes, leave in the tin for 10 minutes and serve.

artichoke & pancetta tartlets

ingredients

MAKES 6

pastry

75 g/2³/4 oz cold butter,
    cut into pieces, plus extra
    for greasing
100 g/3¹/2 oz plain flour, plus
    extra for dusting
pinch of salt
cold water

filling

5 tbsp double cream
4 tbsp bottled artichoke purée
400 g/14 oz canned artichoke
    hearts, drained
12 thin-cut pancetta slices
generous handful rocket
    leaves
50 g/1³/4 oz Parmesan cheese
    or pecorino cheese
salt and pepper
2 tbsp olive oil, for drizzling

method

1 Grease six 9-cm/3¹/2-inch loose-based fluted tart tins. Sift the flour and salt into a food processor, add the butter, and process until the mixture resembles fine breadcrumbs. Tip the mixture into a large bowl and add a little cold water, just enough to bring the pastry together. Turn out onto a floured work surface and divide into six equal-sized pieces. Roll each piece to fit the tart tins. Carefully fit each piece of pastry in its tin and press well to fit, trimming the excess. Cut six pieces of baking paper and fit a piece into each tart, fill with baking beans and chill in the refrigerator for 30 minutes. Meanwhile, preheat the oven to 200°C/ 400°F/Gas Mark 6.

2 Bake the pastry cases in the preheated oven for 10 minutes, then remove the beans and baking paper.

3 Meanwhile, stir the cream and the artichoke purée together and season well with salt and pepper. Divide between the pastry cases, spreading out to cover the base of each tart. Cut each artichoke heart into three pieces and divide between the tarts, then curl 2 slices of the pancetta into each tart and bake in the preheated oven for 10 minutes. To serve, top each tart with a good amount of rocket then, using a potato peeler, sprinkle shavings of the Parmesan cheese over the tarts, drizzle with olive oil and serve at once.

smoked salmon, dill & horseradish tartlets

ingredients

MAKES 6

pastry

75 g/2³/4 oz cold butter, cut into pieces, plus extra for greasing

100 g/3¹/2 oz plain flour, plus extra for dusting

pinch of salt

cold water

filling

125 ml/4 fl oz soured cream

1 tsp creamed horseradish

¹/2 tsp lemon juice

1 tsp Spanish capers, chopped

3 egg yolks

200 g/7 oz smoked salmon trimmings

bunch fresh dill, chopped

salt and pepper

method

1 Grease six 9-cm/3¹/2-inch loose-based fluted tart tins. Sift the flour and salt into a food processor, add the butter, and process until the mixture resembles fine breadcrumbs. Tip the mixture into a large bowl and add a little cold water, just enough to bring the pastry together. Turn out onto a floured work surface and divide into six equal-sized pieces. Roll each piece to fit the tart tins. Carefully fit each piece of pastry in its tin and press well to fit, trimming the excess. Cut six pieces of baking paper and fit a piece into each tart, fill with baking beans and chill in the refrigerator for 30 minutes. Meanwhile, preheat the oven to 200°C/ 400°F/Gas Mark 6.

2 Bake the pastry cases in the preheated oven for 10 minutes, then remove the beans and baking paper.

3 Meanwhile, put the soured cream, horseradish, lemon juice, capers and salt and pepper into a bowl and mix well. Add the egg yolks, smoked salmon and dill and carefully mix again. Divide this mixture between the tart cases and return to the oven for 10 minutes. Cool in the tins for 5 minutes before serving.

blue cheese & walnut tartlets

ingredients

MAKES 12

pastry

100 g/3^1/$_2$ oz cold butter, cut into pieces, plus extra for greasing

200 g/7 oz plain flour

pinch of celery salt

25 g/1 oz walnut halves, chopped in a food processor

cold water

flour, for dusting

filling

25 g/1 oz butter

2 celery sticks, trimmed and finely chopped

1 small leek, trimmed and finely chopped

225 ml/8 fl oz double cream, plus 2 tbsp extra

200 g/7 oz blue cheese

3 egg yolks

salt and pepper

chopped fresh parsley, to garnish

method

1 Lightly grease a 12-hole muffin tin. Sift the flour and celery salt into a food processor, add the butter and process until the mixture resembles fine breadcrumbs. Tip the mixture into a bowl and add the walnuts and a little cold water. Turn out onto a floured work surface and cut in half. Roll out the first piece and cut out six 9-cm/3^1/$_2$-inch circles. Take each circle and roll out to 12 cm/4^1/$_2$ inches diameter and fit into the muffin holes, pressing to fill the holes. Repeat with the remaining pastry. Put a piece of baking paper in each hole, fill with baking beans, then chill for 30 minutes. Meanwhile, preheat the oven to 200°C/400°F/Gas Mark 6.

2 Remove the tin from the refrigerator and bake the tartlets blind in the preheated oven for 10 minutes, then remove the paper and beans.

3 For the filling, melt the butter in a frying pan, add the celery and leek and cook for 15 minutes, until soft. Add 2 tablespoons of the cream, crumble in the cheese, mix well and season with salt and pepper. Bring the remaining cream to simmering point in another saucepan, then pour onto the egg yolks, stirring. Mix in the cheese mixture and spoon into the pastry cases. Bake for 10 minutes, then turn the tin round in the oven and bake for a further 5 minutes. Leave to cool in the tin for 5 minutes and sprinkle with parsley.

feta & spinach tartlets

ingredients

MAKES 6

250 g/9 oz ready-made
   shortcrust pastry
300 g/10½ oz baby spinach
25 g/1 oz butter, plus extra for
   greasing
flour for dusting
150 ml/5 fl oz double cream
3 egg yolks
125 g/4½ oz feta cheese
25 g/1 oz pine kernels
salt and pepper

method

1 Grease six 9-cm/3½-inch loose-based fluted tart tins. Roll out the pastry on a floured work surface and divide into 6 equal-sized pieces. Roll each piece to fit the tart tins. Carefully fit each piece of pastry in its tin and press well to fit. Roll the rolling pin over each tin to neaten the edges and trim the excess pastry. Cut six pieces of baking paper and fit a piece into each pastry case, fill with baking beans and chill in the refrigerator for 30 minutes. Meanwhile, preheat the oven to 200°C/400°F/Gas Mark 6.

2 Bake the pastry cases blind in the preheated oven for 10 minutes, then remove the beans and paper.

3 Bring a saucepan of water to the boil, add the spinach and blanch for 1 minute, then drain and press to squeeze all the water out. Chop the spinach. Melt the butter in a frying pan, add the spinach and cook gently to evaporate any remaining liquid. Season well with salt and pepper. Stir in the cream and egg yolks. Crumble the cheese and divide between the tarts, top with the creamed spinach and bake for 10 minutes. Sprinkle the pine kernels over the tartlets and cook for a further 5 minutes.

cherry tomato & poppy seed tartlets

ingredients

MAKES 12

pastry

200 g/7 oz plain flour, plus
    extra for dusting
pinch of salt
100 g/3¹/₂ oz cold butter,
    cut into pieces, plus extra
    for greasing
2 tsp poppy seeds
cold water

filling

24 cherry tomatoes
1 tbsp olive oil
2 tbsp unsalted butter
2 tbsp plain flour
225 ml/8 fl oz milk
50 g/1³/₄ oz mature Cheddar
    cheese
100 g/3¹/₂ oz cream cheese
salt and pepper
12 fresh basil leaves,
    to garnish

method

1 Lightly grease a 12-hole muffin tin. Sift the flour and salt into a food processor, add the butter and process until the mixture resembles fine breadcrumbs. Tip the mixture into a large bowl and add the poppy seeds and a little cold water. Turn out onto a floured work surface and cut in half. Roll out the first piece and cut out six 9-cm/3¹/₂-inch rounds. Roll out each one to 12 cm/4¹/₂ inches diameter and fit into the muffin holes. Repeat with the remaining pastry. Put a piece of baking paper in each hole and fill with baking beans, then chill for 30 minutes. Meanwhile, preheat the oven to 200°C/400°F/Gas Mark 6.

2 Remove the tin from the refrigerator and bake the tartlets blind in the preheated oven for 10 minutes, then remove the paper and beans. Put the tomatoes in an ovenproof dish, drizzle with oil and roast for 5 minutes.

3 Melt the butter in a saucepan, stir in the flour, and cook for 5–8 minutes. Gradually add the milk, stirring to combine into a white sauce. Cook for a further 5 minutes. Season well with salt and pepper and stir in the cheeses until well combined. Put 2 tomatoes in each tart case and spoon in the cheese sauce, then return to the oven for 15 minutes. Remove from the oven and top each tartlet with a basil leaf.

aubergine & pesto tartlets

ingredients

MAKES 6

flour, for dusting

250 g/9 oz ready-made puff
    pastry

1 large or 2 small aubergines,
    trimmed and thinly sliced

5 tbsp olive oil

3 buffalo mozzarella cheeses,
    sliced

6 tbsp pesto

1 egg yolk

pepper

method

1 Cut the pastry into six pieces, and roll into either circles or rectangles, then place on two baking sheets, three on each. Preheat the oven to 190°C/375°F/Gas Mark 5.

2 Brush the aubergine slices with 2 tablespoons of the oil and cook briefly in a non-stick frying pan, in batches, then arrange the slices neatly overlapping on each pastry base, leaving a 2.5-cm/1-inch margin. Lay the cheese slices over the aubergine slices and spoon over the pesto. Drizzle with the remaining olive oil and season with pepper. Brush the edges of the pastry with egg yolk and bake in the preheated oven for 15 minutes. Remove from the oven and serve.

potato, fontina & rosemary tart

ingredients

SERVES 4

250 g/9 oz ready-made puff
    pastry
plain flour, for dusting
3–4 waxy potatoes
300 g/10½ oz fontina cheese,
    cut into cubes
1 red onion, thinly sliced
3 large fresh rosemary sprigs
2 tbsp olive oil
1 egg yolk
salt and pepper

method

1 Preheat the oven to 190°C/375°F/Gas Mark 5. Roll out the dough on a lightly floured work surface into a circle about 25 cm/10 inches in diameter and place on a baking sheet.

2 Slice the potatoes as thinly as possible so that they are almost transparent – use a mandolin if you have one. Arrange the potato slices in a spiral, overlapping the slices to cover the pastry, leaving a 2-cm/¾-inch margin.

3 Arrange the cheese and onion over the potatoes, sprinkle with the rosemary and drizzle over the oil. Season to taste with salt and pepper and brush the edges of the pastry with the egg yolk to glaze.

4 Bake in the preheated oven for 25 minutes, or until the potatoes are tender and the pastry is brown and crisp. Serve hot.

caramelized onion tart

ingredients

SERVES 4–6

butter, for greasing

100 g/3½ oz unsalted butter

600 g/1 lb 5 oz onions,
    thinly sliced

2 eggs

100 ml/3½ fl oz double cream

100 g/3½ oz Gruyère cheese,
    grated, plus extra to
    garnish

20-cm/8-inch ready-baked
    pastry case

100 g/3½ oz Parmesan
    cheese, coarsely grated

salt and pepper

method

1 Melt the butter in a heavy-based frying pan over a medium heat. Add the onions and cook, stirring frequently to avoid burning, for 30 minutes, or until well-browned and caramelized. Remove the onions from the pan and set aside.

2 Preheat the oven to 190°C/375°F/Gas Mark 5. Beat the eggs in a large bowl, stir in the cream and season to taste with salt and pepper. Add the Gruyère cheese and mix well. Stir in the cooked onions.

3 Pour the egg and onion mixture into the baked pastry case and sprinkle with the Parmesan cheese. Place on a baking sheet. Bake in the preheated oven for 15–20 minutes, until the filling has set and begun to brown.

4 Remove from the oven and leave to rest for at least 10 minutes. The tart can be served hot or left to cool to room temperature, then garnish with Gruyère cheese.

cherry tomato clafoutis

ingredients

SERVES 4–6

400 g/14 oz cherry tomatoes

3 tbsp chopped fresh flat-leaf parsley, snipped fresh chives, or finely shredded fresh basil

100 g/3^1/$_2$ oz Gruyère cheese, grated

55 g/2 oz plain flour

4 large eggs, lightly beaten

3 tbsp soured cream

225 ml/8 fl oz milk

salt and pepper

method

1 Preheat the oven to 190°C/375°F/Gas Mark 5. Lightly grease an oval ovenproof dish. Arrange the cherry tomatoes in the dish and sprinkle with the herbs and half the cheese.

2 Put the flour in a mixing bowl, then slowly add the eggs, whisking until smooth. Whisk in the soured cream, then slowly whisk in the milk to make a thin, smooth batter. Season with salt and pepper.

3 Gently pour the batter over the tomatoes, then sprinkle the top with the remaining cheese. Bake in the preheated oven for 40–45 minutes, or until set and puffy, covering the top with foil if it browns too much before the batter sets. If serving hot, cool the clafoutis for a few minutes before cutting, or cool to room temperature.

courgette & cheese gratin

ingredients

SERVES 4–6

55 g/2 oz unsalted butter

6 courgettes, sliced

2 tbsp chopped fresh tarragon
or a mixture of mint,
tarragon and flat-leaf
parsley

200 g/7 oz Gruyère or
Parmesan cheese, grated

125 ml/4fl oz milk

125 ml/4 fl oz double cream

2 eggs

freshly grated nutmeg

salt and pepper

method

1 Melt the butter in a large sauté pan or frying pan over a medium–high heat. Add the courgettes and sauté for 4–6 minutes, turning the slices over occasionally, until coloured on both sides. Remove from the pan and drain on kitchen paper, then season to taste with salt and pepper.

2 Preheat the oven to 180°C/350°F/Gas Mark 4. Spread half the courgettes over the base of a greased ovenproof serving dish. Sprinkle with half the herbs and 55 g/2 oz of the cheese. Repeat these layers once more.

3 Mix the milk, cream and eggs together and add nutmeg and salt and pepper. Pour this liquid over the courgettes, then sprinkle the top with the remaining cheese.

4 Bake the gratin in the preheated oven for 35–45 minutes, or until set in the centre and golden brown. Remove from the oven and leave to stand for 5 minutes before serving straight from the dish.

baked eggs with cream, spinach & parmesan

ingredients

SERVES 2

25 g/1 oz butter, plus extra
    for greasing
125 g/4 1/2 oz baby spinach
1/2 tsp freshly grated nutmeg
4 small eggs
50 ml/2 fl oz single cream
2 tbsp freshly grated
    Parmesan cheese
salt and pepper

method

1 Preheat the oven to 160°C/325°F/Gas Mark 3. Lightly grease two individual ceramic gratin dishes, or similar.

2 Melt the butter in a large frying pan over a low heat and add the spinach. Cook for 1 minute, stirring with a wooden spoon until the spinach starts to wilt. Season with a little nutmeg, then divide between the prepared dishes.

3 Gently break 2 eggs into each dish. Pour over the cream and sprinkle with grated Parmesan cheese, then season with salt and pepper. Bake in the preheated oven for 10 minutes, or until the whites of the eggs have set but the yolks remain runny. Serve at once.

celeriac, chestnut, spinach & feta filo pies

ingredients

SERVES 4

4 tbsp olive oil

2 garlic cloves, crushed

1/2 large or 1 whole small head celeriac, cut into short thin sticks

250 g/9 oz baby spinach leaves

85 g/3 oz cooked, peeled chestnuts, coarsely chopped

200 g/7 oz feta cheese (drained weight), crumbled

1 egg

2 tbsp pesto sauce

1 tbsp finely chopped fresh parsley

4 sheets filo pastry, about 33 x 18 cm/13 x 7 inches each

pepper

method

1 Preheat the oven to 190°C/375°F/Gas Mark 5. Heat 1 tablespoon of the oil in a large frying pan over a medium heat, add the garlic and cook for 1 minute, stirring constantly. Add the celeriac and cook for 5 minutes, or until soft and browned. Remove from the pan and keep warm.

2 Add 1 tablespoon of the remaining oil to the pan, then add the spinach, cover and cook for 2–3 minutes, or until the spinach has wilted. Uncover and cook until any liquid has evaporated.

3 Mix the garlic and celeriac, spinach, chestnuts, cheese, egg, pesto, parsley and pepper in a large bowl. Divide the mixture between four individual gratin dishes or put it all into a medium gratin dish.

4 Brush each sheet of filo with the remaining oil and arrange, slightly scrunched, on top of the celeriac mixture. Bake in the preheated oven for 15–20 minutes, or until browned. Serve at once.

cheese & tomato pizza

ingredients

SERVES 2

dough

200 g/7 oz plain flour, plus
    extra for dusting

1 tsp salt

1 tsp easy-blend dried yeast

1 tbsp olive oil, plus extra for
    brushing

6 tbsp lukewarm water

topping

6 tomatoes, sliced thinly

6 oz mozzarella cheese,
    drained and thinly sliced

2 tbsp shredded fresh basil
    leaves

2 tbsp olive oil

salt and pepper

method

1 To make the dough, sift the flour and salt into a bowl and stir in the yeast. Make a well in the centre and pour in the oil and water. Gradually incorporate the dry ingredients into the liquid, using a wooden spoon or floured hands.

2 Turn out the dough onto a lightly floured work surface and knead well for 5 minutes, until smooth and elastic. Return to the clean bowl, cover with lightly oiled clingfilm, and set aside to rise in a warm place for about 1 hour, or until doubled in size.

3 Turn out the dough onto a lightly floured work surface and knock back. Knead briefly, then cut it in half and roll out each piece into a circle about 5 mm/1/4 inch thick. Transfer to a lightly oiled baking sheet and push up the edges with your fingers to form a small rim.

4 Preheat the oven to 230°C/450°F/Gas Mark 8. For the topping, arrange the tomato and mozzarella slices alternately over the pizza bases. Season to taste with salt and pepper, sprinkle with the basil and drizzle with oil.

5 Bake in the preheated oven for 15–20 minutes, until the crust is crisp and the cheese has melted. Serve immediately.